P9-DDE-047

FRED ALLEN'S LETTERS

fred allen's
LETTERS

edited by

JOE McCARTHY

garden city, n.y.

DOUBLEDAY & COMPANY, INC.

1965

FOREWORD

Fred Allen passed through this life masquerading as a vaudeville and radio comedian, and he became one of the most popular entertainers of the century.

In truth he was a classic humorist, one of those rare spirits who see the world as it is, and who laugh in order not to weep. His letters sparkle with his gay, bitter style, and overflow with comic invention. They are funny as hell; they re-create a colorful era; they make a remarkable American live again.

The lucky people who received letters from Fred Allen have treasured them to this day. Thanks to this volume, everyone can now own the best letters he wrote.

HERMAN WOUK

CONTENTS

INTRODUCTION

The thing about Fred Allen which set him apart from such other popular comedians as Jack Benny and Bob Hope when he was shining as a radio star in the 1930s and '40s was his unique ability to delight intellectual high brows with the same humor that pleased his vast audience of middle brows and low brows. He seemed to be received with equal pleasure by truck drivers, traveling salesmen, housewives addicted to daytime soap operas, sophisticated wits and professors of literature, who seriously compared his satire to that of Jonathan Swift and Mark Twain. Benny and Hope, great entertainers, could hardly claim such wide appeal. Allen's brand of wit captivated both the hard-boiled professional show business people around the tables at Lindy's and James Thurber and Harold Ross, the grouchy and demanding editor of *The New Yorker*, who often said that Allen was the only performer on the radio worth listening to. Thurber's all-time favorite joke was Allen's line about the crows so badly frightened by a farmer's scarecrow that they brought back corn they had stolen two years before. "You can count on the thumb of one hand the American who is at once a comedian, a humorist, a wit and a satirist, and his name is Fred Allen," Thurber wrote.

Allen was also a prodigious writer of funny letters and his friends felt that the wit and humor in his letters was much sharper and zanier and more entertaining than in his radio scripts because it was more relaxed and outspoken. "When Fred was writing his radio scripts," H. Allen Smith said recently, "two dozen invisible goons stood behind him, each with a blue pencil. A thing that might amuse the sponsor would possibly enrage the sponsor's wife or brother or cousin. A scripted situation hilarious to the account executive might give one of the network's vice-presidents the green fantods. So he always wrote for radio under wraps. When Fred finished his weekly script and turned to his correspondence, he pulled out all the stops and spoke his mind freely and happily."

Letters from Allen were carried in coat pockets for months after they were received and passed from hand to hand at luncheon tables and parties. A great many of them were carefully saved. Several years after Allen's death when his widow and co-starring partner on the stage and radio, Portland Hoffa, started to collect his letters for the selection in this book, her appeals brought thousands of them out of attics and cellars. Many more thousands of Fred's letters, which had been preserved, and often reread, for many years, had only recently been thrown away or lost. Portland's task would have been much more simple and her collection much more enormous if Allen had kept carbon copies. But he typed all of his letters himself on a portable typewriter, never dictating to a secretary, and he seldom bothered to insert carbon paper.

If Allen had filed copies of all of his letters, he would have filled almost as many filing cabinets as General Motors or the Pentagon. His output of letters was amazing. Allen's weekly working schedule was long and harder than that of other radio comics because, unlike all the others, he wrote, revised, and cut his own scripts, in addition to rehearsing and performing. Despite this work load, he devoted two days a week, when he could have been relaxing, to his letterwriting. He wrote to all kinds of people —close friends and relatives, show business associates, old vaudevillians whom he had not seen in years, childhood neighbors in Boston. He answered much of his show's heavy fan mail. During World War II, he wrote regularly to many friends serving in the armed forces.

Allen's letters flowed from his portable typewriter quickly and easily, without much premeditation, but with deftly skilled wit and irony. Wildly comic images popped up on his stationery as they often did in his casual conversation, spontaneous and effortless. "Those mosquitoes in New Jersey are so big," Allen once remarked. "One of them stung a Greyhound bus the other night and it swelled up so badly they couldn't get it into the Lincoln Tunnel." Ray Bolger was so thin, Fred observed on another occasion, if he had an ulcer he would have to carry it in his hand. Only Allen would visualize a British gentleman nudist, as he describes one in a letter, wearing a monocle in his navel.

Typing with two fingers, Allen rarely made a typographical error; nowhere in any of his letters are words xed-out or erased. On the few occasions when his typing did go astray, he would let it stand and go into a comic aside in parentheses, denouncing the typewriter for butting in on his literary efforts. "this is the new comedy typewriter," he complained after a funny misspelling in a letter to Groucho Marx. "you don't have to think, you keep typing along and the typewriter makes up puns and gags by itself. i will come home some night and find that the typewriter is gone and is working as a writer for jackie gleason."

As all the world already knows, Allen typed his letters, as Don Marquis' archy did, in lower case. It was often explained by magazine biographers in Allen profiles that he acquired the habit as a touring vaudevillian in the early '20s when the shift key on his portable was broken. However, as the letters in this selection show, Allen did not actually begin to swear off the use of capital letters until 1934, after he had left his stage career. Curiously enough, and perhaps a psychiatrist could do something with this one, although Allen typed his rollicking letters without capital letters, he always wrote the more inhibited scripts of his radio show in pencil and entirely in capital letters. His stationery displayed a caricature of him by Al Hirschfeld, some letterheads showed him being crushed between the pages of Joe Miller's Joke Book and others, in his later years when he was unhappily involved in television, had him scowling from a TV screen. Before his radio period, around the time when he was playing in the memorable revue, *Three's a Crowd,* with Libby Holman and Clifton Webb, Allen acquired a large quantity of discarded business stationery bearing the professional letterhead of a Chicago cesspool and septic tank cleaner named Matthew Stift. For a long time afterward, Fred happily used the Stift stationery when writing to friends.

None of Allen's letters are dull; even his brief notes to dentists or doctors requesting an appointment have unexpected twists in them. Many letters were excluded from this selection because they were too personal or too concerned with inside show business shop talk to interest the average reader, or simply to keep this book from extending to the length of the transcript of the Army-McCarthy hearings. Other letters were left out because their text has little meaning without the newspaper clippings, scraps of silly fan mail, unsolicited contributions from would-be comedy writers or greeting card poetry that Allen enclosed with them. The necessary enclosures were either missing or too difficult to reproduce in a book of this type. Allen's favorite indoor sport was sending such gleanings, with wry comments, to his friends, especially to Nunnally Johnson, the Hollywood film writer and producer, with whom he exchanged entertaining clippings and various other tidbits for many years.

In November 1955, for example, Johnson mailed to Allen an obituary of a New Yorker named Roy Forkum. Acknowledging this valuable information, Allen forwarded to Johnson a news item about the eccentric Foster Baker who had recently confessed every major crime committed in New York City over the previous two years, without, according to the police, ever actually being involved in any of them. Allen wrote:

dear nunnally:

the passing of roy forkum went unnoticed here. you have done new york city a great service in calling it to our attention. i showed your note to mayor wagner and he is planning a plaque to be placed near the grandstand in central park. this tablet will read simply

FORKUM MALL

am enclosing a clipping that may be helpful. if you are writing a mystery at the moment and are having plot trouble in working out a solution of your crime, foster baker may be the answer. foster has confessed committing every major crime in new york for the past two years. you can use him in the last reel. foster can walk in and confess whatever it is. regards.

On another occasion, Allen hastened to airmail, without comment, an item from Leonard Lyons' column describing the religious fervor of Jane Russell. "I love God," Miss Russell was quoted as saying, "and when you get to know Him, you find He's a Livin' Doll." Another Allen communiqué to Johnson enclosed a clipping from a Cape Cod newspaper reporting that a special tribute had been paid at a banquet in Yarmouth to a town road department employee named Harry Allen who had dumped the first load of gravel on Flying Point Road when construction of that highway was started in 1924 and also dropped the last load when the thoroughfare was finally completed in 1950. A second enclosure was an offer from a man named Ecker in Milan, Italy, to supply Allen with jokes and comedy ideas from the Italian press. As a sample of his wares, Ecker submitted an Italian newspaper cartoon showing a sailor pulling up his shirt to display to a youngster his chest, tattooed with a picture of a battleship. "What fun is that?" the urchin is saying. "Now if you were Lana Turner—" A third exhibit was a poem that Allen had received from an unknown New England poet, a lament for the death of a three-year-old boy named Kendall Miller in a town called Cushing. The poem ended:

> Now a robin sings again.
> Down in Cushing, spring again,
> But—no Kendall in the yard
> And his parents find it hard.

Concerning this assortment, Allen wrote to Johnson:

through a leak in the sidney skolsky column i have learned you are in germany preparing to direct a picture. i am sending some items you maybe can use.

1 . . . for a banquet scene which you must surely have in the story, a special tribute paid at yarmouth to harry allen, veteran town employee who dumped the first load.

2 . . . you will certainly need some laughs in the picture. m. ecker,

via manzoni 30, milano, italy, is your man. this sample joke will sell
you on m. ecker's service.
3 . . . a dramatic reading that involves the death of a small boy. if
you have a small boy dying in the picture, this may come in handy.

Allen received many homemade poems of the Kendall Miller
elegy type from his radio and television audiences. He urged
Johnson to consider one of them which he submitted as material
for a dramatic reading tour. "i can get the rights to this property,"
Allen wrote, "and i know that with the rendition you will give
to this rustic epic, you will chase tyrone power, judith anderson
and raymond massey in off the road." The poem suggested by
Allen was composed by a C. L. Dinsmore and was entitled "A
Ballad on the Death of Dennis McLain, who shot his Mother-in-
Law, his Wife and Himself at Waldoboro, Maine." The ballad
begins:

> Once more I lift a heavy pen
> And sing of the death of Dennis McLain—
> Another tragedy here in Maine . . .
> This Monday, the tide came in in the morning,
> And Dennis clammed—and still no warning.
> No one could guess as he filled his hod,
> In an hour's time, he'd meet his God. . . .

Allen often sent Johnson excerpts of fascinating dialogue that
he found in newspapers and books. ("She looked at him ear-
nestly. 'Get out of politics in this stinking town,' she pleaded. 'Get
yourself a decent job . . . Mark, darling, I'm thinking of us, you
and me.'") Allen clipped out of a newspaper a report from
Weatherford, Texas, in 1955 on a jealous husband who shot the
local Baptist minister, the Reverend Chester Stevens, six times in
the head and chest. When he turned himself and his gun in to
the police, the husband was quoted as speaking a line that Allen
circled heavily with a red pencil: "I did wrong over at the parson's
house." He sent the clipping to Johnson with the following note:

dear nunnally—

think you will be interested in the enclosed. in orson bean's next picture you can find a place for the line, "i did wrong over at the parson's house." happy new year if possible.

* * *

Allen's letters are presented here with as few explanatory footnotes and editor's comments as possible. Most of them need no special introductions and the fact that Allen did not bother to date many of them does not matter much because their chronology is not important. Here and there, like a lot of us, Fred misspells proper names but that isn't important either. However, a brief résumé of Allen's career in show business and his personal background may provide his correspondence with a helpful setting and off-stage lighting.

A Boston Irishman, born in 1894 and christened John Florence Sullivan, Allen was the son of a bookbinder who earned $19.23 a week. His mother died when he was three years old and he was raised by his Aunt Lizzie ("a wonderful woman") in the Allston and Dorchester sections of the city, working as a youngster in the Boston Public Library and as an errand boy for a piano company. Allen was still in his teens when he broke into vaudeville as a comic juggler who cracked jokes as he juggled, first using the stage name of Fred St. James and later Freddy James. His routine soon began to feature more jokes than juggling, including such sure-fire howlers as, "Condensed milk is wonderful but how can they get a cow to sit down on those little cans?" and "She was so old when they lit the candles on her birthday cake six people were overcome by the heat."

Freddy James became Fred Allen when he was breaking into big-time vaudeville as a comedy monologuist; with a new name and new jokes he could ask for a higher salary than the $75 a week that Freddy James had been getting in small-time theaters. In 1919, Fred Allen made a smashingly successful debut at B. F. Keith's Palace on Broadway, the highest pinnacle of vaudeville. Any performer who had played the Palace in those days could be assured of being booked by the manager of any important theater in the country, sight unseen. By 1922, after touring as a headliner on the Keith circuit, Allen was playing in Shubert vaudeville on the same bills with such big stars as Lew Fields and Nora Bayes and earning the then astronomical salary of $400 a week. Writing his own highly original comedy lines—which were often borrowed by Al Jolson and other greats—he was already identified in show business as a performer with a classy following. Three times in one season he was brought back for return engagements at the Shubert Theater in New Haven by demands from admiring Yale undergraduates.

From vaudeville Allen moved to the musical comedy legitimate theater in the Shuberts' Winter Garden attraction, *The Passing Show of 1922,* where he became acquainted with Portland Hoffa, one of the girls in the chorus. They were married in 1927 after Allen had made a vaudeville tour in partnership with a comedian named Bert Yorke. It was while he was appearing with Yorke in Toledo on a dreary Christmas Day that Allen ad-libbed his most famous, and most widely plagiarized, wisecrack. The orchestra leader was a gloomy little man who never laughed as he listened to Allen's witticisms during three shows a day. Finally Allen could stand the musician's unsmiling acidity no longer. Leaning across the footlights, he asked, "What would you charge to haunt a house?"

Most of Allen's letters in this collection cover the last twenty-five years of his life, beginning in the early 1930s when he was playing on the stage in the depression-stricken *Three's a Crowd.* When that show closed in 1932, Fred and Portland rented a cottage for the summer at their favorite vacation resort, Old Orchard Beach in Maine, expecting to go into another Broadway musical in the fall. The promised venture never materialized because of lack of money. Fred took a job instead, which he thought would be only temporary, as the writer and star of a weekly radio comedy program, sponsored by Linit starch. He remained in radio for next seventeen years and never appeared on the stage again.

Linit gave him up in 1933 but Hellman's mayonnaise pounced upon him a few months later and, to his surprise, renewed his contract after the summer salad season was over. Then he was established on the air as a popular comedian with a following and there was never a lack of sponsors from then on—Sal Hepatica and Ipana, Texaco and Ford. The grind of turning out a weekly show often annoyed him, as his letters show, but he stayed on the radio treadmill, begrudgingly, until 1949 when television became popular, with Milton Berle as its king, using gags that Allen had used in *The Passing Show of 1922*.

Once, during the war, Allen gave up his show for a year on the advice of his doctor and found himself working almost as steadily making guest appearances on other radio shows. Now and then he went to Hollywood to play in a movie but movie acting, as a regular line of occupation, never appealed to him. "The only role they want to give me is the part of the publicity agent in a backstage story about a musical comedy," he once said. Allen could see himself doomed in Hollywood to become a Ned Sparks type of comedian.

Although he was one of the big show business celebrities of his time—a top radio star in that golden age of radio was as important as a top movie star—Allen never behaved like a celebrity and never thought of himself as anybody particularly special. He stood out conspicuously in his self-centered profession as a modest and unpretentious man who lived simply and quietly. He and Portland rented an apartment in a non-fashionable neighborhood of Manhattan, between Radio City and Central Park, never owned an automobile, and walked to their rehearsals and shows. On their movie-making visits to Hollywood, they stayed in an inexpensive apartment hotel. Before one of their trips to the Coast, Allen's agent in Hollywood tried to persuade him to lease an elaborate twelve-room house in Beverly Hills. "Don't be afraid," Allen wired the agent in reply, "You don't have to let on that you know us." The Allens were reluctantly forced to leave Old Orchard Beach, the decidedly unexclusive seaside resort in Maine where they summered for many years, because their cottage there was too exposed to autograph seekers and other gawkers. Their vacations after World War II were spent at such staid and quiet saltwater hotels as the old Gurney's Inn at Montauk, where, as Fred claims in one of the letters that follow, the tide came in only at a signal from the lady proprietoress and the guests belched after meals into little clusters of pussywillows that were served with dessert. Allen could have belonged to the swanky athletic clubs in New York but he much preferred to play handball and punch a bag twice a week with cops, firemen, and postal clerks at the West Side YMCA. His friends from the Y often accompanied him to the Friday night fights at Madison Square Garden. He and Portland never went to night clubs. Fred's idea of a pleasant social outing was an evening at the theater or a trip on the subway to Alton Cook's home at Jackson Heights, where he would exchange funny stories and reminiscences with Cook, the radio-television, and later the movie, critic of the New York *World-Telegram,* and H. Allen Smith. Their three wives would sit apart in a separate conversational group.

Allen's simplicity led some smart-aleck columnists to call him a tightwad. Actually, he was always supporting as many as six families of unlucky relatives and friends and sending money to unemployed actors and gag writers. He gave away more than $100 a week in small bills to alcoholic panhandlers. One ragged bum, known as The Whistler, used to put the touch on Allen every Sunday morning when he came out of St. Malachy's, the actors' church on 49th Street, just west of Broadway. On Sundays when he could not make it to the theatrical district, The Whistler would arrange to have a large sign displayed in the window of Mike Jacobs' ticket office, on the same street as the church, which said, "Mr. Allen— The Whistler is out of Bellevue Hospital again and wants to get in touch with you." Allen would go inside and leave two dollars at the counter for his faithful client. A beggar in Hollywood once read in a movie trade paper that Allen was due to arrive that morning from New York to begin work on a picture at Twentieth Century-Fox. Hastening from his boardinghouse to meet Allen's train at the railroad station, he fell and broke his arm. He asked Allen to pay the forty-dollar doctor's bill because he felt that the injury was Allen's fault, and Fred paid it.

When television replaced radio as the dominating entertainment medium, Allen made a few tentative tries at it but he never felt at ease in television and the network executives at NBC wanted no part of the comedy show that he wanted to do, a sort of Allen's Alley with the visual format of Thornton Wilder's play, *Our Town*.

"They claim a comedy show in TV is no good unless it has a lot of singers and dancers," Allen said in 1952. "I haven't been able to relax on a television stage with all those technicians with earphones wandering back and forth in front of me while I'm trying to tell a joke. They've been listening to me and the joke in rehearsals for two days and by the time the performance rolls around they're leaning on their cameras and sound equipment and staring at me with the enthusiasm of a dead trout. Television is a triumph of equipment over people and the minds that control it are so small that you could put them in the navel of a flea and still have enough room beside them for a network vice-president's heart."

Allen was also frustrated during the television age by poor health. He suffered from hypertension and fretted over his strictly salt-free diet, which kept him away from Italian restaurants where he loved to eat spaghetti with white clam sauce. At one point he made a deal to appear in a TV quiz show, designed along the same lines as Groucho Marx's *You Bet Your Life* with the entertainment drawn from ribbing the contestants rather than from the quiz itself. Allen's doctors forced him to give up the project. John Crosby, then a television critic, wondered sadly why television could not provide such gifted comics as Groucho and Allen with something better than asking ladies from Kenosha how their husbands proposed to them. Being restrained by medical advice from playing the clown in such a spectacle in the twilight of his career was probably one of the most fortunate things that ever happened to Allen.

In the last few years of his life, Allen appeared Sunday nights on television as a panelist on *What's My Line?* an easy chore approved by his physicians because it required no rehearsing or script preparation. He spent the rest of the week writing two autobiographical books, *Treadmill to Oblivion*, an account of his years in radio, and *Much Ado About Me*, memoirs of vaudeville and musical comedy days. Allen had always wanted to be a full-time writer; one reason why he devoted so much time to turning out so many letters was the satisfaction that he found at his typewriter. He often said that he enjoyed the preparation of his radio scripts more than the performance of his shows. When he left radio, he seriously considered writing skits and monologues for other comedians like his good friend, Goodman Ace. In his earlier years, he had written comedy material for a fellow Irish Bostonian, Jack Donahue, the famous Ziegfeld comedian-dancer of the 1920s. Allen was greatly encouraged when *Treadmill to Oblivion* won praise from critics and became a best seller in 1954. He plunged into *Much Ado About Me* with relish, working daily in an office without a telephone a few blocks from his Manhattan apartment.

On the night of Saint Patrick's Day, 1956, when *Much Ado About Me* was not quite finished, Allen was stricken with a fatal heart attack while walking his dog on West 57th Street. The next day Herman Wouk wrote a tribute to Allen, hailing him as America's greatest satiric wit of modern times, which appears in its entirety at the end of this book. "Fred's wit lashed and stung," Wouk said. "He could not suffer fools. In this he was like Swift and Twain. But his generosity to the needy, his extraordinary loyalty to his associates (in a field not noted for long loyalties) showed the warmth of heart that made his satire sound and important."

— JOE McCARTHY

I.

AN ASSORTED SAMPLING

MABEL DAWSON*

october
18th
1946

dear miss dawson . . .

thank you for your letter.

you will be glad to learn that the honey arrived in excellent condition. portland had some at breakfast yesterday and reported that it was the best she had ever tasted.

we don't get much honey here in new york. we have had one bee for some time. we have no flowers and have to let him out to sneak into the various florist shops in the neighborhood. i think our bee is nearsighted. it must spend a lot of time on artificial flowers, for the amount of honey it gives some months is negligible.

our bee has no comb. it carries the honey on its person. when we want honey we summon the bee, point to the biscuit, or whatever object we want the honey on, the bee flies to the table, squats and buzzes a little and when it arises we have about enough honey to float a carraway seed.

you can imagine what a boon it is to us to have three large jars of honey. we are sending our bee down to florida for a good rest this winter. i am sure that when it returns, brown and healthy, it will be ready to pick up where it left off and keep us in honey for years to come.

we are having a difficult time finding guests to use on the program but i guess we will manage to keep going some way during the coming season. if not, some week, i may put our bee on the show and there will be a real b on n.b.c.

sincerely . . .

fred allen

* One of the Allen radio show's fans.

december 26th
1947

dear miss dawson . . .

portland and i want to thank you for sending us the wonderful christmas package. we appreciate your kindness even though we must say the usual trite phrase "you shouldn't have done it."

since you sent the honey for our bee i should bring you up to date on wendell. we christened the bee wendell after oliver wendell holmes who left harvard in 1829 with a b.a. degree.

wendell hasn't been doing at all well. last summer he developed an acid condition. when he would sit on portland's costume jewelry things would turn black. worrying about his acid condition brought on an ulcer. this led to arthritis and most of the fall wendell was gimping around in severe pain. finally, we started mixing wheaties in with his pollen and wendell showed some improvement.

no sooner was he cured of his physical ails than he developed amnesia. wendell forgets he is a bee. he thinks he is a man. i catch wendell trying to put on my underwear and lathering his tiny jowl and attempting to shave. we write the word "bumble" on the floor and go around buzzing hoping wendell will remember but he doesn't seem to. we think that chronic amnesia has set in. when your package arrived we showed wendell the honey and he didn't even know what it was.

sincerely . . . and . . . a happy new year.

fred allen

JACK HALEY

gurney's inn
montauk, n.y.
august 10th
1944

dear jack . . .

you could never stand this place. you can not only hear a pin drop here; you can sense the rustle of the fabric of the sleeve as the person's arm is raised to drop the pin. it is so quiet here after meals the guests belch into little clusters of pussywillows that come with desert. the tide comes in noiselessly at a signal given by the woman who owns the place. it is so quiet you can hear a caterpillar backing into a globule of dew. you would go nuts here.

i hope flo has been able to find a woman to work around the house. if that religious woman comes back she'll dent the rugs with all that kneeling. wealth and possessions bring these troubles. a person should never own anything that he can't get into a coffin. it's like that gag . . . don't buy anything in hollywood you can't get on the chief. if you want to own something get a goitre or a hernia, something you won't have to have dusted and something you can carry around with you.

regards . . .

f.a.

GROUCHO MARX

oct. 13th
1950

groucho—

every sunday, after mass, we stop for breakfast at the stage delicatessen. at this hour max, the proprietor, is host to a motley throng. horse players, bookmakers, cream soda lovers and sturgeon gourmets. how i, a gentile, get in there, i don't know. since the same characters meet every sunday there is a friendly atmosphere rampant that no airwick can subdue. when the lox is running good and the cream cheese is spreading easily those assembled, between smacking their chops and wiping their greasy fingers on their vests, will discuss some topic that is currently engaging the general public.

yesterday, the air conditioning not functioning at the stage, there was a gamey flatulent essence dominating the room but the flanken was lean and spirits were high. talk turned to the tallulah show. every tout, every bookie and every questionable customer present had seen the program.

eating was suspended. chicken fat was shaken from fingers to point them. novy was shredded from snags of teeth to make way for encomiums. the countermen stopped slicing to mingle their opinions with those of the chef who looked out of the kitchen door while keeping his eyes on an order of scrambled eggs and onions not too brown. a fat man put down a dr. brown celery tonic bottle and emitted an effervescent burp while he paid his tribute to the hour. a man swung open the men's room door and added his kudo to the acclaim.

everybody in the delicatessen agreed that the tallulah show had been great. this is a cross section that the surveys never reach. i bring you this report to let you know how the man in the street reacted to the show.

i thought the show was excellent. the mechanical miss hurt a little and meredith was winded trying to get the panel bit off but over all portland and i agreed that it had taste, intelligent fun and stature.

regards—

fred allen

may 14/53

dear groucho—

i have just returned from boston. this is an accomplishment. very few actors, who started in boston, were able to leave there. many of my old acquaintances, of the harry latoy, kelly and galvin and kenny and hollis days, are still around boston playing clubs and eating beans three times a day. i can show you twenty smalltime actors in boston who have been eating beans for over forty years. you may have seen some lean years but i can show you boston actors who will make your lean years look like mack gordon. (the former mack gordon.)

when i came back from beverly hills i called goody. he said that he was going to call you immediately. he had been intending to write you but it is the old story in new york—as soon as you pile up enough good intentions the mayor will grab them and pave an intersection with them—this enables the administration to keep the subway fare at its present level. i imagine that goody's intentions were stacked up to the ceiling before he called you. assuming that he did call you.

i have been looking around for a court room without a bath for you. i went down to 43rd street to inquire at yandis court. lou holtz used to own yandis court and i thought i could get you a rate. on the yandis court site i found the times building. i think that yandis court became a mostel (mos tel. this is the new comedy typewriter. you don't have to think, you keep typing along and the typewriter makes up puns and gags by itself. i will come home some night and find that the typewriter is gone and is working as a writer for jackie gleason.)

went down to the bartholdi inn. there were plenty of court rooms down there years ago. it seems that the bartholdi inn became loew's state for a time but there was a fellow sitting in the box-office with a register. i think they are trying to change loew's state back into the bartholdi inn until television blows over.

tried a few other places; mrs. montfort's, the coolidge, the somerset, etc., but court rooms are out of the question. they are all taken by english actors who can't afford to go to the cornonation. (corn-onation. you'll go a long way among your writers to find a man who will beat this typewriter.) these loyal britishers are going to hole up in court rooms until the thing blows over. speaking of "holing up"—in the sequence shown on cinemascope from "the robee" (the frigging typewriter is showing off again) one of the soldiers is discussing the disappearance of the messiah. he says something about "we'll have to find out where he is holing up." the messiah may show up wearing chaps later in the picture. the whole thing may be a western with togas for all i know.

you should be safe here around may 22. leo has the giants out of town. the only news i have is that john cedric craig, the pyrotechnist, died. he left an estate of used roman candles and four bales of burned matches. see you soon. portland joins me in best wishes to eden and to you.

f.a.

MARK LEDDY*

Old Orchard Beach
Maine
July 20, 1932

Dear Mark,

I am in receipt of both of your notes but it is difficult to answer just now. There is a jazz band playing at the local drug store and they rehearse a few cottages from where we live.

* Allen's agent in his vaudeville days.

Right now they are working out a medley containing such numbers as "Put on your old grey Bonnet" and "When we are M A double R I E D" etc. You would enjoy walking into the drug store at night. Just as you get seated at the soda fountain, these six birds let out a blast from the saxophone section that will curdle the milk in your milkshake.

They are versatile and consistent. Versatile in that they all sing and croon through megaphones that look as though they are cardboard containers that have been varnished. Consistent, since everything they attempt is lousy. The band is called Ralph Armstrong and His Arcadians. The dictionary defines an arcade as "a vaulted passageway or street". If there was really anything in a name then these fellows would certainly be playing in a vaulted passageway or in the street.

Mr. Kane, who runs the drug store, came over to me the first night the band opened and said "I don't know about these boys, they seem a little heavy for my place". Mr. Kane told me that he used to play vaudeville but dancing teams took up room and he had to take out tables and on the whole it paid him better to just run a straight musical aggregation.

Now about the "Night at Quigleys" which "Raymond" is running next week. I have spoken to Johnny Quigley and he is ready to appear in his original role of Newsboy Tenor but he says that tabloids have become so popular that he now sings the newsboy songs in a smaller voice. If this will be alright, he will open when you set a figure. His opening song is still "Shine 'em up, Shine 'em up", followed by some talk, "I can row a boat, canoe, canoe" after which he will sing the first quarter or the last quarter of Shine on Harvest Moon, according to the season of the year. He also has a recitation but I doubt if you will want any talk at an affair of this sort.

I am enclosing an all star bill, booked by Bert Brennan, for September 26th. He wants me as MC for the affair but I doubt if I shall be in town. You will note the regards from Dave Manley. I have suggested to Bert that if the 26th is a hot night that he let the Whirlwind Trio work all through the show and this will save the cost of turning on the fans. I feel sure that the Whirlwinds can stir up sufficient draught to circulate the air and no doubt cool off the theatre at the same time. This might be the solution of the Arab Act Unemployment situation. Arabs work cheaper than the cost of the electric current and through putting two arab acts on at the overture and let them spin and whirl, at the side of the stage, all through the show the theatre manager would get the same results and achieve a humanitarian result at the same time.

Came across a bit of bad news this week. Lavender and Old Rose got a date but the wardrobe had been stored so long that the costumes had faded. They changed the billing to Heliotrope and Thorn but were cancelled after their first show. The manager said he wouldn't have an act break in anything at his theatre —not even a new name.

I can't accept any dates now but when I return we can go into conference at the nearest Coffee Pot. I can't get back to New York until after September first and then to play any dates I will have to get organized and talk over the talent situation with you. We might get a part of Kate Smith for the smaller houses which I could use for a finish. Thanks for the Paramount, thought perhaps I can do it later but I wouldn't want to run into those places cold the way we did with the Unit. It took me two weeks to dig up enough old wheezes to meet my Public half way. Best for now—

F.A.

FRANK ROSENGREN*

Old Orchard Beach
Maine
June 18, 1932

Dear Frank . . .

The normal season here in Maine for vacationists starts on July first and ends after Labor Day. Having nothing better to do this month, we decided to come up ahead of the average tourist and see why nobody comes here until July.

* A book dealer and close friend of Allen's.

And now we know. We have been here at Old Orchard six days and it has been colder than an Eskimo street walker's big toe on a dull night. Goose pimples come to a head here and give off a sort of liquid frost when pressed unduly. The people eat candles and use the wicks for dental floss and business is so bad in fish markets you can hear a fin drop.

We are constantly bothered by nudists who stop at the door begging for an old vest or a sock or any article of clothing to tide them over the chilly period. This morning I heard a knock and found a nudist who is an English gentleman shivering at the front of the house. He was wearing a monocle in his navel.

Being confined to the house, as we have been, has led to interior decoration. A new curtain has been hung on the front door so that my birthmarks and other blemishes will not be common gossip. I, who know nothing of machines, have installed a radio set with a lightning arrester and ground wire. The arrester has sort of an ego complex and seems to be looking up, daring lightning to start something. I hope that the God in charge of the Bolt Delivery Service can take a joke. Otherwise a nance clap of thunder will reduce this place to a decoy for stray dogs. I am sorry now that I wasted so much time on the radio set. All one hears is stale jokes and much ado about certain songs being sung through the special permission of the coffee-right owners. I may demolish the bothersome contraption in a moment given over to a personal antidecibel movement. I'll let you know later.

I have also tacked up soap dishes, coat hangers and put some brads in a quaking chair. I say "tacked up" advisedly. We will only be here two months and I see no reason why I should waste energy, which I am bound to need in later life, actually nailing up fixtures. Should anything collapse, through some faux pas of a guest, one of those "Oh, I didn't know it was tacked up" incidents I shan't feel obliged to worry about it. We are doing our best to discourage guests. My brother spent the weekend with us and left tonight ill from exposure and undernourishment. If he will only get mad enough to talk about his experience around home, we may be able to scare off any prospective cadgers and callers.

I addressed the mice, on the day of arrival. I put it to them squarely that it was up to them to look to the Maine Society for the Preservation and Culture of Rodents for sustenance. I have no intention of having a lot of those sneaky mice pimping in the kitchen. I'll keep them out if I have to go downstairs at night and mew for an hour or so before going to bed. I have put a scarecrow in front of the package of bran since learning that crows, faced with a corn shortage, have turned to puffed rice, and other breakfast foods. If you can conveniently send me a copy of the Dunciad I would appreciate it.

Now that I am reading so many books, my brain is polka dotted with dabs of mis-information and false knowledge and I am too befuddled to concentrate on any one thing. If I was to adopt a child, I would return with twins, but this has been done with girls who went away to attend boarding school. Always a plagiarist I!

I hoped to write several scenes here but my aunts are coming for a rest which I need more than they do and then Portland's kid sisters are coming which means a period of bedlam and waiting to get into the bathroom. Life is futile and the man who wears a toupee should take his hat off to no one.

I rest my case, as the French Horn player said when he missed the last bus.

Portland sends her rural regards to Florence and we will out yokel you two for twenty dollars a side, any time after September first. Best for now. Send the Dunciad before I succumb to an offer to drive a baker's wagon here.

f.a.

sunday night.

dear f. . . .

let me know if you are interested in making suttee. i have a dead hindu lying around the place here. there are so many fire-eaters out of work just now that i have been afraid to kindle a blaze in the yard lest these brimstone munchers gobble up the flame before i can get the hindu kindled. i think that a good pyre would be a business getter here at the moment. there are so many frozen street-walkers around that any one of them would gladly leap into the flame posing as the hindu's mistress.

if you are interested, let me know, and when i have an opportunity i shall wrap the cadaver and come out, with a box of matches, for a week-end. suttee-making is rather antiquated but someone will eventually bring it back at the fair and we may as well reap the profits if there are any profits in using defunct hindus for fuel.

now that the army is carrying the mail it looks as though the confederate soldiers will deliver letters in the south. as long as they still have the suits we may as well make use of them. things are picking up here . . . they caught a communist speaking from atop a mahogany soap-box last week.

hoping this finds you the same and with best lenten wishes to florence . . . i am . . .

fred allen
"as far as i know"

JOHN KIERAN

december
30
1954.

dear john—

we cannot match the reports of your bird activities in westchester. we have no flying squirrels zooming through the air around 58th street. we do have an old slate-colored junco who flies in from long island occasionally. this slate-colored junco is owned by a real estate man, building a development to be called o'brientown. o'brientown is going to be the irish answer to levittown. the houses are put together hurriedly and when one of the slate shingles falls off of a roof the real estate man releases the slate-colored junco who flies up and covers the hole in the roof until the real estate man gets the first payment on the house. the only other ornithology note we have available involves two school teachers who went into birdland the other afternoon thinking it was the audubon society office. regards—

F.A.

JOHN J. MCCARTHY

march
14th
1941

mr. john j. mccarthy
fire department headquarters
municipal building
new york city

dear mr. mccarthy—

mr. kershaw, of the texas company, has spoken to me about your kind invitation to dampen the ardor of four thousand uniformed men, who will attend the holy name communion breakfast on april 20th, through subjecting said four thousand uniformed men to an outburst of oratorical pyrotechnics using my mouth as the rocket base.

unfortunately, my radio chores keep me going sixteen and more hours daily seven days per week. this flagrant violation of the existing labor laws not only keeps me in hot water with the wagner act officials but the many hours required for the preparation and presentation of the weekly radio programs take up the slack in my days which might otherwise be devoted to writing and memorizing talks to be given at assorted gala functions. for this reason i am compelled to forego appearances at the many festive events to which i am invited.

i realize that it would improve my social status to be found in good company for a change. i know that the mayor's speech would be an inspiration to me in my future work. i have heard that the combination breakfast at the astor is excellent. but, even these temptations on the one hand will not shorten my days nor lighten my labors on the other. i am sure that if you were out squirting a hose sixteen and eighteen hours a day you couldn't find time to operate a sideline that involved watering lawns.

sorry that i cannot attend but know you will appreciate my position. you can get even. if i ever have a fire you can send your regrets. i will understand.

sincerely . . .

fred allen

DORIS BEECHER*

november 26th 1936

dear miss b. . . .

am in receipt of your letter requesting a letter to add to your collection which . . . as i understand . . . boasts such sterling artists as mr. fred stone and mr. randolph scott.

i am rather particular about the company kept by my letters after they have quit my typewriter but since these men appear to be sober, industrious and reliable i feel that no harm can come to any missive of mine through coming in contact with the letters you have from these above-named merry fellows.

and so . . . complying with your request . . . here is your letter;

dear doris. . . .

your letter received! happy to know that you have recovered from your automobile accident.

oh boy!

sincerely . . .

fred allen
n.b.c. studios
new york city

* One of Allen's radio fans.

this letter can be cut out and pasted beside your others or this entire manuscript can be kept and the first and last parts ignored . . . or you can fold the letter four times and it will make an excellent covering for the floor of any room in a doll house.

the office advises me that your request for tickets will be granted. if you do not receive them all of a sudden let me know and i shall attend to the matter personally.

best wishes . . . only ?? more days to do your xmas shopping!

DANIEL MARSH

Allen was often plagued by requests like the following one and sometimes they made him rather testy.

april
17th
1948

dear mr. marsh . . .

i am in receipt of your letter dated april 16th.

when a radio comedian wins an award it seems always to be contingent upon the comedian performing some function in return.

i have won several awards that entailed taking costly adverts in obscure magazines.

one year, i was given a "peabody award." this involved engaging a taxidermist to stuff me into a dress suit, and writing a speech—which later i had to deliver to a group that looked like an insolvent rotary club that rented itself out to attend drab gatherings of this sort.

now—boston university has voted me "the american comedian of the year." (year not given) to accept this honor you ask me to come to boston, with some forty musicians and actors, and broadcast, on sunday may 2nd, from the b.u. campus.

unfortunately, we cannot broadcast away from new york

city. our orchestra plays the "prudential hour" earlier on sunday evening. our actors have commitments on other programs and cannot leave the city. our guest on may 2nd is bing crosby who is coming to new york for one day to appear with us.

i am afraid you will have to take back the award and give it to someone who is less involved than . . .
yours sincerely . . .

fred allen

JACK MULCAHY

old orchard beach
maine
august 30th

dear jack. . . .

your letter was sent up here to maine and i am sure that the envelope enjoyed the trip. the climate here works wonders with postage stamps and tourists. i have seen a letter arrive with washington looking pretty anemic on a two cent stamp. after the mail has laid around in this invigorating air for a couple of days you wouldn't know george. his cheeks fill out, his adam's apple is straining at the skin in his throat and his white wig turns a cack-colored brown . . . a tribute to the all powerful infra-red rays of our native maine sun.

we saw all of the spreads you managed for shirley temple while she was sick in boston during her new england tour.* i sent one picture out to harry tugend. it was the one where hundreds of little kiddies were standing on arlington street reacting to that unforgettable dramatic moment when little germ-infested shirley staggered to her window to wave a fever-wracked greeting to her little fans below. i thought that you were coming up through here and waited for the date to send you a wire. this town is enroute

* Mulcahy, a movie publicist, was beating drums for a Shirley Temple picture.

to portland and we thought you might stop off for a lobster or a preview of a mess of crabs. finally, the local paper said that shirley was going back and i didn't bother you.

i waited in new york hoping that the entourage would arrive before we finished. i had the sponsor in accord with your wishes and he promised to give up one of the client's private rooms should mr. zanuck's tyke attend. you wasted so much time around dirty navel, iowa, and torn prune, nevada, that i realized you couldn't possibly get to new york before the radio season was over. i hope you have retained some notes on the trip for i would like to go over the entire trek with you when we come out again . . . if! with the material loose on a journey of that sort you should have enough data to make a book. the next time . . . should you take the little ritz brother or jane withers across the country . . . for gosh sake let me know. i will be glad to drop everything and join you for the laughs.

we start back on the air october 5th. i don't know what we are going to use for jokes but i guess after we get started the knack will return and we can continue to pound out the weekly tripe. i was all in when we finished but feel better now. i am still nervous but portland has been sick and my aunt was taken to the hospital yesterday and the tax men have been heckling me to the point where i really haven't been able to relax. i have a few more weeks and am going to stay here as long as possible.

i may be out next summer. it is too early to tell yet. mr. z has an option to be exercised before december 31st. if he doesn't take it up i have two other propositions supposedly open at any time and when i see what happens to the radio problem this coming year i will know better what i can do. if you have occasion to come to new york during the fall or winter let me know. we will be at the dorset, the address you have, and for a slight fee, should you attend a broadcast, i can see that the mulcahy name once again echoes through the loud speakers from coast to coast.

if harry brand came back with an english accent give him my limey regards. hope all is well and that the studio had enough ice left over from the henie pictures to melt down for a canal for suez. also, trust that sol has enough guns left over from his westerns to lend darryl for jesse james. best for the moment and convey my bronzed regards to sammy my favorite wardrobe genius.

f.a.

ED SIMMONS AND NORMAN LEAR

The following letter is a reply to a hoax perpetrated by Simmons and Lear, the Hollywood comedy writers, who delighted in goading Allen into such daffy correspondence. On another occasion, after the Polish girls' Fred Allen Fan Club had disbanded, Simmons and Lear acquired several sheets of business stationery bearing the letterhead of an ironmonger named Harry Saminow and used it to involve Allen in a highly complicated series of charges and countercharges concerning a set of andirons and some ingots which they claimed he had ordered from Saminow. A few highlights of that exchange are also exhibited here.

november

11

dear barbara—

i am in receipt of your letter asking my permission to start a polish fan club, dedicated to my many accomplishments and carrying my name.

for many years, i have been against fan clubs. i remember back in 1902 a group of girls got together in littleton, new hampshire, to form a guy kibbee fan club. mr. kibbee, even at that early age was as bald as a boy scout's knee, and the girls all shaved their heads to look like their idol. all through the summer the little baldheaded girls had a jolly time. they had guy kibbee meetings, they talked like guy kibbee and when field days were held the fan club would rush out and spell guy kibbee in different formations and in different languages. with their little bald heads they were a shiny sight. when the cold weather arrived, however, it was another story. thirty of the baldheaded girls contracted pneumonia and within three months the entire guy kibbee fan club was wiped out.

that is only one reason i hesitate to sponsor a fan club. if beri beri or scurvy breaks out in your group how is it going to look with little emaciated bodies lying around the streets of california wearing my fan club buttons.

another thing, i don't think that my popularity will last until you can get a good-sized fan club assembled. if you have the enthusiasm why not forget a fan club for me. why not use this energy forming a vegetarian group in your polish neighborhood? to help you get started i am closing a copy of the official vegetarian song.

as you girls march along singing—
"oh how saintly you feel
and how sprightly you feel
on the right vegetarian meal
leave out fish fowl and meat
and you'll find that what you eat
adds to something sacred and sweet"
you will feel the yogurt coursing through your veins and you will know that you are saving the lives of cows, lambs and pigs. running a fan club for me you will only be saving an old ham.

fred allen

March 9, 1953

Dear Fred,

Sorry this whole business with the andirons ever started—but it never fails when you try to be a good guy and do favors.

Harry Saminow was never a close friend of ours and the foul-mouthed things he's been saying since this affair started—well, it just isn't worth it.

If you wanted to swap the andirons for ingots, it was OK to mention it to us—but why did you have to tell Gert? Now the whole thing is in the open. She told it to the oldest Bender girl (the one with the bad skin) and she in turn has been blabbing it all over town—and with you 3000 miles away—well, we've got enough on our minds.

Look, why don't you write directly to Harry? Forget about him cutting you out on that andiron deal and tell him you are willing to let bygones be bygones. Harry's not a bad sort at heart. Maybe he'll swap the ingots and maybe he won't—but at least you'll be getting us out of the middle of this thing.

You know, Fred, friendship is friendship. But, gosh, when a person's whole being is tied up with the incidental welfare of the average relationships as they affect the standards of home and life —well, even for the nonce can they beget the effect of permanent disillusion and heartbreak.

So—write to Harry. You'll feel better for it.

Our very best to you and yours,

Ed and Norman

march
12 . . .
1953

ed and norman—

i never thought the day would come when i had to write this letter to you. you said "so—write to harry. you'll feel better for it." i wrote to harry. the andirons should drop dead. for my thanks what did i get? a snotty letter on kleenex.

how did i know that in the same mail with my letter about the ingot and the andirons a letter came from peppy weiner saying that harry's brother-in-law morty was fired from his job. peppy weiner is the head of the manischewitz wine office in bronxville. it seems that morty has diabetes and didn't tell peppy. morty was out selling all day and when he came back to the office with his diabetes he had sugared two gallons of his samples. peppy said if harry's relatives are maple trees he could go climb them. harry writes back to peppy saying he should live so long until he catches a saminow in his office.

if you don't know morty he is married to the oldest bender girl (not the one with the bad skin—the one with the short arm who played trombone with spitalny and couldn't play any low notes). gert used to call him crazy morton before she married irving. irving had the delicatessen until somebody broke in that night and straightened out 200 bagels. he opened as an italian restaurant and tried to pass off the straight bagels for breadsticks. harry told him he'd never get away with it and sure enough. personally, to me, irving is crazier than morty. how he came to get out of the clothing business he got stuck with 300 suede dinner jackets at the end of the season. he cut the 300 suede dinner jackets into penwipers and that same year the ballpoint pen swept the country. irving had an idea one time to put a wick in waxey gordon and make a candle out of him to use in a cannibal tea room.

with relatives like these you can imagine the mood harry is in when he hears from me about the andirons. i don't want to keep harping on the andirons but if i am going to be stuck i will send the ingot and the andirons back to mrs. bitoff who is harry's mother-in-law. i should tear my heart out when i am not hungry. rather than experience this humiliation i will put a door on the fireplace and make it into a small closet. the kids can play in it when company is in the room.

sylvia says you will be here for seder. maybe you can talk to harry and fix up this andiron dilemma. sophie has been sick. a herring came to life on the dollar dinner at lindy's. sophie fainted and hit her head on the waiter's belt buckle. mama says you-know.

F. Allen

March 16, 1953

Dear Fred:

So instead of facing the problem and tackling it squarely, we find you hedging with the lowdown on a family of whom we care not one solitary damn. Peppy, Morty, Irving, Sophie and Sylvia be damned! This doesn't clear up the situation any more than if we wrote to you about the Zitsers (Morty's in-laws) when what you really wanted to know was how to clear up this situation with Harry.

So, speaking about the Zitsers, you couldn't have heard because it only happened yesterday about Louie Zitser's new car. It's a 1932 Stutz Bearcat and when Louis bought it, it was bad enough—but now it has developed Mishkin's Malady——a serious car problem that starts with a stretching of the fan belt and when it reaches the crisis, the tires turn into sneakers. Louie is taking it rather well, but it is really heartbreaking to see that little car hanging around the tennis courts, trying to get a game.

Of course, Louie's brother Naish doesn't give a damn. He's got his own troubles as he has just come down with a pretty bad case of Lastvogel's Disease, otherwise known as Hardening of the Nostrils. Poor Naish has been sneezing pebbles for six days now. Twelve years ago, Barton MacLane had the same thing, caught a bad cold on top of it and stoned his best friend to death.

Well, with all this trouble going around, what can one say except to be thankful for everything good that comes your way. It is a pity to see the suffering that goes on among those you know and love—even if they deserve it—and heaven knows the Zitsers have had this coming for years!

But let's have no recriminations! Live and let live!

Which reminds us. Fred—if you send the andirons back to Mrs. Bitoff, you'll never hear the end of it! The old lady Bitoff hasn't been too well lately what with her eye trouble and all. You must have heard how her eyelids have slowly turned to sandpaper and she is gradually winking her eyeball down to the size of a pea. Yesterday, she was visiting with the Zitsers and one of them fell out—it took us six hours to find it as it got mixed up with a load of Naish's pebbles. Meanwhile, little Maxie Zitser (eight years old and already with a hernia) plugged his study lamp into her empty eye socket and—well, Mrs. Bitoff has enough to think about.

You said:—"maybe you can talk to Harry and fix up this andiron dilemma." OK, we will, but if it doesn't work *this* time,

YOU better be ready to straighten things out—even if you have to pay for them.

    Best,

Ed and Norman

WESTERN UNION

NEW YORK NY MAY 26 1953

ED SIMMONS AND NORMAN LEAR

PARK SHERATON HOTEL 7 AVE WEST 55 ST NYK

LE SANG EST PLUS DENSE QUE L'EAU. JE SUIS ARRIVE.

MARCEL DE SAMINEAU

JOE KELLY

november 19th
1940

dear mr. kelly . . .

    i am in receipt of your note and the invitation put out by spears murphy futch of washington's mayflower hotel. the minister's upper plate must have slipped at mr. murphy's christening. as i see it, spears was probably leaking, the font was messy and the minister in bending over dislodged his upper plate. after he said, "i christen you spears murphy," spears no doubt voided and the minister said "futch." according to church law, futch became part of mr. murphy's name. i am sure, though, that the word is nothing but an obsolete latin imprecation.

best regards . . .

f a

NEW YORK STOCK EXCHANGE

Charged with slandering Wall Street on one of his radio shows, Allen
wrote this apology to the president of the New York Stock Exchange,
who put it up on the exchange's bulletin board.

gentlemen:

no malice was intended and i am sorry to have incurred the
disfavor of the gentlemen. i have considered committing hari-kari
on the two points recently gained by bethlehem steel. i have also
thought about calling a conference since a conference is a gather-
ing of important people who singly can do nothing but together
can decide that nothing can be done. both ideas were abandoned
in favor of this letter to you.

sincerely

fred allen

LOUIS SOBOL

january 13th
1943

dear louis . . .

in a recent column you said you couldn't recall ever having
seen me in a new york night club. you never have, louis.

during the past twenty years, i have visited but four noc-
turnal pothouses. each visit, i might add, was made under duress
and fraught with event.

in 1923, i went to the old parody club to see clayton, jackson
and durante. the dance floor was smaller than the top of a sugar
barrel and a buxom lady consummating a jazz posture brushed a
plate of soup in my lap. fortunately, it was night club consomme,
a plate of hot water from which a waiter's thumb had been re-

moved, and it didn't stain. but i departed the parody club with a luke warm lap.

in 1934, i went to the hollywood cafe at the behest of rudy vallee. during the show rudy gave an imitation of me and spoiled my entire evening. had i wanted to listen to me i could have stayed home and talked to myself and saved the cover charge.

in 1940, i went to the club 18. after i had ordered some food jack white heckled me until in self-defense i had to take to the floor. i went there to be entertained and ended up entertaining myself. when i returned to the table, one of mr. white's actors had eaten my sandwich and the waiter had finished my drink.

in 1941, i went to the stork club to have some pictures taken with jack benny. this was business. the visit is not recorded in my diary as a night club outing.

after the above experiences i abandoned the night club. why should i go to a night club? i can get better air in a closet. i can cook better food myself. i can hear better music on a portable phonograph. and i can meet a better class of people in the sub-way.

sincerely . . .

fred allen

H. ALLEN SMITH

hollywood
july 11th
1940

dear allen . . .

life here is an eternal siesta. nothing has happened since you left. that is, nothing has happened to alter my opinion of the place or to speed my departure. the picture has been postponed three days and now we start on the 17th. that means we shall arrive back three days later which makes me madder by the minute.

i am working on a saroyan play for my own amazement. it

concerns a mild fellow with a super-inferiority-complex. he is born in hollywood. he lives in hollywood. he dies in hollywood. all through life he hates hollywood but his timorous nature forbids him to criticize or give vent to his true feelings about the place. two months after he is buried a little bush grown up through the dried soil on his bare grave. the bush thrives and in the fall produces a colossal fruit . . a single raspberry . . . the posthumous opinion the little man had of hollywood.

f. allen smith

old orchard beach,
maine
august
16th
1945

dear h.a.

the tide is high today. since i have stopped associating with people and things that cannot hold their liquor i am ignoring the beach today. each night i resolve to answer some letters on the following morn but nothing comes of it. i seldom have the desire to do anything. i could become a bum if only i had enough will power to keep me from returning to work. i don't know whether it is the maine air or whether the pictures of dr. townsend and alf landon one sees in every house tend to bring home to a transient the futility of existence. i think that is the reason most people in maine have wrinkled faces. they sit so much a lot of loose skin forms around the abdomen. when they comb their hair this skin is pulled up around the scalp where it sags awhile and then finally corduroys or settles into wrinkles.

i received my decameron some weeks back. i read it at once. i think you have an excellent collection and i certainly enjoyed those brann pieces and the joe mitchell and street pieces. the assortment should meet the approval of all of your ardent followers and i hope the sales exceed what you are using for expectations.

old roaring brook road sounds like the lane i would expect the wilkins family to take enroute home after a hard day at the whiskey vats. roaring brook. there must have been powerful waters in your section years ago, if a brook could roar a stream could raise a bloody din as g.k. chesterton might say. from your building ventures, sawbuck making (i always thought a sawbuck was ten dollars) cement mixing and mortising you should be equipped to turn out a book in rebuttal that would chase louis bromfield's "pleasant valley" out of print.

i think doc rockwell intimated that buying a house was not unlike going out with a virgin . . . you never know how the gamble will turn out. we are going up to see doc this saturday. he is very busy with his lobster business and as a special treat he is going to take me out with him sunday morning to help him "pull his pots." this sounds like some chambermaid sport but it is a term used by lobstermen. i may have some exciting notes for my diary after i return from the rockwell manse.

harry tugend wrote me last week. life still goes on at paramount. joe sistrom was sick and ordered away by the medical men. ginsberg and harry seem to be doing all of the work. abe burrows, who formerly wrote duffy's tavern, had a ten week deal at paramount but he is leaving this month and returning to new york. harry didn't mention anything about buddy but i read last week that he was in a wheelchair and expected to attend the sneak of his new picture "stork club." three or four guys have dropped dead on that lot and i don't think it pays to drop dead trying to make a star out of eddie bracken.

i read the woolcott book. i thought it was somewhat like its subject . . . shallow. alec always impressed me as being what he was . . . a bloated poseur. shortly before he died he wrote me a letter saying that he recalled with pleasure that he had given me my start in radio and he also hinted that he would accept a guest shot on our program. the texas co. had employed him one season and he had insulted most of the executives. they wouldn't let me use him.

wish you would write some sort of a novel you could sell to

a picture company. when you see the dough they throw around plus book sales and magazine fees it seems like a gold mine project. if i could turn out matter of that sort i would abandon my mike activities as of now. after living on roaring brook road you should be able to write of the natives and their lives in that high class dust bowl you are forming.

we will be back in time for me to go on "info please" sept. 10th. our show starts oct. 7th. god knows what will happen. all of the old stooges are in hollywood. i still have mrs. nussbaum and the right of way. portland sends her rustic good wishes to nelle. trust that god's big acre is under control and that you have started to work. the trotting races left town last week. all that remains of the racing season is countless hundreds of mutual tickets and several tons of manure.

regards . . .

> until sept. 3rd

> f. allen
> old orchard
> beach . . . maine

CHAIN LETTER

A

CHAIN LETTER
to end all
CHAIN LETTERS

on the east bank of the nile, one day recently, an arabian oyster-shucker was seen to slump over an oyster he was shucking. a british army officer, who rushed to the oyster-shucker's aid, found that the little arab was not dying. he was chanting a prayer in his native tongue to R the god of oysters.

the little arab did not intend that his prayer should be dispatched around the world at your expense. you do not have to send copies of the oyster-shucker's supplication to ten friends within twenty-four hours. a woman, in ohio, who broke the chain is still happily married, and two more payments and the trailer in which she is living is hers.

the oyster-shucker's petition was not meant for the eyes or ears of the world. translated, the little bivalve-artisan's chant to R consisted of five simple words "spare me until october second."

why did the little arab want to be spared until october second? what momentous event was to take place on that date? the british army officer, whose curiosity was aroused, said to the oyster-shucker in broken arabic "why you wantem be spared until october second?"

the arab raised his turbaned head and in perfect english replied, "on october second the texaco company is starting its new program over the columbia network. from nine to ten p.m., eastern standard time, the texaco star theatre will present fred allen, kenny baker, portland hoffa, jimmy wallington, the texaco singers, the texaco comedy workshop players and al goodman's orchestra. it looks like a great show. i don't want to miss it."

"nor i," said the british army officer. with this he saluted and left the arabian oyster-shucker to his shucking.

do you want to share this magic hour with the little arab and the british army officer? if you do . . . tear this letter into five equal parts. put these five pieces in your pocket today! on september 28th, at nine p.m., throw the first piece of this letter away. the next night at nine p.m. discard the second piece. repeat each night at the same time. on the fifth night, as you consign the last fragment of this letter to the winds, it will be nine p.m. october second. turn your radio to your local columbia station. the texaco star theatre will present its first program.

then you will know why the little arabian oyster-shucker prayed to R, the god of oysters; "spare me until october second."

PHILADELPHIA PUBLIC LEDGER

Allen said he once checked into a hotel in Philadelphia and the rooms were so small even the mice were humpbacked. Allen was denounced by the Philadelphia Chamber of Commerce, the Convention of Tourist Committee, and the All Philadelphia Citizens Committee. The *Public Ledger* attacked him in an editorial, headed: PHILADELPHIA FIGHTS BACK. Allen replied as follows:

dr. editor,

the remarks made on my program concerned a small theatrical hotel in phila. twenty-five years ago. no mention was made on my program and no aspersions cast on the many excellent hotels in phila. today. i know that the benjamin franklin hotel is so named because you can fly a kite in any room. i know that the rooms at the walton are so large the world's fair is stopping there when it goes on the road next fall. i know that the rooms at the bellevue-stratford are so spacious that the army-navy game can be played in a closet. and i know that billy rose rehearsed his aquacade in a sink in one of mr. lamaze's mastodonic bathrooms at the warwick.

yrs., fred allen

LAWRENCE E. SPIVAK

december
20th

lawrence e. spivak—

i am in receipt of a letter from the "meet the press" headquarters signed by a man who was either in a decompression chamber or in a hurry.

the signature may have been fashioned by an old hieroglyphic demonstrator who had lost his touch.

after several hours spent deciphering, working with my strong glass, i arrived at the name above.

if you are the party who wrote the letter i am sorry to have to inform you that i am leaving for california after the holidays and will not be available for a "meet the press" session in the immediate future.

sincerely—

Fred Allen
(if you can't read this, here it is again)

fred allen
180 west 58

HAL KANTER*

april 25th
1955

dear hal—

i want to point out the enclosed faye emerson column. this purports to reproduce some actual banter engaged in by your employer, george gobel, and miss marlene dietrich aloft in a plane. if miss emerson is to be believed, miss d's gambit got under way with the trite opening "mr. gobel, i'm marlene etc, etc, etc,. i'm a great fan of yours." if miss emerson is to be further believed george parried with "thanks, uh, uh . . . well, are you going to new york?" if this exchange is counterfeit crossfire i suggest that you warn your lawyer to whisk that boiled beef out of his briefcase and stand by. if this altitude smalltalk is verbatum then i think you should lash george to a writer when he makes his future trips.

if you and the other show writers are not hep to the social routines that are generally used by comedians when columnists of miss emerson's stature are eavesdropping i am sure that goody ace will come up with three or four routines that george can use on buses, trains, planes and when he is abroad on foot. if goody

* Then the creator of George Gobel's TV comedy show.

is tied up i might have time to send on some stuff to keep george going until goody can get to it.

your letter was a relief. i have been getting some fan mail on "whats my line." one this week reads—"who do you think you are that you can insult arthur godfrey every program you are ever on? you should be half as popular and the third as smart or have one tenth the following that mr. godfrey has. what's the matter? it is jealousy or ignorance that you think it is humorous to get personal on the air. it's a great way to make friends. you work hard for a laugh, don't you? sincerely mrs. i.s. jones." if mrs. jones stops buying "poof" i may be finished. stand by for the big show. life is only the overture.

regards.

fred allen

BILL MORROW*

august 10
1944

dear bill . . .

received your letter and that new yorker piece on the reverend mr. james jefferson davis hall. it is wonderful. i have seen the reverend around broadway mumbling and shouting but i always thought he was some old bird who got his money-belt picked at roseland. if i had known he was such a colorful old bastard i would have stopped him and made his acquaintance. i think a fin would win a potential penitent a place in the rev. hall's heart. the rev's first joust with sin is a dandy. even in 1888 actors were getting the finger. what the devil was doing in anniston, alabama that year no one will ever know. i like the way the reverend co-operated with the devil in an effort to make contact with sin. that night, after the dixieland grand opera company had finished its performance and the girls had returned to the hotel, the rev had his door open. otherwise he would never have heard the girls a-giggling and a-carrying on nor would he have seen

* Writer and producer of Bing Crosby's radio show.

that girl a-tiptoeing down the hall in her nightshift. fields will get a hell of a kick out of the piece as it is certainly written well and i think the reverend hall is the man to speak at field's funeral. if they bury him. of course if, after bill dies, they just let him lie around it would be a waste of dough to bring the reverend on from the east with his eating onion and his drinking water.

i hope you don't go out to the coast until after we return. i would like to catch up on the 52nd street cultural exhibits. i think we should see frisco and hyers and harrington off on their fall seasons. i think the hyer's club is the only spot on the street that owns its mousetrap outright. most of those joints are so far in hock they rent their mousetraps and generally use no cheese. they try to get the mice in on speculation. i hope we can catch up socially with the 52nd street trend before you have to leave. welch will be worried if you get out there and can't tell him who is held over at leon and eddie's. most of the acts have to be held over. they can't pay them at the end of the first week.

don't bother answering this letter. i know you have been spoiled. once a person writes for money you can't expect him to write for nothing. toots shor is in difficulties with the opa. he has had more trouble with points. the normandie is being raised. i think it is morganthau propaganda. his slogan will probably be "if america can raise the normandie, america can raise another 13 billion dollars in taxes and war bonds."

i imagine jack benny will have a lot of stories to tell when he gets back from africa. i read yesterday that he and hope were both there. i had a letter from adolph menjou written from a hospital where he was listening to one of the transcriptions we made with some thirty wounded americans. menjou says if people could see what he has seen there would be no strikes, absenteeism, etc. jack will probably see a lot of things, too, before he finally gets back here. if jack gets back first he can beat hope to a release in sullivan's column. i guess the sigh of relief that will sweep through the ranks of jack's relatives when he gets back will air-condition the san fernando valley.

"my name is daddy hall, and i love you one and all"

gurney's inn
montauk, n.y.

ARNOLD AUERBACH*

june
30th
1943

dear arnold . . .

i have just finished the final script of the season. if i had sufficient strength i would project my head out of the nearest window and give three rousing cheers. since i haven't the strength to even open the window i cannot project my head and if i gave the three cheers in my room i alone will hear them. i have abandoned the whole thing and will use the time i might have frittered away trying the accoustics to send you a communique.

portland and i were surprised to learn that you were at upton. i knew you were going soon but i have lost all track of dates. we are happy to learn that the baby approved of the junior utensils. why not have justine rear the little one with a fork, a silver fork, in her mouth. a child brought up with a silver fork in its mouth should make many pointed remarks in later life. you see how the chief is slipping.

i was sitting in the capitol the other night, next to me were a middle-aged couple apparently from the west. the picture "bataan" had been on about twenty minutes. robert taylor, george murphy and many other m-g-m actors were engaged in jungle warfare coming out from under logs and various tropical plants. finally, one soldier started to creep over a log. this was too much for the man. he said, "well, mother, i guess we've seen enough of this picture." the woman said "yes, there's too much crawlin in it." m-g-m spends a million dollars and with all of the wonderful effects and scenes all it meant was "too much crawlin" to this bloated madam. that will probably explain why skelton has a higher crossley than we have.

f.a.

* One of Allen's writers who later became a Broadway musical comedy and revue librettist.

PAT WEAVER

september fifth
1939

mr. p. sylvester weaver
american tobacco co.
new york city.

dear p. sylvester:

gone the halcyon, devil-may-care days when we were expected to hail you as "weaver!", "dear pat," "p.w." and "Sir!" now that you have moved from the agency to become a client, all fraternal salutations must give over to greetings that smack of the dignity accorded the man who sports the furrowed brow, the "tums" packet peeping out of his upper waistcoat pocket and the look of neurotic importance and other outward vestiges we associate with clients in general.*

portland and i are happy to learn that you have sanded the butter on your insteps and that you have started to climb the ladder of success with a vim. we sensed that something was agog "on the street," as we call the sidewalk afront the young & rubicam catacombe. a lean and frowsy gypsy stopped here one evening under a sickle moon. she carried a large ball of kelp into which she was not above peering, for a small pittance and a small pittance is less than a pittance so you can see she was willing to function for less than a guest star on the vitalis show . . . but this is beside the point, p. sylvester . . . the stale daughter of the bush insisted on telling our fortunes. a deal was made, the gypsy who appeared to be nearsighted buried her nose in the ball of kelp in an effort to see what the dank offing held in store for us. the kelp must have finally given up its soggy secret for with a sharp exhale the gypsy withdrew both nostrils, spat out a periwinkle, and said "you are going to lose a friend."

* Weaver had just left Young and Rubicam, an advertising agency, to join the American Tobacco Company, an advertiser.

"one has no friends in the radio game," i ventured. i was not phil baker, and after all i assumed that i could "top a gypsy." i had no script but she was reading from a ball of kelp. "you are right," the gypsy answered, "the man who departs has no friend but he was an enemy who didn't do anything about it and in radio this, to a gypsy, is a friend." well, sir! i was stumped but i sent out for two artificial legs and carried on. "what is the destination of the departing friend," i queried. "this i cannot tell you at these prices" the gypsy answered, "but decipher this message and you will know." with this the tattered seeress crept into the night. looking down at the message i saw a memo bearing a motley array of messy hieroglyphics. "decipher this and you will know." the gypsy's warning bid fair to make a tread-mill of my mind. what to do?

morpheus and i had it out that night. i counted sheep in wolves' clothing. i took off the wolf pelts and counted straight sheep. i counted the wolf-skins with no sheep in them. nothing helped! morpheus gave me his vaporous finger to the hilt. as dawn cracked i waited for the echo and dragged my tired body from the bed. taking my hieroglyphics i raced to an old herb practitioner who has a branch office abutting a rutabaga here in town. the herb doctor was busy brewing a wormwood and gall consomme to cast the devil out of some deviled ham he had found in back of a tourist camp. he stopped his steeping just long enough to fathom the gypsy's memo that concerned our loss. when i returned to portland and showed her what the message allowed we knew then that you had gone . . . never to return. the fatal message was a limerick. it read;

> "he who sics his
> transit sunday . . .
> will live to gloria his mundi."

reading between the lines i know you will get it.

we are sorry to have you leave our conference table, p. sylvester. this is an age of progress and noisy decisions and know-ing that you had shicked-off the fuzz of executive puberty with your electric razor, we somehow were expecting this blow. we trust that your future path will be a proverbial road of roses with no inter-office hay fever to mar your progress.

since you are now a client there are one or two things i should call to your attention; to wit;

> never talk in your sleep at a conference. you will not only wake up the other members of the board but you may say something that will turn up as a blackertsemple and hummert program.

> never point, when you have a hangnail, or two minions will leave the room instead of one.

> never attempt to quaff your phenobarbitol from a dixie cup. the sodium salycilate in the phenobarbitol works havoc with the glue in dixie cups. surer than hell the bottom of your dixie cup will fly open and you will have to sit around the office with an effervescing lap for an indefinite time.

also! am enclosing one special client cork swivel guard. the guard sewed into your drawers prevents swivel-piercing, a great menace to most clients. sitting in a chair day upon day, the swivel is apt to run through the wood and enter the lower colon without so much as a "touche." chet bowles, of benton & bowles, once found himself impaled in a naked swivel and spun around in his chair for several hours before being unswivelled and medicated.

yes, p. sylvester, we are coming back with "the same old stuff." we have said "good-bye" to you as an associate. now, with the news reels, people you didn't expect, etc., we take our leave of you as a listener.

"avoir, p. sylvester!"

Fred Allen

EARL WILSON

dear earl . . .

sorry i can't write a guest column for you. column writing isn't my metier. (metier is french for racket) i could never be a bistro balzac, a saloon sandburg or a diva de maupassant.

an m.c. on a quiz program once told me that einstein knows more about space than any columnist. i told him that a columnist fills more space in a week than einstein can hope to fill in a lifetime. einstein keeps going for years with one lousy theory. to weather a day, you need two columns of facts.

and what facts! i could never take your place.

with gay abandon you write of falsies and girdles and elaborate on their contents. i blush when i see breast of chicken on a menu. the first time i saw jane russell i wondered how she got her kneecaps up in her sweater.

press agents date hedy lamarr, lana turner and paulette goddard for you to interview.

the last blind date i had i opened one eye and it was broadway rose.

you are welcomed at all of the fine eating places. mr. billingsly, they say, carries you over the threshold of his stork club nightly.

the last time i ate in lindy's the tongue in my sandwich gave me the raspberry through a small hole in the top slice of bread. when i complained to lindy he put his head in the sandwich and gave me another raspberry through a small hole in the bottom slice of bread.

when you walk down broadway, you meet scores of interesting people.

when i walk down broadway i meet jack benny or some other actor who is out of work.

the nights you go into toots shor's, oscar levant, between sips of coffee, is bellowing epigrams. to wit: "i ran myself through an adding machine today and found that i didn't amount to much."

the nights i go into shor's toots is generally talking to himself in a low voice. i can't even hear what he is saying. the only time i could hear him, toots was mumbling "why you big crum bum, you're so stupid you think yellow jack is chinese money."

when you go to an opening, noel coward stops you at intermission and regales you with the story that is currently sweeping london. to wit: the one about the young innocent girl whose father told her about the flowers but neglected to tell her about the b's. the girl went to hollywood and made three bad pictures.

the last opening i attended (life with father) a guy named dwight gristle, who was selling black market tassels, told me a broken-down gag about a new cheese store—it was called "limberger heaven."

how could i ever get enough good jokes together to be "earl for a day?"

last night, i walked around town. here's what happened to me.

at the health food store, on 50th street, i saw a sign "hubert frend has switched to yogurt."

at the copa, jack eigan told me about the latest in hollywood styles: an undertaker is featuring a suede coffin.

at the automat, jack haley told me about the picture star who thought he was a banana. his psychiatrist found the picture star had a split personality. his is the first banana split personality on record.

you can see, earl, the whole thing is futile. i can never be a columnist. i know the wrong people. i hear the wrong things. i go to the wrong places.

i will end up like the old man who lived in the cannon for twenty years—he was always hoping to be a big shot, but he never quite made it.

sorry to have to let you down with the guest column.

regards . . .

fred allen

ABE BURROWS*

may 3rd
1945

dear freelance . . .

we read that you had resigned from the duffy's tavern enterprises. i think you have made a smart move. like the infantry
frank loesser mentions in his song about roger young, there is no
glory in radio. if norman corwin had done the work he has
done in radio in any other medium he would have morganthau's
hand in his pocket and a standing in the theatre or in hollywood
that would be enviable. the excellent work you have done in
radio, apart from the satisfaction you have gotten, the money
you have earned and the opportunity you have had to experiment
with ideas to perfect your technique, is transient. in pictures, or
in the theatre, you can work less, make as much money and
acquire a reputation that will mean something. a radio writer
can only hope for ulcers or a heart attack in his early forties.
with few exceptions radio is a bog of mediocrity where little men
with carbon minds wallow in sluice of their own making. for
writers with talent and ideas, after it has served its purpose as a
training ground, radio is a waste of creative time. good luck to
you in new fields of endeavor, mr. b., long may you gambol!

recently a hollywood reporter mentioned that a mr. abe
burrows was cutting a social dove-wing out there and that
claudette colbert wouldn't think of giving a party without a
caterer and this burroughs. we assume that with this nature spell-
ing you are attending claudette incognito. i hope you have the
piano shawl in the act. if you can't get one of those shawls
you might get a navajo blanket. an indian blanket with a. burrows sewed on in birchbark would attract attention before you
gained the piano. i am working on a new cellophane sheet of
music. this will enable the pianist to look through his music

* The Broadway director and hit comedy writer, who had been a gag creator
on the Duffy's Tavern show.

and see how people are reacting to his efforts. many times an entertainer is singing his heart out and behind his music guests are holding their noses or doing acrostics. with the cellophane music sheet the guest will know that the soloist can see him and he will act accordingly. i have another invention you may want later. this is a time stink bomb that explodes in the foyer as guests walk out on the singer. the odor drives the guests back into the room until the artist concludes his program. let me know if you are in the market for any of these parlor devices.

yours until hitler's body is found . . .

f. allen
180 west 58th

now that mussolini is dead the devil at last has a straightman.

AL DURANTE*

newagen, maine
july 18th
1953

mons. durante—

i am glad to have your report on the cape. i don't know anything about north falmouth but after you get by buzzards bay the cape looks the same to me. hyannis is getting to look like little far rockaway but the rustic sections, with a native here and a cranberry there, look the same.

we have been up here for two weeks with one to go. it is very quiet and simple and if you are satisfied to do nothing this place can cope with your wants. the guests all look like people who eat in howard johnson stands all winter and they all have the same equipment. they drive up in pontiacs and desotos with the wife wearing woolworth sun glasses and the husband carrying a thermos bottle. they order double portions at all meals and sit around on the veranda and talk to each other about the same subjects. "the car is running well," "we stopped at the cutest

* For many years, Durante was Allen's publicity man.

motel just outside of fumfet harbor," "john's stomach has been acting up," "which way is the shuffleboard court?" etc.

the big talk last week concerned some shrunken character who beat everybody at shuffleboard. through the grapevine somebody received a flash that the old gentleman lived in florida. this seems to imply that all old people who live in florida are champions at shuffleboard.

i can't send you one of our programs. all of our activities are planned and one morning we "hike down the lichen trail" and another a.m. we meet at 10 a.m. for the "auto trip to the lily pond." when the sun goes down they show movies in the lobby. this week we had "pennies from heaven." i never knew that bing crosby had been a young boy but this picture proved it.

maine has one advantage. no matter how hot it is all day it does get cool at night especially near the coast towns. i think all of the summer resorts are the same. there are millions of middle-aged people riding around the country with no destination. during the summer months they check in and out of the motels and hotels. during the winter they infest florida. if medical science continues to prolong the life span the country is going to consist of some 160 millions of tourists living on the highways. we will be back aug. 1st. will call you at the office. alton cook is coming up here to stay with doc rockwell in august. this will be a good month to open a lousy movie in new york while alton is away. hope you have your tribe under control. regards—

f. allen—

THOMAS J. SMITH*

may 2, 1942

dear lieutenant . . .

since i haven't seen you, old thud, since the night we broke it up at the harvard club on jan. 9, 1940, i was quite surprised

* An old hand from Young and Rubicam's radio department on wartime duty in the Navy.

to receive your note. you recall the night of january 9th, old pot-holder, early in the evening we assembled at harvard hall to hear professor samuel hazzard cross give his risque talk on "are we unduly apprehensive of the next aftermath?" then we all came down to the bar. old chisholm was awakened, a spot or two all round and then, as i remember, during a chorus of "fair harvard" a roustabout at the end of the bar burped and we adjourned. later, it was learned that the chap who burped was a yale man. a note to this effect was placed on the bulletin board.

your note brought back an attack of first degree nostalgia which i am attempting to subdue as i write. we live in strange times, smith. here i sit in my cretonne smoking jacket, with frogs latticed, my church warden filled with latakia and perique, and as i puff away, clouds of rich smoke screen my giant pekinese who lies snoring at the far end of my desk. a few friends are here, nick kenny, chet laroche, ed grimm and a man who recently had his name in dorothy kilgallen's column. a bottle of champagne stands bubbling on the table. it is the bottle the navy was going to use to rechristen the normandie. the liquor man got tired of waiting around and let me have it cheap. all here is peace and contentment. it is life as we envisioned life at harvard.

you, on the otherhand, find yourself coping with life as it was pictured at annapolis. as you sit each morning mulling over your new world of scuttlebutt, hold and crow's nest you must wonder at the prank the divinity that is shaping your end is up to. when you leave the navy you will be the pride of the young and rubicam outfit as you pace your cubicle with a rolling gate trying to work out some "sell" copy for navy cut plug. i am sure that chet will put you on a naval orange, navy cut plug, mum, the destroyer, or some other account that will enable the agency to take advantage of your experience.

everything in radio is just as lousy as when you sat at our conference board on wednesdays, years ago. this week the police call in the mystery skit which read "calling all cars, etc. if you are short of gas, stop at the nearest service station. you can get five gallons. that is all," has been cut. the reference to mr. cameron, of the ford symphony program that implied mr. c was a political speaker is out. the client sent over a new song. "care for your car for your country" and hired a quartet to sing it. we have four commercials now and this would have made five. one of my writers doesn't know whether he is in the army or the navy. meantime, he is taking a flying course nightly. the other writer has bad eyes. he can't see the punctuation the aviator uses on those i.j. fox sky-writing ads. he was put in four f but has been reclassified and put in one a. without his glasses he won't be able to see the war if he goes to the front. the doctor wants me to go to some clinic this summer to have my essential hypertension lowered and the agency is taking up my option. yes, lieutenant, all is the same in radio.

while executive bombs break about me i sit here with my giant pekinese and a few friends pounding out jokes for oscar levant who will grace our festivities tomorrow night. next week . . . marlene dietrich. i will start worrying about marlene after the show tomorrow night. your routine sounds more hectic than a day with bob welch. portland and i hope that you get the intelligence office assignment. chin up, smith. we can't let the wraith of old chisholm down. if there is anything portland and i can send you, let us know. we kept mailing harmon cigarettes until we lost track of him. we know that you formerly smoked a narghile around the office. if you are still sucking on your water pipe at quonset, let us know, we can send you some fresh water. if you want to pick up some extra curricular nautical knowledge, i used to know the yacht club boys and can get any information you might want. we trust that all goes well, lieutenant. let us hear from you. best wishes.

> ye chieffe

JOHN ROYAL

This letter to a vice-president of the National Broadcasting Company became something of a collector's item around Radio City and Madison Avenue in 1940. It reports on the misbehavior of an eagle named

Mr. Ramshaw while the bird was appearing as a guest star on the Allen show in Studio 8-H at the RCA Building.

march 25th
1940

dear mr. royal . . .

am in receipt of your letter commenting on l'affaire eagle as they are calling it around the young and rubicam office.

i thought i had seen about everything in radio but the eagle had a trick up his feathered colon that was new to me. i thought, for a minute, i was back on the bill with lamont's cockatoos.

an acolyte from your quarters brought news to us, following the nine o'clock broadcast, that the eagle was to be grounded at the midnight show. it was quite obvious that mr. ramshaw, as the eagle is known around the falcon lounge at the audubon society rooms, resented your dictatorial order. when his cue came to fly, and he was still bound to captain knight's wrist, mr. ramshaw, deprived by nature of the organs essential in the voicing of an audible complaint, called upon his bowels to wreck upon us his reaction to your martinet ban.

toscanini, your house man, has foistered some movements on studio audiences in 8 h, the bulova company has praised its movement over your network but when radio city is being torn down to make way for another mcguiness restaurant, in years to come, the one movement that will be recalled by the older radio fans will be the eagle's movement on wednesday last. if you have never seen a ghost's beret you might have viewed one on mr. rockefeller's carpet during our sterling performance.

i know you await with trepidation the announcement that i am going to interview sabu with his elephant some week.

yours for a wet broom in 8 h on wednesday nights.

fred allen

2.

THE EARLY DAYS

SIDNEY L. KAYE

sidney l. kaye—

thanx a lot for the pen portrait of the boston public library.

as you know i worked in the library for several years. my salary was 20 cents per hour. for three hours each night i received 60 cents. when work was over i was hungry. an egg sandwich and a piece of pie cost 10 cents. another nickel went for carfare home. on the remainder i started to build my fortune. you can appreciate why this wealth is nonexistent today.

　　　　　　　　　　sincerely—

　　　　　　　　　　　　　　　F.A.

SAMMY TISHMAN

When Allen was touring the Midwest vaudeville theaters for eight months in 1920 and 1921, he wrote weekly reports on the theaters and audiences to Sammy Tishman, one of the tour's booking agents in Chicago. Here are his communiques from Centralia, Illinois, and Mason City, Iowa.

　　　　　　　　　　　　　Centralia, Ill.
　　　　　　　　　　　　　Dec. 25 / 20

Dear Sammie,

Your glad tidings received here regarding "Girls Will Be Girls" just in time to spoil my Xmas. You must have had a fine tooth comb to find that act. It should be called "The Omelet" as that's what a bunch of bad eggs put together makes. I expect to get castrated before going to Davenport so they can't worry me any.

You tell Mr. Mayer that the next agent I get must be lame, so he can't get far away from the Office. Trying to find my Director of Amusements in daylight is like looking for a Virgin in the Follies chorus.

I feel sorry for both you boys in your chosen line of endeavor. You could just as easily have become actors and profit by experience gained through travel. Travel certainly broadens one, and too much of it out here will leave you flat.

Below you will find a synopsis of Centralia. The man who named the theatre, the Grand, certainly had a sense of humor, but must have left here or died without children as the word is obsolete now.

The Theatre

A dandy loving cup. No running water and you wash up with one of those battery outfits (pitcher & catcher). The only two toilets backstage are in the dressing rooms. Any act you like that's booked here, advise them to get rooms 1 or 4 unless they would rather get constipated and dress in rooms 2 and three.

The Orchestra

Five Symphony Cast-offs. They play like Sam Du Fries writes up an act that doesn't advertise in the Chicago Vaudeville.

The Stage Manager

A merry cuss. Takes baggage checks at the depot and the abuse at the theatre. He wouldn't wear a union suit if he was a relative of Gompers. He lets down the asbestos after each act. I asked him why and he said "so that people will have a chance to stretch out and look around between the vaudevilles."

The Audience

You'd have to dig a hole & stand in it to look any of them in the face. They're so low that a dwarf takes tickets to make them feel at home. They look like a thousand Jimmy Barrys and the mgr. puts barbed wire in the lobby to keep them from crawling

into the place. To make sure they get the jokes etc., the picture
changes every day so the people see the acts three times before
you leave, like the Leader in Ottawa.

The Manager

A happy rascal. There are moths in his "street suit" old
enough to vote. His idea of a joke is to see a runaway horse step
on a little baby, or to go home Saturday night and forget to pay the
ushers. He said he wouldn't play Gautiers Bricklayers as he is an
Elk & wouldn't have anything to do with the Masons. He's so nar-
row minded if he fell on a pin point it would stick in both of his
eyes & actually thinks that the show "The Bat" was written by
Babe Ruth. He encouraged the audience to wear padded mittens
so they could sit down and enjoy the show.

Epilogue

You can readily see what you are missing by agenting for a
livelihood.

Again thanking you for putting me on the bill with "The
Pest House," I am

> Yours till Santa Claus
> is in N.V.A.

Fred Allen

Sponsored
 and Abused
 by Mr. A. F. Mayer

The Foster Hotel Company
Mason City, Iowa. Feb 3/21

Friend Sammie,

Am enclosing further proof of my instantaneous success in
Cedar Rapids.

This date is one place where McCarthys Animals couldn't
open.

The audience laughs in the wrong places, the drug store, pool rooms, etc. anywhere but the theatre, by the way it looks.

These jumps will keep me up in show business and I left Cedar Rapids 3:45 Sun & arrived here at 6:15 a.m. today. I guess Rip Van Winkle must have played a season out here & took the 20 yrs. sleep to get used to the mattress.

F.A.

FITZHUGH KNOX, JR.

june
4th
1954

fitzhugh knox, jr.

thank you for the apollo theatre program.

i am the same fred allen. the show that played chicago at the apollo was the passing show of 1922 which had opened at the winter garden in new york the previous year.

if you looked among the "young women of the ensemble" you would have found portland's name. we met in that show and later married. we are still going along after twenty-six years.

looking through the cast i found that many of the cast have gone. willie howard died a few years back. his wife emily miles and many others.

years are all right if you haven't lived through too many of them. i never look back. i just keep breathing. that is the secret of survival and my motto—just keep breathing.

sincerely—

Fred Allen

HERB JENNINGS

October 10
1929

Dear Mr. Jennings: Many thanks for your kindness in making me a member of Euclid Kennel Club. You will go to your grave never knowing how I appreciate this favor.

Had I known, in time, that your son intended joining the Navy, I could have saved you a little something on his equipment. I have a pair of sailor trousers, made to order at Norfolk, Va., which you could have bought very reasonable, Sir. I know that you do not feel that the boy is lost to the Jennings' board for long. It is only a matter of time when Warner Brothers will merge with the Navy, to make a picture for Jolson, and then if your son is qualified he will no doubt appear in Akron as the District Supervisor. You will then be subject to his beck, not Martin, and call. Your box-office will open with Reveille and close with Taps which I'll wager you haven't heard properly done since the Six American Dancer split.

All goes famous with the Little Sho. Business is fine and pending some Nation Wide disaster we hope to be here well into the Winter. I hope so as I have grown corpulent and am slow a mind. I could never rally my faculties to cope with the strong competition now existing in Vaudeville. When one attains my age it is but a step to the grave and why pay excess on my arteries going around the country, when I can merely remain here and disintegrate.

Tom Berry should be back from his vacation this week. Allen Glenn is now associated with the Exhibitors Reliance Corp. Whatever that may be and Asa is an unknown quantity in these parts. Hoping this finds you the same, in your native haunts and with sincere sympathy for Mrs. Jennings and those patient nippers who will soon to able to kick the Hell out of you, I am

Your
Well-Well Wisher,

Mr. Allen

VAL EICHEN

feb. 7th.
1930

Dear Trapper.

Your note came as a great surprise, Sir. I consider it quite a compliment to think that you finally found time to set aside your pelts, puppies and syphons and take up the quill in my behalf. I don't know whether a dog bite, the beer running bad, or a casual glance at the Pantages testimony brought me to your mind but your letter was quite welcome.

I have been busier than Al Gamble in Chalk Factory which accounts for this delayed answer but you know how it is in the "show game," Mr. Eichen.—an actor is "here today and here to-morrow" the way conditions are at present. I have adopted a slogan "Good to the last Buck" and have loaned so much money that Simpson won't even speak to me. I have heard more confessions than a three-eared priest in Chicago and after fifteen years of trying to get in a spot to save some money, I find that it cannot be done. A guy is a sucker to try and become successful for with each step you climb you will find that stronger cheese has been rubbed, by Fate, on your heels so that with each bit of progress a new grade of mouse is found whenever you turn around.

The critic you mentioned Sir, noting an error in your letter, was not in Calgary—it was Regina. I still remember the heading of the column. ONE BAD ACT DOES NOT SPOIL A GOOD SHOW. I still have it at home against the time when I shall go to Regina with my pet dog who will only urinate on statues of Lord Nelson. I shall take my dog and establish headquarters in Regina to be avenged for the bucolic sarcasm and near-wit of that particular lout.

You also mention El Paso. I shall always regret that you were not present on the day that Justice was aborted in that city, Sir. Think of it. Mr. Allen on the defense—sitting alone on the stand

—The plaintiffs—Florence Lorraine et al—smoking in the Judge's private office—My witnesses on the street—allowed in one at a time to testify. And what witnesses—Lucy Bruch—Asaki Japs and McGrath and Deeds. Then my lawyer, secured from the Elks by Mr. McGrath, he having a guilty conscience knowing that he had caused all of the trouble. The Danbury Hatters Case was nothing compared to Allen vs Texas, Sir. The corridors of the court-house still ring with the dialects of my character witnesses and I hope that the presiding Justice has slept with starch in his pillowcases ever since.

I guess that our management learned of your intention to visit the Dog Show this month and fearing that you would bring your "entries" around the theatre, said management bustled the show out of town. We are here this week and open in Boston, next Monday, at the Wilbur Theatre, for four weeks—attendance permitting. There was no reason for us to leave so soon as we made money for forty straight weeks but the man who owns the show was delivered on a kilt by an unskilled mid-wife and he takes no chances even if he is running the raffle.

Sorry that I shan't be able to accept your invitation to visit your Summer Home . . . "Vitaphone by the Sound" in the immediate future but I have you in mind when the show closes. The Mrs. and I may move in bag and banjo if things get too tough. I certainly envy you, Sir, for, show business is a bottomless pit and if you are fortunate you can save plenty with a few good years but the percentage of those able to do so is so small that it seems like a futile struggle for the majority. Thanks for your letter it is such a relief to receive one in which the writer doesn't want anything from "three minutes talk" to "money for the delivery—wife in the polyclinic, etc." Trust that your experience with obesity will prove successful. Best 4 now and hope that your k9s will bring home more depressed ribbons from the show.

                                                            Fred Allen

INSURANCE COMPLAINT

June 18, 1932.

State of New York Insurance Department
Office of the Special Deputy Superintendent
Liquidation of the Southern Surety Company of New York
111 John Street, New York City.

Dear Sir:

The soullessness of corporations is something to stun you. I am myself a victim; and instead of being a man of wealth and honor to the community, I am now a relic of humanity just from the hands of a surgeon who made an honest effort to restore me to the form in which I grew while reaching manhood's estate.

Let me review my case. I carry an accident insurance policy in the . . . Indemnity Company, by terms of which the company agreed to pay me $25 a week during such time as I was prevented from working because of an accident.

I went around last Sunday morning to a new house that is being built for me. I climbed the stairs, or rather the ladder that is there where the stairs will be when the house is finished, and on the top floor I found a pile of bricks which were not needed there. Feeling industrious, I decided to remove the bricks. In the elevator shaft there was a rope and a pulley, and on one end of the rope was a barrel. I pulled the barrel up to the top, after walking down the ladder, and then fastened the rope firmly at the bottom of the shaft. Then I climbed the ladder again and filled the barrel with bricks. Down the ladder I climbed again, five floors, mind you, and untied the rope to let the barrel down. The barrel was heavier than I was and before I had time to study over the proposition, I was going up the shaft with my speed increasing at every floor. I thought of letting go of the rope, but before I had decided to do so I was so high that it seemed more dangerous to let go than hold on, so I held on.

Half way up the elevator shaft I met the barrel of bricks coming down. The encounter was brief and spirited. I got the worst of it but continued on my way toward the roof—that is, most of me went on, but much of my epidermis clung to the barrel and returned to earth. Then I struck the roof the same time the barrel struck the cellar. The shock knocked the breath out of me and the bottom out of the barrel. Then I was heavier than the empty barrel, and I started down while the barrel started up. We went and met in the middle of our journey, and the barrel uppercut me, pounded my solar plexis, barked my shins, bruised my body and skinned my face. When we became untangled, I resumed my downward journey and the barrel went higher. I was soon at the bottom. I stopped so suddenly that I lost my presence of mind and let go of the rope. This released the barrel which was at the top of the elevator shaft and it fell five floors and landed squarely on top of me, and it landed hard too.

Now, here is where the heartlessness of the . . . Indemnity Company comes in. I sustained five accidents in two minutes. One on my way up the shaft, when I met the barrel of bricks, the second when I met the roof, the third when I was descending and I met the empty barrel, the fourth when I struck the barrel, and the fifth when the barrel struck me. But the insurance man said that it was one accident not five and instead of receiving payment for injuries at the rate of five times $25.00, I only get one $25 payment. I, therefore, enclose my policy and ask that you cancel the same as I made up my mind that henceforth I am not to be skinned by either barrel or/and any insurance company.

Yours sincerely and regretfully,

Fred Allen

MARK LEDDY

Leddy was Allen's agent during his vaudeville days.

MATTHEW STIFT

odorless cleaning of

PRIVY VAULTS and CATCH BASINS

chemical toilets and septic tanks

Office: 1700–1 Burnham Building

160 N. La Salle Street

CHICAGO, ILL.*

Old Orchard Beach
Maine
Saturday, July 10
1931

Dear Mark,

This is housecleaning day and since there is only one broom in the house I have to wait until Mrs. A purges the room of their elusive dust particles whereupon I take the broom and retire to the backyard and give the mats a half-hearted treatment. We had our choice, renting this place, we could have had two brooms and no fly-swatter or one broom and the swatter. I thought it would be rather cumbersome rushing after insects and mosquitoes with a broom and consequently took the single broom combination. It has wrought havoc with my Saturday routine but today I am installing a period for letters which will permit cleaning up the correspondence along with the house.

Libby Holman certainly managed to keep my face before the public during the off season with those headlines about her husband shooting himself—now if Webb will only run amok, around the first of August, and brain his Mother with a sachet bag I can

---

* On a vaudeville tour, Allen acquired a quantity of stationery bearing this business letterhead, which he used for a few years.

perhaps remain in the limelight until such a time as I can get back to New York.*

I don't know whether Jack Haley is my agent or not. He wired me that Louis Shurr had a proposition for me with Billy Rose. I don't know whether Louis didn't have money enough to send a telegram or if it is a new system and actors are trying to get part of the commission through advising you before the agent can find out the actor's whereabouts. Since I have my aunts coming here for vacations, I can't get back to New York until Labor Day and naturally must forego such splendid opportunities as afforded by Messrs. Leslie and Rose.

There is quite a bit of local action rampant here. Professor T. H. Flowers, of Boston, presented Daredevil Steele doing his famous parachute jumps here for three performances last week. I didn't manage to get a look at the Professor himself but the Daredevil looked anything but the type. The Board of Trade financed the exhibit and it caused plenty of excitement. Immediately, upon arrival, Prof. Flower's crew tore up the middle of the main street. This confused the parking problem but it seems that it was imperative that a large fire be built, in the center of the town, to inflate the Daredevil's balloon. It was an interesting sight to watch half of the inhabitants holding the giant bag for many minutes until sufficient hot air had been formed to permit the balloon to rise. It helped out the unemployment problem quite a bit. Once the inflation was climaxed, Daredevil Steele rushed around to his back and looked the crowd in it's collective face. This completed he retired to the confines of what was heralded to be a cannon but which upon inspection proved to be nothing but a section of large stove pipe. Without a word of warning the cannon was quickly attached to the bag and quicker than you could say "Elliot and Mullen" the whole contraption was sailing over Kane's drug store and out to sea.

When the balloon reached the advertised height of 3000 feet a cannon was fired altogether too close for the convenience of the crowd, which shrieked and yelled, but this warning was part of

* Miss Holman and Webb were appearing that year with Allen in *Three's a Crowd.*

the show and served as a signal for the Daredevil. No sooner had the report faded into insignificance acoustically than an immense puff of smoke emerged from the flying cannon quickly followed by a smaller explosion and the Daredevil, cannon and balloon descended to the water in the order named. The direction of the gale decided Daredevil's wardrobe. When it blew towards the sea he appeared clad in bathing suit, rubber shoes and parachute. When the gusts were landwards he made a much nattier appearance in white flannels, sport shirt and shoes. The only hitch in the entire proceeding had to do with the crowd reaction.

The authorities were hoping that the crowd would remain here, after the demonstration, and spend their monies at the shrines of the various concessionaires. But the Board of Trade reckoned without knowledge of the working of the moronic mind. No sooner had the parachute opened and the apparent direction of the landing ascertained than the entire throng rushed to the Fords and sped off in the direction of the Daredevil. The only one to profit through the whole business was Prof. Flowers and since his cannon sunk on Sunday, after the performance, it is possible that he only broke even on the venture.

A fan writes me from Providence saying that Mr. Savoy is still using several bon mots formerly my property. I have received an assortment of complaints regarding his routine but I haven't the time, or inclination, to bother with him.

I am sorry that I can't take the Palisades offer through your Mr. Fauer. A friend of mine, a Mr. Fletcher, who is quite a favorite at the park has already spoken to the management about me. I might be there next season the way things look. Louise Groody is billed at the Scollay Sq. next week so if you see Al and Belle Dow give them my regards also Sherman of Philadelphia.

Nothing else exciting here except on account of the increased postal rates, the Biddeford Light and Power Company has hired a marathon runner to deliver its gas bills. The department stores will soon be using a discus thrower to hurl packages to out-of-town mail order customers.

Yours—

F.

Old Orchard Beach
Maine
July 15, 1931

Dear Mark,

It is with a sense of pleasure that I again find the name of
Julius Klein, world famous cymbalon player, before me. It is only
you, the fortunate idle rich, who are able to bask in the presence
of Mr. Klein and his cymbalon at one of your Rye Beach soirees.
We, the less fortunate, have to recall Mr. Klein through his
brilliant and fleeting performance as a musical stooge for Miss
Swanson in "Tonight or Never" and through his sterling rendition
of the manhole cover obligato in Caprice Eduardo Smith.

Mr. Klein has been a student of the manhole cover since his
early days when he was on his pratt. Feeling a draught while
sitting in the middle of the main street in Carbondale, Pa., the
eminent Klein sought the cause and learned that the manhole
cover had an aperture in the center. "A natural native instrument,
as yet undiscovered" mused Mr. Klein as he removed the cover
from the manhole. Striking the cover with his mallet he was over-
joyed to notice a vibrant tone, new to his ears, and foreign to the
musical sense of an embryonic cymbalon player. Borrowing a red
lantern to leave as a flickering guard over the hole in the street,
Mr. Klein hurried away to his studio with his prize.

The rest is history Mr. Leddy. Mr. Klein played the sewer-
top from Coast to Coast under the name of the DePace ensemble and when he foresaw the coming economic depression and
acknowledging his duty as a public citizen prior to his innate
feelings as an artist, he duly presented the manhole cover to
Mayor Walker in an effort to curb the City's expense.

Shorn of his instrument, his first love, Mr. Klein turned to the
cymbalon for consolation and it is indeed gratifying, Mr. Leddy,
to find that he has made such rapid strides with his instrument
intact. The Six Musical Spillers could learn much from Mr. Klein
not to mention the Four Banta Brothers and the Three White

Kuhns but it is not our place to eulogize a man who has made good at a Bath and Tennis Club Dinner Dance.

If the Shuberts have controlling interest in the new Webb show, I would like to be around when Clifton demands silk drapes for the girls and Mother Simmons, the Joan of Arc of the store-house, arrives with cretonne for the chorus. That should make a classy layout with Webb, Butterworth and Patsy Kelly.

Nothing else exciting except that Charlie Althoff went through here the other day all made up. He said that he was on his way to Washington to ask for Farm Relief. Mrs. Allen sends her regards.

F.A.

Chicago
Dec. 10
1931

Dear Mark,

Don't be too promiscuous with those $125 offers. If you knew what has been going on with this show, "Three's A Crowd," with Clifton Webb and Libby Holman, you wouldn't be surprised if I took the first open spot you can find in vaudeville. We have been on a percentage arrangement, to keep the show going, and business has been terrible everywhere. Last week, we waived our salaries instead of laying off and, when all of the bills were paid, my bit was around two hundred and eighty dollars. Out of this I have to pay Portland, commission, valet, laundry, etc., so you can see that I was a fool to split with Yorke and leave vaude-ville.

Yorke, by the way, is doing fine and sent me an alarm clock for xmas. Of course, he hasn't paid any royalty on my act for three years but it is nice of him to wipe out all obligations in one generous sweep of his spending hand. He's alright, though, and just because you don't think that Lane, Drohan, and the other acts in my stable can live up to the material is no reason why you shouldn't remember Harry Dobson at this festive season of the year.

We opened very big here Sunday night and with the help of God—and some business—we should get a few weeks out of it. We had better show a profit soon or I know that Mr. Gordon will put the show "Among His Souvenirs." We have lost every week, since opening, and with the assorted salaries, and Mr. Webb astride his lavender high horse, there is no telling our end.

Rumor has it that Ted Healy has lost his monkey and that his ex-partner, Joe Mendi, is living at the Stanley. This is really funny. The monkey has a room there and wakes up in the morning and yells like Hell but the guests all owe so much back rent that no one can complain to the management.

Hope your new apartment comes up to expectations and that things are humming in that little Bee Hive, which I so laughingly call your Office.

Portland and I hope that you and Mrs. Leddy will enjoy whatever New York is using for a Merry Xmas. If you want a carol to sing around the Office—how about—"There is a Happy Land Fauer, Fauer Away?"

Best for now—

F. Allen

Erlanger Theatre, Chicago.
  Indefinitely?

FORTY EAST OAK APARTMENTS
Forty East Oak Street
Chicago

Feb. 6, 1932

Dear Mark,

If I ever get time, I'll be glad to try to find new material for some of your clients. Eddie Stanley asked me about the Disappointments act, I used with Portland. I don't want to sell that as I may want to use it in a hurry in the event that the show closes.

Gordon and the Erlanger people, I think I told you, walked out on the show. They will not be responsible for further losses. We are running it ourselves and have booked St. Louis and Kansas City and if it isn't too disastrous we may continue to the Coast. Webb wants to go there to autograph the scenery and leave it in Joan Crawford's backyard, I guess. Louis Lipstone saw the show last night and made us an offer to condense it, if we close, and play the picture theaters around here. Girl Crazy, which they say is awful, has been packing them in at the picture houses and our show would make a much better offering for them.

The whole thing is so mixed up I don't know where I am but I know that I'm not in Torrington. I shall keep you advised though and in the event that everything falls apart I may be able to take a couple of your embryonic stars on approval.

Holtz, they say, is so conceited that he can't play Jersey City —they can't get his head through the Holland Tunnel. All those birds make me laugh with the money they ask and the mythical value they place on their ability.

This is a fine town. The Union of Drivers of Funeral Cars has decreed that no private car can get in the line on the way to the grave. Yesterday they walked out on a funeral and left the hearse and other vehicles standing in the street. If this keeps up the first one to open a parking space for bodies will clean up.

F.A.

Old Orchard Beach
Maine
June 18, 1932

Dear Mark,

Since I am continually doing the wrong thing at the proper moment, you will not be amazed to learn that I have eloped to the above address with Mrs. Allen. It wasn't really an elopement. You never can tell when a stooge will pop up and sure enough, after closing in St. Louis and returning to Boston and then here, I turned around and there she was and here she still is.

The season doesn't open here until July fourth. I wondered why and I figured that whoever set the opening dates for beaches and resorts had a Hell of a nerve. Why should one person say that hotels shall not open, ferris wheels shall not start, hot dogs shall not be taken out of their kennels and bath-houses not open until a given date. Well, we have been here nearly two weeks and I now know why the season opens on July fourth.

It has been so cold that I have sprouted a light coat of fur something like you might expect to find on a nance bear. The only road stand doing any business is a place selling barbarcued blubber. Today is the coldest yet but I sort of suspected it when a man rang the bell at eleven last night and put a cake of ice on the front steps. As he stumbled down the road I hollered "Hey, what's the idea of leaving ice at this time of night." "Ice, Hell" he flung back, "That's the dew for your flowers in the morning." People who venture into the water are using their goose pimples for water wings and as they pass the house shivering, from the after effects of the swim, the pimples make them appear to be people standing in a cluster of cantaloupes.

Mrs. Allen, with an Alice Foots MacDougall complex, is continually in front of a broken down oil stove in the kitchen. My stomach has turned into sort of a clinic and I don't know how much longer my tapeworm will stand for the cuisine.

I have taken the place until the last of August and since it can't get any worse I think that we shall enjoy it once we are able to swim and shed our heavy nether-garments. It is quite healthy here and the exercise I get going to the front door to tell Real Silk salesmen that I'm from the South and wear nothing but cotton and the brisk run to the back to tell the oil man that we have already made arrangements, is beginning to strengthen my legs and also help my wind.

After the Publix Tour, I was all in, what with my aunt in the hospital and Portland having a cyst. I figured that if I kept working the Government would take all of the money with the Income Tax next fall and if I didn't work I would have nothing just the same. With this economic bit of strategy in mind I decided to come up here and read and possibly try to write two or three scenes in the event that the Irving Trust puts out any shows in the Fall.

Thanx for calling me about Mr. Rolfe's radio program. Ordinarily, I would have been glad to talk with him about it but, after last season, with twenty-eight weeks work and salary paid for only eight weeks I thought it better to default for the present.

The only excitement we have had is a wire that arrived early this morning. It was from home where Richy Craig had wired to find my address. My aunt all agog phoned my brother who sent a wire to me at 7:30 this morning. You see agents aren't the only ones who lose sleep over actors. In cases of this sort actors suffer as well and haven't even the chance to get the subsequent ten percent.

I shall be back in New York around September first. I have nothing definite. Batchelor has several things on the fire but so have the frankfurt vendors down here which means nothing. The Little Church is the only thing around the corner in New York. Prosperity has been deported. Hope that all goes well with you Sir. Mrs. Allen wants to be remembered which is sort of silly after you have seen her on the stage. Best for now—

F.A.

Old Orchard Beach
Maine
Aug. 2, 1932

Dear Mark,

I am a little behind with the outgoing mail thanks to several of my relatives mistaking my place for a Tourist Camp. They have been running in and out of here using my dental floss, after each meal, and neglecting to contribute to the community chest. It appears that I shall have to leave here shortly lest I host myself into financial difficulties. We have run the gamut of my family and are now down to my wife's two sisters. If we get any bows, on our work for the season, they will be taken when the two closing guests check out.

You will be upset to learn that the piano player with Ralph Armstrong's Arcadians, that drug store band, was taken ill the other day and the other boys couldn't play with any other pianist. None of them read music and it seems that certain daring flies have been stealing past the screen door, in the drug store, to light on the music and hear themselves played after which they give vent to a sly insect chuckle and leave with the next outgoing banana split customer. A new band was pressed into service for one night lead by a nondescript musician who played a hot nail-file.

I was going to speak to the owner about your second edition of the Norman Thomas quartet but didn't think that you would take your commission in aspirin.

Your graphic description of conditions around New York would lead one to believe that you were looking into the Holland Tunnel at midnight wearing Jack Potsdam's glasses. Things couldn't be that lousy in a fine comb factory and I shall try to prove that you, instead of gilding the lily, have merely charcoaled the Powell.

With the Coast Time out of the RKO Time, it is a wonder that some of the Horace Greeley ancestors don't rise up and revise his slogan. They still could use the "Go West—young man" part of it and put a P.S. saying "but if you do, see Fanchon and Marco." As Abe Thalheimer used to say "A bird in the hand made Lucille and Cockie."

I see that DeCalion is playing the Met in Boston this week. I guess the Publix people had to book him to see if there is anyone sitting in the balconies around the circuit. He can check up on the upstairs business as he goes over the top of the ladder just before his finish. Haley finished his Brooklyn week and is making another picture for Warner. He signed for twelve shorts, I think, after the first baseball short turned out so well for the first. As the author, my bit was five hundred, and he wanted me to do some others but when Murray Roth left over there, my only intimate acquaintance with the plant ceased apparently for all time.

Have managed to finish two sketches so far and have hopes of getting three, or four, more done before we leave here. They won't be perfect but the ideas at least will be on paper and if they look half-way decent they can be developed at rehearsals. I have some ideas I think are funny but not having anything definite it is difficult to work them out.

The only difference between Milton Berle and Ted Healy is that Berle reminds you of someone when he bows whereas Healy seldom bows. Wynn is billed at the Shubert, in Boston, opening Labor Day and I hope that means that Mr. Powell's commission will start for a long season. With the Fire Chief and radio publicity Wynn should pick up a lot of additional business especially as he starts out West.

We leave here the 28th and I shall report to you.

F.A.

Old Orchard Beach
Maine
August 26, 1932

Dear Mark,

After reading the propaganda for the Keewaydin Camps, I feel that my Summer has been wasted and that I really haven't lived. It must be great to wake up, after a night in the open, to find crickets in your pockets and lake trout in your underwear. Those guys get so far into the woods that they think a Davey Tree Surgeon is a Man About Town and that a hermit should know all of the latest dirty stories.

We are leaving here, this coming Sunday, and I expect to be in New York late next week. I haven't definitely decided what I shall do. Walter Batchelor has written me about several things but I haven't done anything definite as yet. I haven't heard from Walter this week so far. He has Geva, in the Webb Show, and was to go to Philadelphia for the opening Monday night. Naturally, I haven't heard how it opened but since Dietz has been planning the show, and working on it, since last season there is every reason to believe that it will be a hit. I hope so for a couple of hits will put some life in the theatres before ivy starts growing over the doors.

I have written out a couple of scenes and have several ideas for others which I hope to do within the next week or so. I have myself in mind for most of the material but you never can tell about scenes. What we think is funny doesn't mean a thing when the nervous producer takes a look at the script.

When Leslie's show was in Chicago, I heard that the music was excellent and that if the comedy element was bolstered up it should have a good chance. I have been away from your City for the past season, with the exception of the Paramount week, and hardly know where I stand. Working with fellows like Hassard Short and Howard Dietz is one thing and trying to concoct something that would appeal to White, Carroll or Leslie is another.

You say that talent is scarce but I think that material is the hardest ingredient to find. The "little show" had no outstanding names, at the time it was produced, and it probably made more money than any of the recent musical shows. That happened because no one knew what it was all about with the result that different things were attempted. The average so-called "Broadway" producer thinks that he has one finger on the pulse of the theatregoer and that he alone knows what material should be used.

After a couple of months up here I feel sort of out of touch with current matters. It is only imagination, I know, and when I return to find that Flippen's nails are still eclipsed and that Buddy Doyle is giving an audition for radio it is only then that I shall know that all is normal and my confidence will return. I guess if a person remained here long enough he would be afraid to come back but when I see Minnevitch billed at the State I know that all is well.

The Orpheum, in Boston, is featuring "Big Name" vaudeville so I guess that Vic Morris's eyes were getting bad and he wanted to be able to see who was billed outside of the theatre. With three houses playing the same policy perhaps the Loew house started to feel the competition. With Wheeler and Woolsey pictures playing the RKO theatres, though, there is no real reason why Loew should strengthen the bills.

I shall be home part of next week but will stop in to see you when I get back Friday, or early the following week. If worst comes to Sablotsky though, we can put a blonde wig on Ethel and book her up here in these towns, as Jean Harlow. The pictures are always out of focus and anyone can make a personal appearance using any name you see fit. Even the managers can't tell what Garbo looks like.

F.A.

Old Orchard Beach
Maine
Thursday
July 15, 1933

Dear Mr. Leddy . . .

The nearest I have come to show business, during the past few weeks, is seeing a copy of Billboard sticking out of the pocket of a stooge who passed through here looking for his comedian.

I hope that you have arranged to break that jump for Deltorelli Glissandos. I would hate to think of the boys missing the Century of Progress through any laxity on your part. How can you tell when a clown isn't clowning these days? Nine times out of ten, I guess would be the answer on one of your books.

There have been a couple of attractions here lately that would lead me to believe that vaudeville isn't coming back. If it is going anyplace it is in the wrong direction. Hank Penny and His Cronies. I knew the minute I saw the act that it must be a radio attraction. And even in radio I imagine they are only coming in on the crystal sets. The comedian had no teeth and he was as funny as a letter from the Income Tax Dept. Hank was the life of the party and the bags in the knees of his overalls would have made a dandy set of brassierres for Margaret Padula.

I was forced to miss an exhibition of legerdemain given by a Truxton Holmes. He was at the New Theatre last Saturday evening. His banners showed a set of mangey pigeons escaping from a sleeve that looked like one of Sam Curtis's pants legs. I wanted to report on this act for you but Walter Batchelor was here with Gilda Gray, playing at a dance place, and I couldn't get away to see Truxton. One of the major attractions I have been able to find, though, I came across, quite by accident, last Sunday. I went down to a little place called Camp Ellis. It is one of those towns that look like the first act set in any of Eugene O'Neill's plays. There is nothing there but a few fishermen and plenty of bait. The population, exclusive of worms and clams, is about forty. In the Winter this total shrinks to a weathervane and a lamplighter. But, set up in the center of this bleak looking center was a tent advertising the appearance of a ventriloquist. He had a lot of kitchen chairs in the tent and was ogling little boys, from the flap, trying to get them to give up their candy money to see his extravaganza.

I don't know how he did on the day. I looked into the tent and he had several dummies that looked as though they could have told of Alf Ripon's boyhood days had they been encouraged. The vent didn't like my looks and he hastily closed the tent crevice until such a time as I went away.

It looks as though Bangor had taken out vaudeville. We haven't seen a road show since my last letter. Our vacation is cut short and we are returning to New York next week. I open August 4th on the Tom Howard program for a short series. If everything is satisfactory and the company decided to continue with radio there is a strong possibility that we shall run into the Winter with it. Jokes permitting, of course.

There aren't many jokes left to tell and most of the comedy programs are pretty bad, as usual, but I can't be any worse than most of the others so I may as well see if I can get Mr. Atwell and the rest of the sterling company and again make the air unfit for the better class of bird. Some of the loud speakers were throwing up before the Baron got off and I know that I couldn't write programs as bad as his . . . on purpose.

If you haven't left for the Fair, with the Musical Clowns, I may see you next week. Best for now . . .

mr. a

JAMES R. NAULTY

April 15
1933

Dear Jimmie,

I am staggering around here up to my birthmark in joke books, fan-mail, and bills and doubt if I shall ever see the carefree days, we once knew, again. I took the radio thing to make expenses on Sunday nights, hoping to get a Broadway show meantime. The way it has turned out, there is no time for anything but the broadcast and I have lost two shows on account of becoming a radio star.

Portland and I have about six more weeks to go and then I don't know what will happen. All of the other comedians have a budget for gag writers, and staffs of men to help write the broadcasts, but, this is one of those Morris Green Hours and I have been doing everything alone. How long I can last, is a mystery up to now, but I figure the first bad program will see the two of us flying up Madison Avenue with the Linit people right behind us.

Things are pretty quiet around. The papers are full of news about the City's financial troubles and still Tammany won't agree to cut the budget or the salaries of the big office holders. I don't know how it will come out but the bankers have refused to lend the City any money until certain things are remedied so it looks as though Al Jones might be Mayor any day. He could put some blue lights on the City Hall and after all of those Follies he should know something about Greenwich Village which would help a little.

We are glad that you and Dolly like the Sunday night affairs and I hope that I can keep them good so that I can last until something else turns up. I used to be able to put an act together, when things were bad, but now there isn't enough vaudeville to tire out a trained pigeon act flying from town to town.

Hope that your school is thriving and I wish that I could sneak away to Marion or someplace until the depression makes a farewell appearance. Port wants to be remembered to Dolly and we both hope that the goose is off of the ground even though it isn't hanging high.

Thanx for your letter and best for now—

F

RED PEARSON*

Aug. 20, 1933

Dear Red . . .

Your letter arrived Monday. I had been wondering if you had gone Hollywood. I didn't know whether, or not, you had your name on the back of a chair or I thought that perhaps they had named a sandwich after you. A lot of guys who had sandwiches named after them a couple of years ago wish they could get one to autograph with their teeth the way things are. There are a lot of Blue Eagles in windows but there are more blue pusses on 47th St. than I have ever seen before.

It doesn't look as though Gertie Marcus signed the code for she is permitting lounging to run overtime outside of the Tavern there. I haven't been on the street since you left. I used to go to get a haircut at the Somerset but I found an unemployed barber who had a pair of scissors that Wynn used for cutting out jokes and I figured I might as well get a comedy haircut independently. If you want any hot horse news, or any message sent out along the street I'll be glad to go down and step over Shorty some afternoon to deliver any tidings. Let me know. God forbid!

Am glad that you have had a chance to put the eagle eye on the lay-out there. I think if you can keep from saying anything until you see a spot that you will end up living in a Spanish Castle there with Ted Healy. It isn't hard to take inventory of

* A comedy writer who sometimes contributed jokes to Allen.

most of the gag-men around and then when you see what the best ones are doing you can act accordingly. It only takes a couple of good connections to keep a butler in your joint and I hope everything will come out okay. Everyone around here says that Ted is a big hit in some pictures that will be released soon. I hope he is for the good of everyone concerned.

I imagine that Eddie probably knows more about jokes than most of those guys who have nothing on their minds but a beret but naturally if they're going to keep those soft jobs they've got to keep anyone with the least bit of intelligence in the closet. I don't know what the situation is but he should be worth a lot of money to any firm if he is behaving himself.

Lahr got back this week, I talked to Buddy on the phone but I haven't seen him yet. Harry isn't with Bert now. I don't know what happened but I think Harry wanted to work under the code and he asked for some more dough or something that split up that Old Gang of Yours. I have just listened to Bert do the dentist scene . . . "roots go down to there" and the other choice bulls and blunders which we know so well. He'll out Baron the Baron when he gets going good on his own program again.

I will be waiting for those two super-super features with the Chief and the Baron. I can imagine what they will be like. The Baron starts back on the air next week, I think. Well, the more the merrier. A lot of new ones are starting but it's always the same—everyone who starts doesn't finish. I had a nice letter from the agency this week saying they are well pleased with the programs so far and that they're going to start checking around the country and if everything is okay it looks as though we may continue for another 13. I hope so as I haven't heard about any shows except that circus that plays the Stanley occasionally and I wouldn't last through an audition for that.

If you find any budgets or if Eddie wants to do any business later you can let me know. I've been lucky so far. I haven't had to go to the joke books at all. I've been doing Portland's lines out of the skull and the other stuff I've been slapping together from the newspapers and odd things that come up. I am going to try and keep away from those Lahr specials as long as I can but at least I've got them all if it gets tough. Buddy said that he would send me down some clippings later on but I know he'll be busy until Bert gets the new show going. I think Bert has hired the author of Good-Bye Again . . . a fellow named Haight . . . I don't think that Good-Bye Again will mean anything at the end of thirteen weeks but I guess everything will come okay.

I can't think of anything else, Red. It's the same routine with me here. Atwell disappeared this week and I didn't hear from him until today. The actors all want more money and none is ever satisfied but if I can only keep the thing going that's all I care about. If you use any mayonnaise out there be sure to order Best Foods, on the Coast, as every bottle helps as Eddie can tell you.

Best for now and I hope that everything will break even better than you expect. If anything happens you can always come back on the Old Master's payroll as long as the Old Master has one. Milton Berle is the new sensation of the air . . . according to Milton Berle.

Portland sends her best and while we're pulling for you I'm digging for myself.

F.A

Old Orchard Beach
Maine
Friday
July 3, 1933

Dear Red . . .

Well, it looks as though I shall be back on your list around the first of August. While I fear that you will never peek in the door and see a duck on the table, while you are delivering, I shall guarantee you a hearty welcome and "spot" cash at the hearth. You can't ask for better conditions, Mr. Pearson.

The whole thing isn't set for sure but it is practically in the bag. The show is to start on August 4th or 11th and from then on I am going to ask various colleges to use a larger type in their humor magazines. My eyes barely got through last season and around April I found that the fine print used by Danbury Newsman was too much for me. The bon mots of Foote and Jerrold contained in some of the earlier first editions also became nothing but blurs in my study. For this reason then, I shall have to ask you to be on the watch for comedy matter printed in 12 point PICA type.

You may not be familiar with the different sizes of printing-types but anything from the 3½ point . . . brilliant type to the 6 point . . . nonpareil . . . is out. From now on . . . no type smaller than 7 point . . . and up to Billboard signs will be okay. Keep this in mind, Pearson, as you don't want to have to open a new field of humor and start going around to the Blind Asylums to pry jokes out of those raised-letter books.

There is a magician billed here this coming Saturday, and next week there is an all star cast called the Gladstone Manor Players, "direct from Broadway," appearing at the Capitol Theatre for three days. The managers here want "flesh," Mr. Pearson. Not "Flesh" on the stage so much as "flesh" in the audience. The actors who have worked here for years have played to empty seats so much that they take bows going by a chair factory. This is no good as chairs don't pay off as you know.

I'll let you know if anything comes up to crab the present deal and otherwise I'll be back in two weeks and give you a ring at 202 which as we know is the Sunden-Brentano headquarters. If you are preparing the Life and Loves of Coffee Bill, I am in the market for a copy of the limited edition.

Give my regards to Buddy. If Lahr has signed up for a year it looks as though you should get back on the pay-roll over there. Best for now . . .

mr. a.

Monday . . . September 18th . . . 1933

Dear Red . . .

Well, I was glad to get your letter on Saturday. I had been worrying about your position on the long trek and I thought that perhaps some real estate man, or a sudden wire from Slim Sully had touted you off of Hollywood and that perhaps you had left for Oklahoma. As long as you arrived safely that is the main thing.

I am glad you told me about the hitch-hiking conditions enroute. I have it all figured out if the programs go stale I can make a little dough writing original material for hitch-hikers signs. They could use a snappy gag and then through printing the gags in small type the motorist will have to slow up to read the puns and then the hiker can jump in the rumble seat before the driver can do anything about it. I know a guy who started to the Coast with about ten oil paintings. The last we heard from him he was in Little Rock and he had twenty bucks more than when he left and he had also sold three of his paintings. I think that a guy with pottery would do well on the road. No one has used pottery yet and don't be surprised to see me coming into town with a few busts of Mussolini or Jack Pearl under my arm.

I haven't heard anything from Buddy. He came up and left me some clippings and said he'd be back before they left for Chicago. They're in Detroit this week and I think they get back here Saturday. I haven't heard anything about them at all. Harry is still with me and I don't know whether he is going back with Bert Lahr or not. I haven't said anything about it as under the new code you know, one employer can't dicker with another man's worker. I know that Lahr tired him out and he looks swell now.

I have Harry going up to the Y and we play handball every day. I have also been taking some boxing lessons which will help me to open a protected material department of my own as soon as I perfect my left jab. When I figure I'm ready, I'll let you know and if you want a punch taken at anyone around 47th St. let me know. I'll guarantee one punch but after that it may be nip and tuck.

Things are just the same with me. I'm still up here pounding my head on the floor to try and keep the scripts going. They took up one option for thirteen weeks and now I am all set until the first of December. They said if the mayonnaise sales pick up they will keep it on all Winter. If you can get word around where Ed Wynne can hear it that mayonnaise can be used instead of glue to stick those stale jokes in the books perhaps he will switch from Lepage to Hellmann's and that way I will be all set for the rest of the season.

Am glad to hear that your salary starts and for God's sake don't let the Boss get into you for any dough. If you start off on a strict cash and carry basis perhaps you can save a little pile out there. I don't mean a pile of rare old first editions, I mean a new set of sawbucks. You say you will straighten up . . . which I resent, Mr. Pearson. You don't owe me anything so forget about the whole business. When you come back you can pay me in books or any special stuff I may need. Don't send me any money as I will only send it back to you so if you have all of the bills paid at home, get some postal savings checks or open an account at some lunch wagon out there. I would like to look in your room some day and see a duck on the table for a change. Don't let sex rear it's nasty head out there. I read today that Jean Harlow got married so I'm not worrying so much about you now. I don't know whether the 1st volume of Frank Harris and Gin works on the coast. You may have to switch to Applejack and Captain Devereaux.

If there is anything I can do here . . . except walk down 47th St. . . . for you let me know. I will probably see Buddy this week-end as he is coming to get his clippings and gags he left here. Nothing else I can think of. Berle opened, as you know, but he didn't seem to set anything on fire unless he played with matches after the broadcast.

Say "Hello" to Eddie and I hope you boys will keep The

Chief under control. Amy McPherson opens at the Capitol Friday so it looks as though Billy Sunday will get the Palace soon as business is going to Hell there, too. Portland sends her best wishes and we both hope that everything will be to your liking there.

F.A.

3.

OLD FRIENDS

LEO LINDY

december
3rd
1948

dear leo.

thanks a lot for your note.

i thought i could sneak that routine with georgie jessel in while you weren't listening.

i realize that your business has been too good for a long time. it is keeping you on the job too many hours. if this continues you will never have any time to yourself.

instead of plugging lindy's i thought you might be interested in having me knock the place for a few weeks. that might cause business to fall off and give you some rest. if you are interested— let me know.

there is a rumor around that the mice in lindy's go over to seventh ave and the house of chan for chinese food once a week. they have one mouse in the house who eats with chopsticks.

take care of your health—let the customers get sick.

best wishes—

fred allen

JOE KELLY

Allen exchanged thousands of letters over the years with Joe Kelly, his closest personal friend in Boston and his confidant since boyhood. The letters in this selection were written while Kelly was working in Washington as secretary to Senator David I. Walsh of Massachusetts and later, in Boston, as aide to then Mayor Maurice Tobin. The "Professor" or "Doctor" McGuire referred to in the correspondence is Constantine E. McGuire, a mutual acquaintance who worked with Allen at the Boston Public Library in 1910 and is now an internationally known economist.

March 20, 1931

Dear Mr. Kelly,

Business has been so bad, with our Webb-Holman-Allen attraction, "Three's A Crowd," that this coming Saturday may see me in a position to accept a commission in the Army of the Unemployed— Please advise the Centaur and let me know his reaction.

Last night, the manager informed us that when the cast, musicians, stagehands, etc had been paid that there was hardly anything left for the stars except some possible adulation from a few lovers of celestial bodies. Mr. Webb expressing great concern flew from his room to acquaint the acoustics with the ultimatum that "we might as well be out of work as working for nothing." It is alright with me and I can close my loan and writing business through sealing the purse and dulling the nub of my pen. Presto! It is done. If the business during the coming week—when the closing has been advertised—picks up we may remain until June sixth, but I doubt it.

I am going to see about the passports tomorrow and shall advise you under which name I shall sail. Not trusting the usual birth-certificate and marriage license routine. I am advancing on the Sub-treasury building flanked on the one side by a Somerville mid-wife and on the other by Father Leonard who married us at a hog-Latin Actors' Mass. If this fails, then I am sending to Boston for an attache of the Internal Revenue Squad whose testimony will get me deported to Ireland and then I can meet our party on the continent at a later date.

When these matters have been cleared up, I shall write you anent the proper diplomatic correspondence becoming a person of my station in Society. It is definitely settled that we sail June 26th. Mrs. Allen has charge of the Travel Bureau and I, as usual, function at the Exchequer window. She has met several of the gulls, who follow the Rochambeau, personally and it is better for a bird-lover to know his gull than to risk a chance acquaintance with some mangy feathered friend at sea. These friendships are not lasting and invariably the gull after accepting all favors enroute departs at the dock and seeks new patrons without so much as even dropping you a line or a bit of gull dung. We have our own gull which I hope to train and later use in vaudeville.

Should I experience any difficulties, on the morrow, and I don't mean Dwight, I'll advise and you can set the Giant Wheels of Politics whirling in my behalf.

Notes of Boston Actors: Mr. Charles Lane has just received a new vaudeville vehicle from the pen of that facile wit F. Allen. Mr. Lane says that he will soon know whether there is really a depression as soon as he starts to look for work. Up to now he has been without an act and unable to look for anything but Mr. Allen.

Mr. Drohan has returned from a season of lolling about Hollywood and is at present engaged in painting his house at 42 Baily St. He recently journied to the home of Mrs. Lovely and gave her husband his Summer haircut.

Mr. Joe Donahue has returned to Charlestown, from the Warner lot, to make a series of personal appearances at his Mother's dinner table.

Mr. Walter Donahue is at present appearing for the Loew, Inc. at the National Theatre, 149th St. and 3rd Ave. Mr. Allen, his author, has promised to see the new act on Tuesday.

Best for now—

Mr. A.

May 2, 1931

Dear Mr. Kelly,

You will be pleased to learn that business fell off so badly last week, that the three stars of "Three's A Crowd," who have been playing on percentage, received absolutely nothing for their week of labor. After the stagehands, musicians, chorus, and minor principals had been remunerated, the management informed us that there was nothing remaining. Mr. Webb flew, or glided rather, into a puse and a man from the Mint administered the last financial rites before he was able to give vent to his true feelings.

It seems that Mr. Webb, in making the arrangement to continue the show on a percentage basis, neglected to state a minimum salary which should act as a stop-gap. Business has continued to turn the corner for the worse and last week, he realized his mistake. I don't know what will happen but it burns me up to think of having to spend thirty or forty dollars, on laundry, pressing, help, etc., for the privelege of working eight shows for nothing.

We applied for passports, on Monday last. Everything was fine until the matter of birth certificates was broached. I had a card issued in 1916, when I was caught in Australia, and Port had nothing but a rumor to substantiate her existence. Consternation reigned for a time but we both raised the umbrella of common sense and came off lightly. I had to dispatch a fast post to Charlie Van who returned a certificate bearing the impression seal, which seems to be indispensable if one desires to quit the Country. Port had to drag her Father to a Notary, down where they live, and have him swear that she was the fruit of his loins etc. Everything has been mailed to Mr. Weinstein and we hope to have the passport during the coming week.

I am going to Boston, on June tenth, to apologise to everyone for being in a position to take a vacation. I shall hear the customary lament, peculiar to my aunts, that they never had the chance to do this, etc.

We sail June 27th elements permitting and I hope to arrive in Italy posing as a Methodist in time to put El Duce in his place. He can't make an armory out of the Vatican and my one regret is that I couldn't attend St. Margaret's toady and hear Fr. Bill's fiery sermon relative to the existing hubbub in Rome. It augers ill for the Italian fruitstand owners on Dorchester Avenue unless they come out vs El Duce in no uncertain terms.

Well to Hell with it. Port sends regards and best for now. We hope that Mr. Hoover returned from Valley Forge in excellent spirits.

F.

May 28, 1931

Dear Joe,

Your letter received, at the hotel desk, this a.m. on my way to the Gym. I opened it, on the corner, in front of a fellow who has an apple stand there. Seeing the Senate stationery, and the two bills peeking out, he rushed me and said "Thank God, Senator, you've brought the first installment on my bonus." I replied instantly, "Screw, Bum, you're nothing but a publicity man for some orchard, and these monies are merely a gesture, from Washington, on the part of a Southerner, who wishes to discharge an obligation." At these harsh matutinal words he slunk into his shell, which happened to be a pecan covering, and apologised saying that he rescinded any, and all, derogatory statements made vs Senators, Government et al and that his business would mind him—akin to the lion training racket. The last seen of him he was opening an El on his apple stand in an attempt to sell crab-apples to the unemployed who had nothing but promises from the Baldwin Interests.

I can appreciate the workings of the Senate. There is a flood in the Mississipi—(probably mis-spelled)—regions and an appropriation is in the offing. By the time the Bill passes the Senate, the South is in the throes of the Drought so the money comes in handy, after all.

A publishing firm, one Simon and Schuster, here has approached me with intent to foister a dollar book, on the Public, belittling the Depression. I have been dickering with them for two weeks, and have submitted assorted jokes, and matter, which would tend to replace the feather, in the risibility tickling, at this time. Nothing definite has occured, up to this time, but you may have the pain of parting with a dollar, in the near future, to see what I think of the Depression, it's evils, and remedies.

Nothing new has transpired re The Allens Abroad. The show is still holding up and we have hopes that it will run into the Summer months. There is no telling, though, and I don't even believe what I see let alone the idle prattle of persons who read tea-cups. We still have hopes of going to Europe if for no other reason than to apologize to Mussolini for the fact that we cannot tolerate broccoli.

Metro-Goldwyn-Mayer have offered me a trip, to California, this Summer to work in their studios. Everything is so indefinite that I wouldn't sign a paper to the effect that I would meet the pall-bearers, at a given time, even if I were the corpse.

I am going to Boston on February 15th, for the weekend. There is the matter of the Federal Income Tax to be straightened out not to mention the lack of rye in my aunt's cupboard. I hope to attend to these matters on a flying trip.

Thanks for your installment and hopes that you have both the Senate, and the House, well in hand. From the looks of things, America is a Cinderella Playground and eventually it will be twelve o'clock and everything will turn into a pumpkin— which will be a form of Farm Relief.

Port sends her best and we both hope that you are well and efficient. Let us know, at least a week, ahead when you might come here so that we can arrange another egg-nog festival in your honor. Until then, I am,

America's Tired Idol.

F

April 3rd
1932

Dear Mr. Kelly,

I have been forced to forego the questionable pleasure of writing you for the past few weeks. Manager Milford and I arranged a deal with the Paramount people to present a condensed version of Three's A Crowd in their movie theatres.

Once accepted, and terms satisfactorily adjusted, we had to scurry around to engage girls, and replace the missing people from the original cast. This work was finally completed and after a week of rehearsals we opened at the Paramount in New York. The show runs an hour and there are four and five shows daily and since I am on the stage most of the time it isn't the rest I have been contemplating for some months. The season was so disastrous financially that I am in a position to recoup part of the losses and continue my welfare work.

I don't think that the show is as charming as it was formerly but at least we have twenty-five people working and for these thirty cent audiences I guess it will suffice. At Brooklyn, I was worth 25¢ at the first show, 35¢ from two p.m. until six and from then until closing time it cost 65¢ to see me when I was good and tired. The mentality of the average picture theatre audience is so low you can't call them down unless you are in a sewer but I am slowly adjusting myself and will eventually find their medium of banter. I have inserted such jokes as— Do you know Andy Mellon—and the other fellow says—No but I know his brother Water. That will give you an idea.

My Boston reputation will be ruined after my appearance, next week, at the lowbrow Metropolitan but at the nearby legit Colonial I was getting practically nothing and next week I shall be paid. Or overpaid—perhaps. Another feature attending next week's engagement is the suspension of the FREE LIST. When seats aren't reserved I don't have to buy tickets and, in Boston, this is quite an item. If Uncle Joe and Aunt Alice want to see their nephew they will have to stand in line and take their share of Paramount Service—plus jostling in the lobby which is alright with me. It's better than spending $12 to assure Uncle J and family that they will see the fun at my expense.

Unfortunately, we do not play Washington so that you and the Senator can check up on our exhibit but we go to Boston, Buffalo, Detroit and Chicago. If you have friends, in these towns, you have my permission to warn them. You might also advise Dint, Ellen, Will and Midas that the attraction is apt to be misrepresented and that the folderol isn't strictly kosher. The fact that I am the star should be sufficient warning but the way people flock to the shrine proves that the mentality of the payee is at a low ebb.

I am still carting around sundry volumes and no time to read them. It has gotten so bad that some of the older books are starting to snap at me and I am afraid that some night the ghost of Artemus Ward will run amok through my quarters.

F.

Nov. 1, 1932

Dear Mr. Kelly,

Seated here on my fan mail, with the breezes blowing through the musty areaway, I turn to my personal mail for relaxation. I have been in my mouldy quarters for days pouring over jokebooks and magazines in an effort to rout out forlorn gems of wit that haven't been heard since James Whitcomb Riley stopped whittling.

Radio is quite trying. I am still at the mercy of the sponsors and each Monday we get the reaction from the President of the Corn Products Co. He calls the agency, the agency calls my representative and he in turn phones to let me know Mr. Moffatt's reaction. Last night, for example, Mr. Moffatt thought that I talked a little too long, at the start, also, that there was not enough of the organ music and lastly, that the Guest Star's voice cracked. All in all, it was quite an evening.

As soon as we finished at the station I rushed home to attend a meeting about next week's program. It is to be a jail and I have been writing all day. Now that I scan my efforts it all looks lousy to me, as usual, and I am again ready to quit. I have engaged a co-author, who rushes in when I have all of the work done, makes a few suggestions and then leaves through a crack in the door. I feel that he will not be on my personal payroll very long but I hired him to take some of the load off my shoulders.

You would enjoy my weekly routine. The script is always sent to the advertising agency on Tuesday morning, except this election week which we give over to two other radio personalities, Hoover and Franklin. Tuesday night, the script is returned to me by the program director. He tells me what the executives have decided is funny and then I start to work again until Thursday afternoon when we meet at the radio station for rehearsal. The executives then listen to the whole thing through the amplifiers, to see if it sounds any funnier, and then I leave for home with notes, suggestions, corrections, etc.

I then have from Thursday evening until Friday night to make a master script. This is again delivered to the agency and sent to the Columbia studios where copies are made for the artists to be used on Sunday evening. Sunday, we report at the studio at five and rehearse until six-thirty. Then the orchestra arrives and we are excused until seven-fifteen. At this time we have a full dress rehearsal and then wait until nine to actually do the show. By then everyone is so tired and nervous that no one gives a damn whether people like the program or buy Linit either. Finally, the broadcast is over and I go back to a meeting about the material for the following week and start in again.

I don't know how long I can last but I am going to take it until some decent show comes up or until such a time as Linit goes into the hands of the receiver instead of the tubs of the consumer. Prof. McGuire came one night last week, only for a few minutes. No sooner did he arrive than Mrs. Slim Jackson called, she is an acquaintance of vaudeville days, and she came to tell me that Slim had deserted her. It was quite interesting since she cornered the Doctor and reminded him that when a man had lived with a woman for fifteen years that she was entitled to something. The Doctor reached for his coat and some data listing the illiterate colored population of Little Rock fell out of a pocket. Hastily snatching the memo the Doctor fled through the door saying that he would be back after the election. I have yet to see him for any length of time so you will have to rely on the Senator's predictions until such a time as I can pin the Doctor down to facts.

If there is to be bloodshed, will the Democrats guarantee transfusions? I shall advise later. Meantime, I wallow from corner to cranny stepping on fan letters, joke books, packages of Tucks, and occasional intruders.

Let me know if you are coming the 27th, for sure, and I'll get you a couple of tickets for the studio and you can see a broadcast firsthand before returning to pass bills and take up your Washington season of backslapping.

Port sends regards. The radio stirred up a letter from Mr. Ham who, as you remember brought the groceries to the door at 20 Reggio. We have yet to hear from Bill, the iceman.

Formal regards Sir . . .

F.

MATTHEW STIFT
odorless cleaning of
PRIVY VAULTS and CATCH BASINS
chemical toilets and septic tanks
Office: 1700–1 Burnham Building
160 N. La Salle Street
CHICAGO, ILL.

Dec. 15, 1932

Dear Mr. Kelly,

We are not getting anyplace, with this silly correspondence. Are you and the Senator going to sit idly by and see pyorrhea set in on the industry and commerce of Massachusetts? The Mills of the Gods grind at breakneck speed compared to the functioning of your outfit. Do you realize conditions as they are in our homes and factories? WAKE UP MEN!

Do you know that things are so bad, in the Franklin Park Zoo, that the hyenas have stopped laughing and that the weeping willow is the only shrub that thrives in our Fenway? Do you know that cactus, in seven genera, has been found crowding out the dahlias in the Arnold Arboretum and that itch-mite is found on the vines covering the Longfellow mansion?

Do you know that everything is at such a low ebb, in South Boston, that the tide hasn't come in for three weeks at L St? Father Burke caught two hungry men, at St. Augustine's, trying to scrape the dessert off of a painting of the Last Supper, which hangs in the lower chapel.

Have you heard that the Santa Claus, in Raymond's basement is without underwear and has large holes in his shoes. What times are these when the kiddies trudge from Belmont and points North to have all of their childish notions of prosperity shattered at the first glance of a ragged and ill-kempt Kringle.

You don't know that the Reds have been stealing the pigeons on Boston Common and selling them to near-sighted poulterers for Tom Thumb Turkeys. How can families believe these statements of prosperity and maintain the true Xmas spirit while attempting to split the wishbone of a pigeon, after a scanty feast in which dessert is served right after Grace has been said. Is that a dinner for the man who works eight hours a day if he is working?

These are the things you should look into instead of spending the people's money for holly for the poorhouse windows and name plates for the statue of the Unknown Soldier.

I don't want to complain but you don't have to be in a phone booth to see the handwriting on the wall and a stitch in time would have kept the mills open in Lawrence. I hope that you will look into existing conditions, Mr. Kelly, and also that if you intend coming through here, and want to see the show, that you wire me at least two days ahead as tickets are very scarce and will be even harder to get during the holiday season.

Hope all goes well and that you have the Nation's problems well in hand. Best for now.

F

March 20
1933

Dear Mr. Kelly,

A few lines to advise you that Mr. Miller, the eminent keeper of bad meat, has caused the giant wheels of industry to turn in the right direction.

Some weeks ago, in one of our broadcasts, we had Miller's Market on fire. Mr. Miller wrote us a personal letter saying that he had been heckled in the neighborhood and that many of the coarse wits had functioned the following day. Such brilliant remarks as "Hey, yer rear end was burned out last night" and "What did yer pay to get yer name on the radio," were noted by the Foreign Correspondent of the Dorchester Beacon. Dan Gillis, speaking through a crack in Proctor's door, on account of the inclement weather remarked "Yer ergs are laid by a Technocrat and mine are strictly fresh."

Such mental anguish was suffered by the purveyor of questionable groceries that I stopped in to see him on my last visit home. He was bashful in the presence of a radio personality and hid in the ice-box for the first few minutes of my visit but after whispering discreetly "Here, Miller, Miller" and holding my aunt's bill out as sort of bait he slunk into my presence and told his story. He happened to mention, inadvertently, that he had just ordered a carton of Linit.

Well Sir, when I arrived back here I, forgetting any tact that may have been mine, up to that time, retold the incident to the fellow from the advertising agency. "You mean to say he actually ordered a carton of Linit," the executive said hoarsely. "Yes," I replied "and what is more I feel that he will pay for it, eventually." This was too much for the executive. He rushed to the office and immediately wrote the New England Headquarters to the effect that "Business Man Sees Better Times Ahead Orders Linit." The N.E. manager immediately wrote me and his letter is enclosed. Sorry that I can't send you another message, which has since arrived, telling of a man who walked into the Food Karnival, at Cobb, Bates', and said that he was a personal friend of Fred Allen's and furthermore that he wanted a package of perfumed Linit. The latter note carried a P.S. The gentleman referred to, did not give his name.

Such popularity and confusion must be deserved, Mr. Kelly. If Franklin D. has imported Eddie Dowling as official jester, I suggest that my name be submitted to the Honorable David I.

in the event that he is considering adding a Merry Andrew to his staff.

Mrs. Allen received the invitation to the Coolidge services but, due to lack of funds, was unable to get away. I doubt if she was missed for Gracie Allen and several other "Dumb Girl" portrayers still outrank her in popularity, according to the latest Crossley Survey.

Nothing else exciting. I have a night off, tonight, and am spending it trying to get rid of some personal mail. Best for now.

Mr. A.

Sunday.

Dear Mr. Kelly,

Your scurrilous, scathing and opprobrious missive has arrived at my town house. Your mentally deformed Boston Representative who criticizes my writings should be discharged instanta and in his place you should engage a man whose brain, at least, has been sullied by puberty.

On January tenth, in The New Yorker, an article, entitled Don't Trust Midgets, appeared over my signature. The subsequent week another piece was submitted to the same weekly, and duly returned to it's author. Names aren't necessary here. I later learned that the entire staff, of this publication was a branch of the Shakespeare Lovers. Knowing full well, that if I were to be encouraged with pen, Shakespeare's name would become obsolete, except in corridors, of the Boston Public Library. With this in mind, the second article was returned to me and I have dispatched it to College Humor. They cannot trifle with me in this manner.

I have purposely put on my coat so that I may laugh up my sleeve at the efforts of you, the Senator, and the Boston hireling of the Nye Investigators, to mock at my authoring. I am no Don Quixote and this one admission accounts for the fact that I am not atop my mangy steed riding Washingtonwards to shunt my staff at the wings of the Gubernatorial, Senatorial, Departmental, and Congressional Windmills.

Instead of wasting the tax-payer's time pursing your lips in an effort to launch an uncouth noise in the direction of my ear drums, why do not all of you forensic luminaries do something constructive? Look at your reflections in the Mirror. What have you been doing down there?

I'll tell you.

After eighteen months Mr. Wickersham returns with his report. The minute he turned in his weighty document eleven men were put out of work. A fine how do you do. At least he could have kept the commission working on the report until the depression blew over.

Part of the South is inundated. Terrible floods, suffering, loss of life. What happens. Washington will appropriate. A fund is the only immediate solution. Master minds convene, fume, drink, smoke, harangue. By the time the money is available the South is suffering from the drought. Too late to help the Flood Sufferers the money is returned and the entire process repeated. By the time the Drought Fund is accessible the South will be suffering from normalcy. A fine kettle of fish.

The Red Cross won't accept twenty-five millions and still, each Xmas, they will buy the thinnest red cloth available with which to make suits for their street Santa Clauses. No wonder children have lost faith in the Kringles. How the Hell can a Street Santa Claus smile at whelps when the wind is seeping through his flimsy garment and he has no drawers on to boot? No wonder, even before the depression, Santa Claus had a long puss and snapped at the kiddies. Ringing a bell. Nothing but a come-on for a paper mache chimney or an imitation iron pot. Why shouldn't the men who are supposed to waft joy into the tiny hearts of Young America, why shouldn't these men snarl at their lots, and posterity as well. Make the Red Cross take the money and buy balbriggans for their Santa Clauses next year. Then will the natal day of Our Lord regain the place it once held in the hearts and minds of my countrymen.

If you, as a paid employee of the tax-payer, would spend

your time looking into these vital matters Mr. Kelly, instead of issuing derogatory documents having to do with my honesty, sagacity and ability as an author, then Sir, America would indeed be

> "the Land of the Free
> and the Home of the Braves"
> (Music furnished upon request and 2¢ stamp)

Have you any pamphlets on Interior Decorating for Rabbit Hutches?

Formally,

F

january 15th
1934

mr. k . . .

your letter today and also the calendar arrived earlier. now if the senate is giving out watches so that i can tell what time it is i will be all set for the balance of the season.

i do not envy you the augmented activities. there is enough trouble if you are doing a minimum amount of work but when you are placed in what, in the eyes of others is an exalted position you are open to all sorts of headaches. i have arrived at the conclusion that there is no absolute peace to be found. if you become a bum and sit in one place, near the relief office, you can survive, but if you just decide to sit down and do nothing, the first thing you know you are lousy and you have to scratch. life, in my estimation, is a biological misadventure that we terminate on the shoulders of six strange men whose only objective is to make a hole in one with you.

at the present time i have a little trouble with the federal tax board, the n.y. state tax board, i am bringing charlie flanagan's brother over from dorchester to play his harmonica on the 27th, inky sheehan is after me to be the master of ceremonies at the firemens benefit at the majestic in march. he wants to come over here to discuss it, a million actors want to get on the program. dolph singer is up in saranac and his trunks are held at a hotel down here. bob walters was put out of his hotel and the collection agency is after me because he said that he worked for me when he hired the room. a baby in akron, named after me, was one year old last week. bill mckenney wants to hire the town hall quartet for one appearance at the wool show at the boston statler february 4th. jack benny and i have a weekly feud wrapped in cellophane and i am trying to write another thing with a fellow who comes on the program for several weeks but who keeps forgetting things and can't play.

you, at least, with official business may get someplace in the political hubbub but the kind of non-essential traffic that usurps my hours can only end in some sort of a psychopathic reaction that will have me over in bellevue with my legs strapped to my pratt so that i cannot kick myself for ever leaving the local scene and straying from the polluted air of hodge's. also, tom ryder's kid nephew, in fall river, won't believe that tom knows me and will i send the kid an autographed photo to prove that tom and i are like that.

some leader may catch you making sense out of the assorted mess in the office and reward you with a worthwhile proposition. the best i can look forward to is more trouble and the curses hurled at my skull from the rabble and others whose favors have been overlooked, or denied.

bob sent me the item about us leaving for hollywood. i think the sooner we go the better. i read today that i am to go into a picture called "sally, irene and mary." this was a show that eddie dowling did some years ago and unless it is entirely re-written i think it should wash me up permanently as far as pictures are concerned.

    yours—

                f.a.

wed. night

mons. kelly . . .

have just arrived home. it is 2:30 a.m. i have been at
the wheeze since nine this, or yesterday rather, a.m. if you think
this is an easy racket you are greatly mistaken. i would rather
be a guest star at the spanish inquisition than have to face the
cretins and jerks we have to pander to to survive.

port and i have plane tickets to boston for next thursday,
may first. today, however, something came up that may put us
back a week. amos and andy wrote me that they were coming
to new york and would like to go on the program. they will
only be here a limited time. i wired them tonight and if they
can go on the show, may seventh, i will have to postpone our
trip home until the eighth. we have a little problem at the
moment. cantor passed us on the popularity survey and our outfit is worried. we have an option coming up for next season and
they have asked us to put in some guest stars. if i can get amos
and andy it will help us greatly and perhaps in the ensuing
hubbub the company will sign the show for next season. personally, i don't really care. i am exhausted and the petty trib-
ulations and crum people i have surrounding me aggravate me
more than they help me. i will probably be better off if the
whole thing breaks up and i take it easy for a few months. if i
have time to read and think i may be able to work out something that will enable me to do some other type of program
wherein i can take things a little easier. this is really a gruelling
task and when i look about me at the egotistical prinks who
have been enabled to function through my activities i occasionally
pray for a crooked leg so that i can kick myself in the sphincter
as a lesson to myself.

if amos and andy can't come on the program we will be up
may first. i will have to let you know later. meantime, hope con-
nie is well and that the outlook is okay. with the new tax setup i

will be better off putting a floor show in hodge's grocery store and living on my reputation.

madam sends her regards to you both. hope that all goes well.

Mr. A—

thursday

dear joe . . .

i have been owing you a letter but there is no time for mail, sir. you may be having your troubles with the campaign but i can assure you that your activities stand out like a drop of water at l street compared to my present difficulties.

a week, or so, ago word was whispered around the offices "mr. bowles is back." to you the cry "mr. bowles is back" means nothing. mr. b is the man who, after you have worked all week to concoct a mess of drivel that will barely skim through the loud-speakers without leaving a stench in a radio owner's parlor, rushes in at four p.m. on wednesday afternoon and tears the entire show apart . . . leaving nothing but punctuation marks for you to put some new words between and have it ready to convulse our thirty million listeners, from coast to coast, by nine p.m. eastern standard time.

well . . . mr. b is back after a hard summer of resting first one cheek and then the other on the mahogany deck of his boat. he lit into the old town hall with a will, sir. as a result i have had to eliminate the educational feature, and spend countless hours in research so that i can produce a travelogue weekly. he also has removed the finish of the program and one night insisted that the question box, a feature loved by twenty seven million listeners, according to the same digest poll that showed the wind turning against our beloved f.d.r. in other words he has kept me in hot water until i have begat a permanent red glow like the bottom ember in those fake wooden fire-places the gas company sells its customers around november first.

there has been no time to write . . . think . . . evacuate or function. the idea for the sketch about the future with everyone on a pension is swell but we could never get away with it. since the federal radio commission has swung into action there can be no mention of anything that might tend to draw attention to the radio, sir.

Mr. A

monday eve.
january
1938

dear mr. k . . .

i have been intending to write you for some time. i have been afraid to stop work for mr. morganthau has been known to chide those of us who have been tax-bait for the past few years. i keep my nose to the emery wheel and am considering mailing little tid-bits of skin to washington to prove that i am giving both nostrils in an effort to see the new deal through.

in hollywood, for eight weeks, i discovered that i could function with three and four hours sleep. working at the studio, i had to be up at six and six-thirty. and when i returned at night i still had a radio script to write which kept me up until one and two a.m. in order to present the program in hollywood we had to transport twenty some people out there, musicians, actors, office help, writers, etc. and when the whole thing was paid for all i had was the use of the hall and a chance to let my many fans hear from me. i will have to call you in to work out a way that will enable me to either stop working altogether or to fix it so that i can "ease off" as we say in maine.

i don't know what the hell i am working for except that now there is a mob of people depending on me for their activity and it has almost gotten to the point where i can't stop. something has to be done and unless doc mcguire rears his sedate head on short order you will have to rush to my rescue with a psycho-who-ever it is that checks up on economic lunatics . . . to find out why i should tick at this rate.

the fortunate man of our times must needs be hump-backed. with his head bowed over by nature, he is in a position to contemplate his navel which will prove to be as worthy of attention as the happenings of our times and the man who has spent his life pondering on his navel will find as much therein as the man who has frittered away his life toiling will find in his pocket. i am not a small-time confucious. i am not poor richard. i am merely a resident of dorchester doomed by some evil fairy around moseley street to roam the earth until such a time as my penance has been paid.

F.A—

march 1
1936

dear joe . . .

we have been getting six thousand letters weekly, for the past few weeks, commenting on the prize awards at our amateur nights. does the senator need more proof than this that people on relief have radios, three cent stamps and stationery? it must be fine down there. i am besieged around here. my cousin at station weei, in boston, wants to come here to be an announcer and i am being deluged with requests to pull strings . . . if i heeded all of the letters i would have to run away with some man who has a puppet show to keep my hand in at string pulling.

some son of a bitch around savin hill wrote me about the sad plight of an old savin hill boy who is now living in brooklyn and would like to become a janitor, or porter, at radio city. i guess i am supposed to call john d. up and say . . . "see here, john, you can't let an old savin hill boy down." the funny part of it is that i don't even know the fellow who wants the favor let alone the bird who needs it.

you will be glad to know . . . and advise the senator . . . that cap smith has been equipped from top to toe. i have sent him a suit, shirts, socks and haberdashery so that he will be able to make a nice appearance when he goes to see his friends on relief.

his mother wrote me several times about a suit and finally in a moment of complete insanity i got in touch with the cap. he is all set unless some republican has left a nail sticking out of the bar at beano's place which might play havoc with his blue suit.

i haven't paid my income tax yet. bill thompson is now in newark and he has had my figures for some time but he went home over washington's birthday and last week he was in some minor auto mishap, i think, so i haven't mailed my pittance in to washington yet. i would like to protest the pink slip arrangement. i used a sketch on it weeks back showing how people would have to go on the radio reading their income tax returns from coast to coast. later, i had portland's father protest about it over the air but apparently my efforts have been wasted. am enclosing a clipping showing that my anti-townsend plan made the hearst papers which is another black mark against me.

since we haven't been out of these rooms for eighteen months we are going to atlantic city, this week, for two lousy days. i am so tired of amateurs, mail and other headaches that i feel like quitting but each week i get a show out some way and count one wednesday off on the way to old orchard. i won't know much about when we can leave here but i doubt if it will be before the end of june. regards—

f.a.

old orchard beach
maine
august 25th
1939

dear mr. kelly . . .

you will learn here that in your great haste to flee the hospitality rampant at 5 odena you departed leaving a pair of wormy swimming trunks about the premises.

the moth-eaten girdle hung on the line until twilight set in. i was ashamed to be seen taking this chastity band in the house and it seemed best to wait until night had started its fall before sneaking out on the back veranda to salvage your gear.

i approached your trunks warily as they were surrounded by a busy covey of moths. after a stiff battle the woolen jockstrap was brought indoors; try as i might i could not fend off the moths who formed a flying wedge and bore down on me inside the house.

as i reached around for a late copy of the biddeford journal to fashion a truncheon with which i hoped to rout the closet-butterflies my attention was caught by an undernourished moth who clung to the seam of your garment heaving and wretching no end. closer inspection showed that he was trying to cough up a frayed end of your trunks he had swallowed. as i watched him straining to spew i noticed a strange thing. the little fellow racked with spasm was aiming his oral cavity at a small hole in your neptune drawers. then it dawned on me. this was no truss sabotage. closer inspection showed that each moth had a dusty talon down its tiny throat intent on coughing up shreds of your kelp-knickers. each moth had its oral cavity aimed at a ragged aperture. why? i asked myself. like a veritable flash, mr. kelly, came the answer.

the moths who had sampled your loin wares found that they could not digest them. gastronomic repentance set in and here they were assembled for the collective purpose of coughing up their spoils and fitting their gastric contraband back into the gaping holes they had made in former moments of epicurean weakness. impressed by their good intentions i abandoned the moths to their work of reconstruction and the following morning, when i looked again on your swamp-leotard, i was happy to find the many holes in your garment filled in and hundreds of tired moths lying about the crotch sound asleep.

at the moment your hip-cloth reposes in the lower drawer of the grand rapids portable cupboard that stands southeast of the door as you enter the door of our chamber. if not called for within thirty days this navel awning will be sold at auction . . . or mailed to your next of kin.

F.

november 23rd
1939

mons. kelly . . .

the screen guild program arrived here. it is allegedly a philanthropic enterprise. the gulf oil company pays the guild and the
money is supposedly going into a fund to build a home for screen
actors who have fallen upon hard times in technicolor. actors who
are thriving at the moment donate their services to keep the sunday programs going. i appeared on the program last sunday. my
appearance was prologued by two weeks of headaches, interviews
with conrad nagel, interviews with ralph morgan, conferences
with the oil executives, conferences and sundry meetings with
robert benchley and tallulah bankhead. the blowoff came last
saturday when miss bankhead, without duress, admitted that the
whole thing "stank." i rushed home to write half of a new program and benchley retired to a bistro to write the other half. sunday, miss bankhead disappeared and the program finally went on
with what i had written and what benchley remembered. meantime, i was getting out my own programs, turning down an invitation to speak at the notre dame dinner, at south bend, trying to
find the address of the man who invented the electric milking machine, talking to the mother of a little boy who had to get out of
school two days and come from philadelphia to louse up the show
last night, and getting my ear bent by a woman sent to father
mullen, at old orchard, by bishop mccarthy, of portland, and re-
layed to me via one father burns here on 68th street. i have been
a veritable whirlwind, mr. k, and wouldn't be writing now but for
the fact that this is thanksgiving day here and everything is closed
up but my corona . . .

F.A
180 west 58th st.

new york
december 16th
1938

dear mr. k . . .

am in receipt of your voluminous scroll and the inflation warning. baiting the capitalist will get you nowhere, mr. k. all of you government employees seem to be against the "little fellow" with a million dollars or less. the impertinence of your s.e.c. exchange committee caused the late mr. coster to go to a fatal extreme and i hear that after he had shot himself the connecticut police ran in and arrested the body for having a gun on it without a license. the day will come, mr. k! but when?

dr. mcguire showed up tuesday and insisted on seeing hamlet. it is the uncut version which starts at 6.30 p.m. and runs until 11.30. the audience is taken out on a leash, at 8 p.m. and given fifty minutes to find a tree and eat. the dr. thought we should go to the algonquin and with about half an hour to bolt calories the urge for some nondescript wine seized the dr. the waiters couldn't locate the mosel passe, or whatever the wine was, and the finish was it came, looking like a kindergarten urine test, and we were late returning to hamlet.

the dr. predicts a big year coming up. ultimate inflation will arrive and i think it has to be done before june . . unless a new law is passed. this could happen. stocks will rise and prices keep them company there will be much building and business activity but eventually someone will have to pay and it won't be captain smith. the dr. looked fine and is returning in january when we will probably meet again and journey to the acquarium to catch whatever piscatorial tableaux is running at that time. the dr.'s philosophy can be reduced to one cold statement. you get out of life only what you put into it. the only thing to do is work, preserve your health and let external happenings happen about you without giving them heed. i live with one foot out of the window so i am prepared for the worst.

portland and i are both happy to learn that you are mating, or rather giving the kelly call which may result in connubial affiliation. we will do nothing to hamper any orderly progress nature and cupid may have under way. i will not tell the charmer that her husband is a spider dissector, a half-assed dolphin fisherman and the owner of the haggardest pair of summer trousers extant.

i went home a couple of weeks ago but had to work on a sketch after i left lizzie's and i left at ten a.m. friday and just made it. if i can come up after the first of the year will let you know ahead. port sends her best and we trust that you and dint will have a merry xmas and a satisfying 1939. best for now.

F

december 21st
1939

dear junior . . .

for a person who has asked few favors of people i get in more trouble in my role as foil for others with dull axes to grind. at the moment, i am writing a mrs. hannington, of brookline, to permit her daughter to stay here a few months longer and pursue her career in radio. i am making arrangements with a hospital to continue some narcotic treatments for a gentleman from boston. i just paid for six weeks of treatments and the fellow has been out one week and feels "very nervous". he thinks two more weeks will straighten him out. last night, a friend of mine came to the broadcast after he had eaten some seafood, or someone had given him a mickey. he was deathly sick and at 11.55 p.m. i left him on a toilet seat while i rushed upstairs to regale california with my labored wit. all through the hour bulletins came from the first aid quarters as to my friend's condition and at one a.m., when i finished, he was so weak i had to ask uncle jim to accompany him to a distant point in jersey in a cab. mr. john o. hewitt who hasn't had his rent, since 1935, is after me again and mr. fred lareine, a gentleman with no legs, came in his wheel-chair last night to advise me that the veterans of foreign wars are holding up his pension money and his landlord is holding up a final notice.

nothing else new but just as exciting. hope dint is better and that you and kay will enjoy a pleasant xmas. we rehearse on xmas so it's just another day for us. best 4 now.

F.

february 8th
1940

dear mons. kelly . . .

this, i trust, constitutes an answer to yours of saturday february third. i am flattered to learn that lizzie's check warmed your sacro-iliac. i wish it had been able to heat up mine. i am still going around here looking as though i had just dropped a bag of coke off my back. the doctor says it is lumbago but i have to sit so much from friday to monday that i can't get rid of the damn thing. if i never get straightened up again you may be able to place me on the boston park department harpooning paper around the common. i am just bent at the correct angle to operate one of those broomhandle stilletoes. keep it in mind. the call may come shortly.

i sent the pine point hermit a small check last week. it seems the river bed has been frozen over for weeks and he has been without clam, pelf and provender for some time. he cashed the check and rushed over to old orchard to buy some meat. he returned and made a big stew and the first mouthful made him sick. his stomach had shrunk, or something, and he was sick for a week after his first taste of something solid. he may be putting it on a little for me and i must guard against too intimate an acquaintance since he is a chronic letter-writer and i am sure would move his clam-fork and his three dogs into our backyard if we ever appeared at old orchard again.

three druggists appeared tonight to ask me to come to the pharmaceutical convention in mechanics building in april. the catholic charities are after me to go on some program this month to help the drive. hodge wrote that he missed the program last week through a new maid stepping on his plug at home and futzing up his radio connection. many southerners complained about joe louis calling me fred on the program. wall street is still after me and i guess, after tonight, the republican party will clamp down on me en masse. but, so it goes mr. k. if you have any gas trouble due to bob's absence at the plant let me know. i have a little gas on my stomach that might be of use in an emergency. madam sends her best.

F.A.

hollywood
june 20th
1940

dear mons. kelly . . .

the outgoing mail has gone to hell in these parts. most of my time is spent dodging pests and trying to avoid the mass of chiselers who seem to flourish here. there are all sorts of rackets from taking a page to welcome myself in a jewish newspaper to giving some bird six hundred dollars to buy an independent ambulance to take to france. so far, i have come through with flying colors and lower bags under my eyes. with any luck i shall escape unbilked. after the last radio show things will die down, i hope. when you work at the studios there is no way these bastards can get at you and while i am in the studio i can accidentally finish the picture which will shorten my stay and enable us to get on a plane and get the hell out of here.

we ought to make a note to remind us not to live too long. i meet people out here i haven't seen for twenty years and i don't even know them. their teeth are gone, their navels are hooked onto their vertebrae, their hands tremble, their eyes are squinting behind bi-bi-focals and they show only too well the ravages of time. most of the drinking men i know of yore are worse off than the others although they may have had more fun arriving at the paresis stage. i think if rockwell will put steam heat in his boat we would all be better off living on his scow than trying to fend off the ravages of time and the future legislation that is bound to result when hitler finally convinces all men that atheism and regimentation are the coming things.

i made a test with jack benny tuesday and optimistic reports are rife. i will see it tomorrow. between the studio and the radio shows i haven't been out of conference since we arrived. am enclosing a couple of pictures to show how my arrival was publicized. in one, two paramount "cuties," or contract players as they are called out here, are receiving the egg jack benny laid in new york. in the other i am animating the well-known "no-rain-in-california" gag. these whimsies were worked out by the man who works out the gags for the photographer. they both get on the train at san bernadino and discuss these gags as you ride in to los angeles. when you arrive the people are waiting, the pictures are hastily taken and the next day mussolini goes into the war and the papers don't print the pictures. madam sends her regards. we would both much rather be coming up odena avenue in old orchard beach than hollywood boulevard but the show game makes odd demands of its subjects, mr. k. i hope the legion convention tips over the parker house and that you are enjoying what is called life in our old habitat.

give dint my regards and i hope he is improving. if you want mary martin's autograph or an old pair of garbo's shoes while i am out here, let me know. best for now.

                              Mr. A
                    el royale apts.
                    450 n. rossmore avenue
                    los angeles, california

hollywood
july 27th
1940

dear mons. kelly . . .

am, many days ago, in receipt of your letter. the picture with jack benny, "love thy neighbor" started two weeks ago and i have been rising at seven a.m. and sinking about seven p.m. the story of the picture opens on new year's eve 1941 and at the start i am filmed riding down park avenue in a large packard. to get the shots i have been sitting in the packard the top of which has been sawed off and the interior filled with lights to aid the cameraman. i sat for three days in this general motors inferno dressed in a tuxedo, muffler, derby, gloves and heavy overcoat. when i arrive home nightly i am in no mood for mail or nourishment. after the car sequence was completed my next histrionic caper turned out to be an episode wherein i am found in bed trying to go to sleep. i count sheep, which are superimposed on the screen above my head and finally the sheep turn into little jack bennys, and i go mildly berserk. i spent one whole day getting in and out of bed and doing the thing over and over again to permit the technical departments to get the angles and the right shots to enable them to carry on with the disney stuff that has to be inserted along with what has been photographed. i saw some of what they call "the rushes" (the developed film that has been taken the previous day) and i look like something out of mrs. booker t. washington by sitting bull. if i look as bad in the rest of the scenes as i look in this one bit i will scare millions of kiddies and set the laxative business back twenty years.

re the mayor's, and mr. guild's, requests to speak at a banquet next january; i wouldn't bet that i will be alive next january. we are starting with a new sponsor this year and i can't tell what will happen. the program is still to be an hour and for the past six years the other one kept me going fourteen and sixteen hours daily. i don't mind going to affairs of that sort the only problem is that a great ballyhoo is made and people expect a lot.

with my weekly radio routine i don't have time to prepare talks, or matter, that fit into the proceedings and rather than make a horse's hock out of myself i merely refuse to accept these invitations.

i get so mixed up with everyone trying to promote me for their own purposes that half of the time i feel like telling them all to go to hell and returning to my corner in hodge's. out here it is brutal. i am supposed to show up at a softball game for the mt. sinai hospital today, tonight i am supposed to be at a charity broadcast to get jobs for local people, the pastor at the church here called last night and left his card, the food sale only got $66 at the church and some woman called up for me to make up the difference as they were trying to raise $100. i am supposed to rewrite two scenes for the picture and then get up at seven tomorrow and be ready to work. herman gerrish wired me to be sure to be in old orchard to start the marathon, mullen wanted a wire to read last week on his community sing. it just keeps going and no matter where we go, or what we plan, some son of a bitch is lurking around the corner with intent to grind his stinking axe on our activities.

i shall answer the mayor and mr. guild and if it is possible to attend the convention (which again comes the week before we go on the air when i have to have auditions and get the ball rolling for the season) and the community fund business i suppose i shall be "happy to co-operate".

looking forward to a taste of oblivion and a speedy return home and with brisk regards from the madame . . . i am . . .
"nobody's favorite"

F.A—

450 n. rosemore ave
los angeles, cal.

MIKE PEBBEREZNIAK

A side of Allen's life that Radio City and Hollywood never saw was his close friendship with the locker-room crowd at the West Side

YMCA in Manhattan—the cops, firemen, and retired fighters with whom he played handball and exchanged opinions on boxing, his favorite sport. Allen's chief correspondent at the Y, who kept him informed on the latest locker-room gossip and handball scores and boxing news while he was out of town on vacations and Hollywood assignments, was Mike Pebberezniak, a clerk in the New York Post Office from Ansonia, Connecticut, and a devoted long-distance runner in his spare time. Allen was always warning Mike against his habit of jogging fifteen miles on the Y track.

old orchard beach
maine
august
seventh
1941

dear mr. p . . .

the reports of your recent handball combat vs the professor sound like figments of an egomaniac's imagination. 21 to 14, i'm laughing. if you entered a court with my partner . . . before you could get the door closed the professor would have at least 18 points. he would play circles around you until you thought you were part of a ballantine ale ad. 21 to 14. you wouldn't dare go into court and show these figures. judge lazarus would give you twenty years to work on your backwall weakness.

i do not know mr. davis, the y boy who took advantage of our mutual friend and honest tapster, mr. lagrey. who is this wolf in feigenpan's clothing who dares to mulct a man who cuffed the daylights out of ben jeby? fortunately, i can smell the chick evans technique a mile away. occasionally, using a sympathy approach, the short crutches, soggy plaster cast and pulling a phony tendon gimp one of these shysters has taken advantage of my good nature but i was never in with ben jeby and when these imposters fool with the professor they are placing themselves in a position to become known as potential jeby's.

too bad frankie can't get away on his vacation. it is just as well. if he went to saratoga he would only lose on the horses and with all the dust that flies around that track he might get something in his eye. everything happens for the best and i am sure the old lady had made it possible for frankie to enter september in a far stronger financial position.

my blood pressure was up higher last week than it was on my first visit to the doctor at biddeford. since my first visit showed that my pressure was higher than it had been at any time last winter, either the doctor is a barnyard man, the testing machine is forty points fast or i am getting worse by degrees. have been exercising but a touch of sacro set in last week. it doesn't bother me much. have cut out tea and coffee and down on the chewing tobacco until the next blood pressure test is taken. if that doesn't help i am giving up. have been chewing spruce gum instead of tobacco. i will have a hell of a time stopping the spruce gum this winter.

saw coley welch last week. he has improved a lot and moves around faster and his left is getting better all the time. he stabbed this tony cisco dizzy and won without much trouble. cisco is a wild man but fights in a shell and is hard to tag. am going sunday night to see paul herrick the new bantamweight sensation. will advise when i have seen paul throw a right or two. soose and zivic fooled me but i think when the chips are down they will both come through. soose should beat abrams and kaplan, tippy larkin and about everyone else has beaten red cochrane.

nothing else new here. these letters are a pain in the sarong.

F.

sunday night. (Aug. 1934)

dear mickey . . .

you're lucky to get such good service on your letter. i happened to finish the show a little early tonight so don't think the prompt reply is due to any influence you have with the postal service.

pretty soft for you up there in connecticut with your box of schraffts and your slingshot taking pot shots at winded rabbits and motorists during the day. no wonder you come back with a belly on you that will get you into the police department before you know it.

i can't very well slow down the shows to accomodate your fans there in ansonia. the stuff is always cut and something generally happens to make us lose time and we have to keep it moving along. if you will write a complaint on the side of an ipana tube perhaps they will listen to you and tell us to take it easy but the whole thing is generally a mess on wednesday no matter what our intentions are in the morning. i knew those scripts i showed you would throw you. they are a lot of work but harry tugend and i have been doing them so long that we cut the thing up in sections and before it is put together it looks complicated. i could show you the whole secret but then you would only be up all night writing and you are in bickfords late enough as it is.

i haven't tried to diet but i still don't think i've picked up much weight. i've been working pretty hard and i don't sleep well so there isn't any chance of getting fat on that routine. with the gym i get tired enough to sleep nights but now with the few extra hours i have there is always something to do and at night i am wide awake. i'll start in again right after labor day and perhaps i will get the left hook in shape for the winter season. two good fights this week and i have to miss them both. canzoneri and dublinsky and the belloise fight. i think arismendi punches too hard for belloise and i don't think belloise can hurt him so it looks like a good ten rounds of body punching with the spider packing away with right crosses and flashy footwork. dublinsky is very good but canzoneri knows all of the tricks and if the fight wasn't on wednesday i would go as far as bridgeport to see it.

thanx for the invitation to come up but i can't even get to a beach. i have one day off . . . friday . . . and this week i have to spend it writing a routine for next sunday night when the state of maine sends a broadcast to admiral byrd at 11.30 p.m. over weaf. the whole thing is on the cuff and there is always some politician around to see that you don't have any spare time. a guy in boston got me mixed up in this and i can't quit.

i don't know about the locker. my card runs out in october and i'll see what happens. the boys will think i have gone goof if i move out on them now after my apprenticeship in the tote room. you just want to get somebody in there so you can take a shower and call it a day. you can't wish off that belly so you'd better turn over, not a new leaf, but a new set of times with the medicine ball this fall.

tell my fans to hang on, when burns and allen come back, as the show has picked up a lot of new listeners since they left. you can give me a report on next week and then i shall see you shortly in position number four on the saupios chart.

best for now.

the champ

FRANK ROSENGREN

Allen was an omniverous reader and an avid book collector. He bought most of his books through the mail from Frank Rosengren, a Chicago book dealer whom he met in that city in his vaudeville and musical comedy days. With his book orders, Fred wrote long letters describing his general life and hard times and commenting on the state of the world. The correspondence and book dealing continued in later years when Rosengren and his wife, Florence, and their son, Figgi, moved to Texas and finally ended with Frank's death in 1949. Here are only some of the highlights of the voluminous Rosengren letters.

THE WINDSOR
New York

March 20, 1931

Dear Mr. Rosengren,

The Depression is by no means over. Society families hereabouts are using stumps for family trees and claiming dwarfs for ancestors and most of the letter writers are rubbing pigeon dung on the corners of their missives instead of buying air-mail stamps.

F. Allen

THE WINDSOR
New York

May 6, 1931

Dear Mrs. Rosengren,

Frank should be a little more discreet. The minute he writes an article, that is apt to cause some discussion, he flees to the Dunes. Why not stay and "face the music." Sousa has been facing the music for years, without ill results and who is Frank to fly in the face of dilemma? His article about "gold in Them Sills and Shelves" will have me looking through my collection, when I get back to Boston and then you will be in for more trouble. He said that certain books were worth unprecedented sums. Who pays, the amounts he quoted, for these tomes?

Ask him if there is any edition of Black Beauty, or, Little Women, that will bring me anything and how I can ascertain the value of an unexpurgated edition of Hans Brinker and the Silver Skates. The copy I possess, of the Brinker series, is the one wherein Hans couldn't get the skates on, due to the fact that his feet were swollen, and some of the obsolete terms, such as "oh shucks," "skiddoo," "Twenty-three for you" and other blasphemies, equally as potent are rampant in this manuscript. It must be worth something. Perhaps Frank could get the Dutch Consul to suppress it and then we could share in the profits selling reprints in plain wrapper.

I would appreciate a copy of "Big Money" —P.G. Wodehouse. Also, please send me a bill. I think that I owe for "Re Beards."

There is nothing exciting here. The theatre public is so show-wise that people are demanding new faces in the Breadline, outside of the Paramount Theatre. Conditions are very bad and dwarfs are fighting sparrows, for crumbs, in the street.

Babies are being weaned on aspirin to fortify them for the economic headaches they will certainly face, in years to come. The hyenas, at the local zoo, have stopped laughing and the

City, to keep up appearances, and in a belated effort to aid the unemployed, has hired two men to tickle each hyena in a futile attempt to cause them to chuckle, at least, out of respect to the Republican Administration.

Thanx for your letter and hopes that all goes well at the nook. Sorry I can't be of help re "Dedications," which Frank must have finished ere now. The only amusing one I can recall is about the committee assembled to dedicate a new building in a small South American town. In the midst of the ceremony a junior earthquake caused the edifice to totter on it's foundation. The committee, and those assembled, dispersed immediately and in the paper, the following day, a notice appeared to the effect that a Unanimous Movement had caused the committee and citizens to disperse before the rites had been consumated.

And so to bed

Sincerely—

F. Allen

July 21, 1931

Dear Mr. Rosengren,

I am in receipt of Lady Holland's Memoirs and you were certainly right in bestowing your popular priced sympathy on me. I have started to wade through the first volume and it reads like the diary of a Lame Nun, who had served forty years of solitary confinement, for ogling a gouty Bishop in a moment of post-puberty weakness. Ere it is finished I know that a recent endowment policy will expire which is the only thing I have to which I can look forward.

Sorry that I didn't know that you were passing through New York. I might have shown you through several of the better speakeasies and I know of a steak place where the tenderloin and sirloin are hewn from Sacred Oxen—fried in the blubber of effeminate whales—there is no dish finer, Sir. You might have spent a day at the Acquarium fishing. Things are so bad hereabouts that many of the actors go here each Friday, and using pieces of elastic, for worms, try to cajole near-sighted salmon into becoming an entree.

Am still working on scenes for the new show with some success. When I am trying to think of jokes, for the theatre, all I can get into my head are puzzles—such as—If three ventriloquists sit down for a game of bridge—which one of the three should bring the Dummy? And you know I am never going to get anyplace in the theatre, with matter of this calibre, running through my cerebellum. Also a tourist, in Switzerland, threw a boomerang from the top of a mountain and shortly after two boomerangs came back. Turning to the Guide he said "How do you account for that?" and the Guide retorted—"I don't know, Sir, unless there is an echo here." You know yourself that I am doomed if my mental constipation is not relieved shortly.

The only good news I have heard, of late, is, that the man who wrote "Happy Days are Here Again"—committed suicide last week. The heat is unbearable—at least in Chicago you get an occasional draught caused from some gunman running through the streets—but here they are starting to sell cement flags on account of real bunting not having moved for weeks.

Am enclosing money order for .75. I thought that stamps might stick together, in a letter, and besides I wanted to visit the Post-Office to see if the Government was still in business.

Thanx for past favors and the Memoirs, which will come in handy to balance a table, when the legs warp.

Best for now—

2501 Palisade Ave.,   Fred Allen
Spuyten Duyvil—N.Y.

                                              August 21st
                                              1931

Dear Mr. Rosengren,

Mrs. Allen and I have been away, for a few days, my annual pilgrimage to a deserted spot, near Atlantic City, where

I hide all of my used razor blades and perhaps you can profit through a solution I have employed these many years.

On August 12th, weather regardless, I pack all of the stained Gem blades in a mock gunny sack, which I made out of brown dental floss, procured from a man who chews tobacco to an extreme, and depart the city. A two hour journey, thirty minutes via train, then a forty minute bus ride, brings us to a steam roller depot where we crawl in the rumble seat of a waiting roller and ride for forty minutes to a depot of the Central New Jersey Piggy Back Transportation Co. Here Mrs. Allen and I mount, for transportation purposes only, a set of Siamese Twins and Piggy Back to our destination. It is a mere ten minutes "as the twins fly" when we are safely landed and ready for action.

The place has no name and is really a yard where smoking cars are stored, by the many Railroad Companies, from April first until Labor Day. Harbored here, during the rainy season, the smoking car windows swell to the point where Ajax couldn't possibly open them, whereupon they are put back into service commuter-proof, as it were, Mrs. Allen and I open the gunny sack and place the razor blades end to end. It being still August 12th, when we arrive at the yards, there is still a small crevise remaining between the lower part of the smoking car window and the sill. This is timed to permit the grand swell which occurs over Labor Day. Everyone knows how it invariably rains, at that time annually, and few have been able to ascertain why this should—this yearly prank of Pluvius—take place with inerring precision. The Weather Bureau is controlled by the Illinois Central and other large rail corporations which will come to light when Mr. Zuta's effects have been thoroughly searched.

This, however, is irrelevant. Into these small spaces I place my razor blades, at the rate of a gross a day, you can see, then, that I am finished in some ten days and knowing that no one will ever be able to open the windows, Mrs. Allen and I summon the Twins and begin our return trip. We are safely home again this year only to find that a canary we had bought in Chicago had gotten out of it's cage and consumed the major portion of our house cat.

All of which should explain why your letters have not been answered, both of them are here and placed in camphor until the Winter when I do most of my reading.

Fred Allen

Friday night
July 2, 1932

Dear "Back-Number" . . .

You will be glad to learn that your Number ⚤1 Customer "Spot-Cash" Allen is still going strong up here. Things are so tough that people who have been living on the cuff are moving farther up the sleeve for the Summer.

I am leaving tomorrow for Maine and will be glad to hear from you at my Summer Home, Fringe on the Neck, as soon as you can get away from Mr. Lahr's conferences long enough to send a word of encouragement.

My attention was called to a blackface act whose case is pitiful. The fellow has been sitting in his room made up for three weeks waiting for a date. He's afraid to wash for if he catches a job he hasn't enough dough to buy enough cork to blacken up again.

F. Allen

December 29, 1932

Dear Mr. Rosengren,

I have been so damn busy stealing childrens' banks to further the depression, and advance juvenile pessimism, that I haven't been near the Corona—lo—these many nights. I have things fairly well in order—two banks have closed and if you have anything near the Banks of the Wabash—I suggest giving it immediate attention since the Wabash institution is not a member of the Federal Reserve.

Have read nothing but the obituary column in the Times,

for several weeks. Too bad about Kin Hubbard. I enjoyed his stuff immensely and shall miss his pithy writings. The books, you last mailed, remain unsullied by my eyes, and, from all appearances, I shall have to engage someone to do my reading for me. The days fly by, like Fords, in Gary, Ind. and before I know it my life shall have been spent in a maronic stupor. My brain cries for sustenance, but my relatives, and dependents demand material things and in the scurry for appease all I am the sufferer. Why should I visit an aging relative, who has never done anything for me but sneak out from under the same pelvic arch as one of my parents? Why should I spend an hour listening to the ticking of an uncle's arteries—when sixty minutes could be better spent in the company of Sis Willner. Mentally, of course, I could have said Shakespeare and have a better phrase but topical things seem to be in demand.

I am taking singing and banjo lessons. Having seen the show last year, you know that this is essential. I am running a crumb line for midgets and have had two nasty letters from the Salvation Army for helping bums, at the stage door of the theatre. My life is a faux pas and louts, oafs and dull-wits are spending my precious minutes. It seems that being in "the Public Eye" isn't all that it is supposed to be. Everyone running a benefit, or opening a pay toilet feels that you are duty bound to assist in making the event a success, through your presence and "a few words," of course, "everyone there has seen you." Yes, the bastards, but they haven't seen me properly. I am waiting for the Chicago Worlds Fair, at which time I shall assemble all of these pests, at different radio stores and at a given hour I, Fred Allen, shall deliver to the World a resonant raspberry the like of which has never been heard since the day that Solomon suffered a change of Life.

Xmas was sort of a disappointment. My finances were so bad that four of my Xmas cards bounced back.

With one arm in the straight-jacket,

Fred Allen

December 11th
1933

dear frank . . .

Your letter just caught me in time. I am leaving for Boston shortly and I would hate to have it known that I had fled the City owing five dollars in the Middle West. I am enclosing check so that I can board the flyer without a weight on my conscience.

I am sorry that you went to the expense of buying a new radio set. The jokes coming over the air, these days, will age the tubes in no time at all and you will have an antique as soon as I have been on for a few weeks. Figgi, your son, will be sorry to learn that Mr. Atwell will not be on the program when we start. For some reason they asked me to change the people around and not to use Roy. I guess they don't want it to appear to be the same group that made the well-dressed salad what it is today . . . the forgotten dish.

You will be glad to learn that, after a week of work, I have all of the fan-mail answered and my desk is as clean as Gandhi's teeth after the thirtieth day of any of his hunger strikes. I am going home for a few days and then Portland and I are going to Atlantic City for the following week. Here the phone keeps going and I am so nervous that I want to get a little rest before we start off on another series. I have so many books to read that I figure we can go to Atlantic City, where it is freezing now, and none will catch me there. I have fortified myself through sewing a bit of mink on my fly to brave the ocean gusts which are so strong the flounders and mackerel are blown through the air like dust along the Atlantic Coast.

We start January second and I shall be back here about December 23rd to get things going once more. I hope that the new programs will turn out well for it is important these days when there is nothing left of the theatre but ghosts of Booth and Barrett running through their parts in the deserted wings.

I think that Tales and Mythology are okay. I am taking them on the train with me to look over but I know they are okay.

You are too late to stunt Figgi's growth. He should have been weaned on black coffee and grown up with a weight on his mind. At the age of puberty you would have had a wrinkled son but he would have been well under three feet in height. You should have told me before if you contemplated shrinking the size of your family and your possessions. I could have arranged the whole business through inventing a reverse thyroid gland for you and Florence and through putting alum in the furniture polish . . . you could have moved into a doll house and had plenty of room. See me before you make another important move and you won't be sorry . . . or perhaps you will be . . . I can't tell at this writing.

Shall write you when I get back. Meantime . . . hope that you will manage a festive Xmas . . . how . . . I don't know. Best for now . . .

F.A.

february 28th
1934

dear frank . . .

god knows what will happen if you ever go into business in mexico. between siestas and hiding catholics in the store, as the mexican rabble rushes by with tiny altar-boys dangling from bayonets, you are going to have a hell of a time showing a profit at the end of whatever they are using for a fiscal year in mexico.

F.A.

december 4th
1936

collector rosengren . . .

i am eliminating the "dear" in all future letters. it is effeminate and i write so many letters to strangers, and pests who seem to be a part of the radio comedian's life, that i see no reason why i should start letters as though i am glad to have the opportunity to waste the time it takes to concoct a note saying that i am sorry that the person doesn't like the program as well as major bowes . . . etc.

from now on . . . in my letters . . . i shall get down to brass tacks. the person will be hailed in print . . . merely so that he will know that the letter is for him . . . and from then on i shall reduce all correspondence to facts.

fred allen

old orchard beach
maine
september ninth
1938

dear mr. rosengren . . .

as i prepare to close my fiscal year at this kelp-strewn resort, i find that you are owed one letter, since i have cleaned up my accounts at the taffy store, the graphologist's, the frozen custard emporium and had my last ride on the sky-swing it is but fair that i send you the letter and officially close everything including the front door of the cottage.

i shall be back in new york around september 15th and will advise if there are any books to be added to my gargantuan collection. if i collect many more volumes i am going to have trouble hauling my library in and out of new york. i am about three books away from having to use the empire state building and the chrysler building for book-ends and don't know how much farther i can go without losing my reputation as the "portable bibliophile." you, and other scheming tome-venders have stocked me up with about as worthless a mass of bound trivia as man could find combing the book-shelves of the moron population of the far south. any sane barrister looking over my estate, when the end finally arrives, will be inclined to beam on the first relative to suggest contesting the will on grounds of insanity.

we are both rested but trouble looms in the offing. two members of our cast have been working in pictures and it looks as though i shall have to audition sundry actors to effect replacements. the program resumes . . . with a bang! i hope . . . on october seventh and from then on i can rave through the winter.

my time has not been wasted here. i am sending a new "nature alarm clock" to washington in hopes that i can sell the idea for lighthousekeepers. as you may suspect lighthousekeepers seldom sleep during the night. the light keeps revolving and what with flashes going into the bedroom every few seconds it is practically impossible for the keeper to doze off. the result is that the average keeper doesn't get to sleep until four or five a.m. he wakes up at ten and the light has been burning during four hours of broad daylight at the expense of the government. my idea is simple. before the lighthousekeeper goes to bed he sets out a mackerel on top of the lighthouse. in the dead fish he has placed a flatiron. the minute he has closed the little door at the top of his beacon a stray gull swoops down and bolts the mackerel. when the gull tries to rise the flatiron holds it down. Dr. R. E. Lee of the vallee program contends that nature works swiftly with the gull and that the process of evacuation completes its cycle in this type of bird in five hours. if the lighthousekeeper sets his mackerel out at midnight and goes right to bed, without piddling around, nature will start to have its internal fun with the gull immediately. promptly at five a.m., as dawn breaks, the gull foals its movement as it struggles to fly away . . . the flatiron comes down with a hell of a thump on top of the lighthouse . . . the keeper is awakened . . . it is dawn and he turns out the light and goes back to bed. millions of dollars will be saved and outside of the wear and tear on the gull's lower colon no effort or expense is involved. i am sending out sample mackerel and flatiron and if the government accepts my "nature alarm clock" i will be covered with glory and gull dung as soon as the experimental tests are completed.

am also working on a correspondence school course . . . "how to become a bum in ten easy lessons." one of these ideas is bound to catch on and then i can sit back and lead the life of james whitcomb and if he didn't lead the life of riley i don't know who did.

bronzed regards to florence and figgi . . .

F.A.

30 west 54th st
new york city
(september 15)

october 5th
1938

dear mr. r . . .

am enclosing check for $27.50. the dictionary arrived on saturday last. the postman started using several three syllabled words so i take it that he peeked in the package on the way over. it is certainly the last word in this sized volume and i feel that it will help to ruin my eyes much sooner than i had anticipated. the paper is very thin, which is good, for, when i have no further use for the book i can get some bull durham and roll cigarettes in my old age.

there is nothing exciting around here. i was trying to work last saturday when the phone rang and some gentleman, i know vaguely, said that he was in a predicament. he had been at some party that had been going on for three days. he had started to tell a story on the third day and was doing very well, with its development, until he realized that he had forgotten the finish. he excused himself in the middle of the tale and called me up to see if i could tell him how it ended. fortunately, it was a very old story that has been told in assorted versions and i gave him the ending. afterwards—i thought that perhaps here might be an idea for fellows who own large collections or others who know many jokes. you could just sit by the phone and whenever an after-dinner speaker, or a house guest, found himself with no finish to his yarns he could call up and, for a nominal sum, be supplied with an ending happy, or otherwise, as the occasion demanded.

you might open a chain of these haunts, thousands of little men sitting at phones. thousands of after-dinner speakers demanding that phones be installed on the dais in the event that they forget stories, gags, or biographical data. if you are interested let me know for i would much rather spend my declining years sitting at the phone in preference to sitting at this damn corona.

the proust set looks and sounds interesting but not for me at the moment. give my harried regards to florence and i hope that things are booming in the store and i don't mean your abdominal repercussions as a result of swigging our sal hepatica. best for now.

F.A.

feb. 2, 1939

dear mr. r . . .

am enclosing check for two dollars for "postman rings twice." it arrived with one ring since our postman is no mental epicure.

i have been thinking about opening a book-worm track here for people too old to stand the strain of watching whippets. i have enough books to open a mile track and race my book worms through some of the better volumes laid end to end. i could make a steeplechase through having a Modern Encyclopedia set in every hundred yards or so to make a decent-sized obstacle for the worms to hurdle.

the copy of "hobbies" arrived and it is quite a publication. there should be a lot of interest in your book collecting columns for everyone has an old copy of Silas Marner around the house that he hopes is worth something. dealing with people in whole-sale lots, as i have been in my new profession, i am horrified to learn the small amount of mentality that has been divided among so many souls who blissfully wander through life getting more en-joyment, out of the experience, i fear, than i do. it makes it all the more miraculous that one person can sell another a book or anything that would tend to help the person mentally. practically all people are "belly-conscious" and it requires a certain amount of optimism to embark in a business that reaches as high, or as low, as the mind of the mass.

well . . . posterity can worry about that. i have enough trouble with the hour program. there will be a sixty foot dummy of me at the world's fair built by the ipana people. i just wanted to warn you. best to florence and i hope that all goes well. best for now.

                                                    fred allen

                                                    may
                                                    fifth
                                                    1945

dear frank . . .

received your letter re the wealth attributed to me by time magazine. time neglected to mention the two operations my brother had last year. the scars are on him but surgery was on me. sundry relatives, also, were supplied with sustenance and garb and many old performers, and other dated acquaintances, had ac-cess to the residue.

after taking a gander at what finally remained you would agree with me when i intimate that the only book dealer i can traffic with is the head of the haldeman-julius five cent book de-partment.

what the hell would i do with the rheims testament? if i need any literature at the moment i require the latest work of doctor fishbein's if he has written anything on essential hyper-tension of late. my blood pressure finally went so high the doctor advised me to give up the radio for a season. the doctor may have heard some of the programs but he looked up from his sphygmo-monometer as he made the suggestion so i assume that he was concerned with my pressure.

the last twelve years in radio have been drudgery. so much drivel succeeds on the air that it is a waste of time to try and maintain a standard. i have written and done over 500 shows and i defy you, or anyone in texas, to life what i have foaled. i am not a quality writer but if you want quantity . . . i am your man.

met an anonymous party in hollywood two years ago who claimed to have seen you and florence. this chap said that you had been ill. i trust that you are well again and able to sit in the front of the store and insult customers. we have been in new york for so many years that i have lost all track of most of our out of town friends. i made a picture last fall which turned out to be a clinker. if you happen to meet anyone who sees it down there in texas . . . deny that you know me.

trust that all goes well "deep in the heart of" and that you and florence are real natives by now. i have hundreds of books around here. if you are in the market, kindly advise.

portland joins me in regards . . .

> fred allen
> 180 west 58th st.
> new york city

ARNOLD RATTRAY

Arnold and Jeannette Rattray, publishers and editors of the weekly East Hampton, Long Island, *Star,* became acquainted with Allen through his old friend, Val Eichen, their neighbor at that seaside resort. Fred carried on a steady correspondence with the Rattrays and their two sons, David and Everett, for many years.

May 15, 1933

Dear Mr. Rattray . . .

This is in answer to yours of April 9th. It just goes to show you how that damn Daylight Saving Time slows things up. In ordinary times, your letter would have been answered the same month.

It is so long since you wrote your letter that no doubt you have forgotten the contents. There is no sane way of judging the value of a radio program. The popularity of it, I mean. If the sales increases, the sponsor is satisfied and the type of product you are trying to sell should determine the class of audience to be attracted. Selling a bath preparation, naturally, you would have to appeal to a slightly more intelligent public than you would have to point for if selling coffee or some staple product. That is why I tried to keep the material fresh and as good as possible.

Radio popularity doesn't last long and you can get arguments on any phase of the business and the way I feel about it is . . . the people who are in power don't seem to know a great deal about it and so then your opinion, and mine, is as good as theirs . . . for argument's sake anyway.

If Mrs. Rattray's book, "Whale Off" hasn't won the Pulitzer prize, I would enjoy reading it. Each Summer, I catch up with all of my reading and, when possible, endeavor to go through all of the worthwhile books I have collected over the Winter period. If my eyes hold out I'll eventually become too intelligent to make a living in what is left of show business. The way things look in radio, and in the theatre, it will soon be necessary to undergo mental castration if one is to meet his public on level ground. The entire problem is too great for me to handle. I believe that the administration's CCC Reforestation campaign will only end in millions of woodpeckers being unemployed. As they say in Paris "One man's herring is another fellow's poison."

Large Val has received an answer from me in this mail and since I expect to repair to Boston shortly, it may prove to be my Swan Song, in seasonal correspondence. Up home, I am so far removed from affairs of the moment that the typewriter often pouts in it's case feeling that I have taken up a new love. In the Fall, however, it is surprised to have me fling off it's pod and start another Winter of pummeling.

Thanx for your kind letter and comment and as soon as I am located I'll advise King Kong Eichen and perhaps we can resume our occasional exchange of pleasantries.

Best wishes . . .

Fred Allen

November
15th
1934

Dear Mr. Rattray . . .

My answers get farther and farther apart but I am still in business here and constantly ignoring the Blue Eagle. The longer I stay in radio the more things pile up to keep me from attending to my private correspondence. We have written over fifty programs and naturally they require more thought now for the things I used to think of, at the drop of an anvil, have all been used.

Tell Mrs. R. that her book, "Whale Off," inspired our recent burlesque of the Admiral Byrd broadcast. I had been looking over her book again recently and thought that with the Admiral and Seth Parker broadcasting from boats . . . something would be done about it. I put three and three together and the program came off well . . . if you didn't hear it I could speak of it in glowing terms.

The critic on the Post is a friend of Atwell's and he has mentioned Roy's absence. I wanted to keep him with us but the firm thought that the show would sound the same as the Salad Bowl and since we are now involved with the Toilet Bowl I didn't have a cheek left to sit on. Should I do another series later, I shall try and get Roy back for he is very popular with listeners and he is an excellent balance for my shows. He was a great favorite of Val's and I have been hoping that Val would write to General Johnson and get things started in Atwell's favor.

Am happy to learn that the "vets" are doing so well on the town there. When things get a little tough with me I shall let the pants out on my boy scout suit, touch up my bugle with a bit of brass polish, and move right in on Val's land. I guess the Government will uphold my squatter rights especially if I call the Interstate Commerce Commission's attention to that act Val took from one state to another around 1918. If the Income Tax people can catch me, after ten years, I guess they can still get Val for that propaganda he spread especially through Canada where they are still not laughing at his monologue.

Give Mr. Eichen my hurried regards and tell him that the 60¢ dollar will not affect the Latin Quarters as far as I know. Also convey my kind regards to Mrs. R and if she liked the Admiral show, two weeks ago, tell her she can take a bow as coauthor. Remind Val of my cloth lollypop for moths, to keep them out of your clothes, and let me know if you have any complaints.

Best for now . . .

f.a.

May 6th
1934

dear mr. rattray . . .

just a few lines to thank you for your wire. i have been owing you a letter for some time, but the events of the days just passed have been almost too much for even me. have had to make two trips to boston as my aunt is sailing for ireland tonight.

she is 77 and all of her life has magnified the stories she heard as a girl, tales of the old country told by grandmothers and other ancestors to whom america looked good as they lived in cow-sheds at home. since i have been a puberty-stricken lad i have heard her say that she hoped that she would be able to visit ireland before she died. well, sir, her dreams became a passport tonight and she sails from boston at nine p.m. i had to go up home to make arrangements for everything in advance since it was impossible for me to be there as the gangplank was lifted back into the s.s. scythia.

it has put me way behind in my work but for such a worthy cause i know that the correspondents won't mind. to add fuel to the fires, the agency has been conducting a campaign for the program and the little time i have had left has been spent in turning out stuff for drug magazines and stunts to get space in the newspapers for the show. i have been up to carnera's camp to box with the champion. i spent all day yesterday in a loft on 65th street making a newsreel of the ipana man, a papier mache dummy that leaves for the world's fair tonight. the dummy yells in my voice at the people all day long, thanx to a special record i made for the man's intestines. around the middle of august i should be generally disliked by all of those who work within hearing radius of the ipana exhibit. the record plays over and over again and mechanical eyes move while stiff-jointed arms wave at the people so you can realize that i am in a way to enjoy some of hitler's unpopularity before labor day.

the reports on our new hour show have been almost one hundred percent "aye." the listening audience has gone up, in the charts, and one of the executives just back from a survey, around the country, reports that the show is very popular. naturally, you would think that i could sit back on your wire and my fading laurels and feel good about it. but . . . if you think this way then i am afraid that you are not familiar with the workings of radio. this coming tuesday we are to audition a new version of the show. it is to be a weekly drug store with a laughing neighborhood druggist running everything. i know that val will get a great kick out of a chuckling old gentleman with no jokes laughing the songs and numbers down his throat.

F.A.

august
4th
1945

dear mrs. rattray . . .

this is a victory typewriter. the letters jump around and i doubt if it will endure the duration. if it gets much worse i will probably have to use a small pool-cue to hit the keys to get them to contact the paper.

correspondence made more sense in the stone age. a person with a lot of mail to throw out could assemble his granite billet-doux and stone bills for dinossaur feed in the backyard and build a small hut. today, there is nothing to do with old mail. you either answer it or ignore it.

since we answer mail portland and i want to thank you and arnold for the gala day at east hampton. where else can you get a field day, a fashion show, the excitement that attends the misplacing of a child and a lobster dinner all in one afternoon?

we also want to thank you for the montauk brochure which came yesterday. we went into new york monday which has sort of mixed up our week. we seem to have lost a day.

portland has asked me to enclose some data on dehydration. there are methods, time charts and pictures. if you dry out the products of your victory garden you should have enough water to open a small pond and put the town pond out of business. if you have nothing else to do with the water you can put it under your father's whale boat.

we may see you again later in the month. convey our best wishes to mr. rattray.

sincerely . . .

fred allen

ALTON COOK

Allen and his good friend, Alton Cook, radio, TV, and moving picture critic of the New York *World-Telegram,* saw each other so frequently that they had little need to write letters. Cook received the following reports during a few summers when Fred was out of town.

> old orchard beach
> maine
> july 19th
> 1938

dear alton . . .

   you will no doubt be relieved to learn that i have done approximately nothing about my annual column. the interest this should add to your daily space cannot be computed. some year the groundhog will not come out and only then will word get around that in 1938 allen didn't come out either.*

   my intentions have been good but the events of each day prove too much for me. i started in new york but mr. batchelor arrived and there were so many business matters to be taken up that he finally remained with us through our last four days in the city right up to train time. when i arrived home in boston, my income tax was up for inspection, my aunt wanted to move and assorted relatives wanted to unload their troubles.

   arriving here at the beach we spent two days unpacking and getting the haven in order. then rain set in. then laston came to make sure that portland wasn't lonesome, i guess. then my brother, his wife and a friend arrived for the weekend to see that i had no time to become a hermit. in between times small boys came to the door for autographs. a man arrived in a car with a trained duck. he wanted to audition the duck for the program in the fall. i happened to be in the toilet when he called. i heard

---

* Allen gave Cook a day off from work every year by presenting him with a column.

mrs. allen say that i was out. this necessitated my remaining in the toilet for over half an hour until the duck man had his say and departed. we have only had two sunny days since we arrived. both of these days we had company on the beach and i couldn't think. yesterday, it started to rain again, today it is raining. it is impossible to think in the house. the waring mixer hums noisily in the kitchen, laston is continually being called to task for not putting enough flour into something. mrs. allen has engaged a maid. the maid comes at one but she has a baby and leaves at three. then she returns at four and cooks dinner. there is sweeping, conversation, doors closing and sundry other noises following one another in rapid succession through the day. today, a wire arrived from bill rousseau asking if he could stop in thursday. if the rain doesn't stop i am afraid that he will find the place deserted.

portland's other sister is arriving sunday then laston will be leaving. then the other sister will be leaving. there is a little girl here who has a car. she calls on the hour to see if portland wants anything downtown. you can see, mr. cook, that had shakespeare been in my shoes the merchant of venice would never have been written.

when the column will be done i can never tell you. i looked over the last year effort. there do not seem to be as many topics ripe for comment this year. radio seems to have slumped back to join the major in raising a large abdominal sac. i thought about another type of column. a radio alphabet. if this would do i might be able to get going.

it doesn't look as though we will be able to get up to see doc rockwell this year. no column and now no trek to the rockwell shrine! gad! what a year! forgot to mention that somehow i got on a committee to judge a contest in esquire. esquire is sending me 100 contest answers to judge. it won't be long now. if you will consider a part-time baby-watcher and full-time lodger i shall be glad to engage one of your rooms where i will not only guarantee to get out my column but i will positively guarantee to get a few minutes to myself.

portland sends her spattered best wishes to bertie from the calorie lab. if the boat gets grounded during the summer will be happy to rush portland on with kidneys complete. best for now!

"The Lone Ranger"

old orchard beach
september ninth
1938

dear alton . . .

no doubt you, aboard your floating privy, have been wondering how the other half has been making out on land. i wrote you some time ago explaining that i had laid out a mess of punctuation for a column but had not been able to find the necessary jibes and blunders to fill in between comma, colon, semi-ditto and period. too many things have been going on here, sir.

portland was abed for one week with an infected throat. we had several horse doctors in to see her but they couldn't diagnose the case unless she agreed to put on a harness and get down on all fours. this she refused to do and finally she found a tree surgeon who treated tourists as a sideline during the summer. this gentleman prescribed a caterpillar spray and finally mrs. a's bark responded and her throat slunk back into organic oblivion.

my aunt came for a short stay and the trip must have been too much for her. when she returned home her blood pressure went so high that a slight shock ensued and she is now in the hospital. i have been going down there and we are waiting for her now until she can leave for home. when she is able to go i am going to boston to make arrangements for her over the winter. i am calling the doctor at the hospital tonight and will know more about our plans when i hear what progress she is making. she is 81 and naturally cannot throw off her ailments as she has done for many years.

we made our annual trek to the shrine rockwell. you will be pleased to know that pandemonium still dominates the household. last year, the little rockwell art group was radio-mad. the boys had built a set and the grounds were a network of wires and old radio parts. this year radio has been forgotten and doc and the boys are camera fiends. the three of them have those candid cameras and all of them snap anything that moves. when one focuses on an object the other two raise their cameras and everything is taken in triplicate. we went fishing again and as usual caught nothing. during the trip assorted snaps were taken of me impaling a clam, spitting into the wind, dropping my line, a close-up of my hand holding a herring before cutting it up for bait, etc. gulls were snapped on the wing, innocent bystanders on the wharf were taken by doc and the boys at all angles. doc said he would send me some of the pictures but several days later i received a terse note saying that nothing had come of his squinting and posturing. the reel hadn't been attached to the spool it seems and some 25 pictures were taken on one piece of film. this you will agree is economical but will not enable posterity to know how i appeared on my fatal day at sea.

portland and i are still living in the summer cottage. if it gets any colder we will probably have to start eating candles and blubber. the sun is warm during the day and if we can last here another week we ought to be well-chapped and healthy. we are staying until next friday. port is going to new york and i will stop over in boston for a week to attend to my aunt's needs and accomodations over the winter.

nothing exciting here. portland sends her chattering good wishes to mrs. c and we both hope that the baby weathered his stay on the boat without sprouting fins. see you soon!

Mr. A

hollywood
july 12th
1940

dear alton . . .

as you no doubt know we arrived in hollywood as per schedule. we have been attempting to carry on in this enervating section without much success. we are both tired and since we do nothing we can only echo the cry of the tourist and blame our fatigue on the climate. the sun comes out daily and shines with monotonous regularity. i am getting to hate the sight of the solar ball and am considering asking the n.b.c. soundman over some day, with his equipment, to let a few claps of thunder and a rainstorm loose around the apartment. if the government wants to help the cotton growers i am submitting an idea that may be worth something. hundreds of easterners come here annually and after staying a few weeks get homesick for the sight of a cloud. if the government will send cotton out here people can make portable clouds and keep them around the house. when a person gets a cloud-yen the cloud can be taken out of the closet and tacked to the ceiling until such a time as the visitor is resigned to return and face the eternal ultra-violet body suspended above by something einstein hasn't figured out yet and the chamber of commerce.

upon arrival i received some sage advice from an actor acquaintance. he told me to speak only to pale people. pale people are the ones who are working. the man with the deep bronze tan obviously spends his days in the open and consequently is inactive and prone to panhandle.

mr. benny went to honolulu to have a two week rest. paramount learned that he was going and his picture was held for a grand opening to take place upon jack's arrival. he was met at the boat by some 20,000 people and made a personal appearance at the theatre and later participated in a gala red cross drive. that constitutes a benny rest. he is expected back tuesday to buckle down.

i haven't heard anything from doc. madelyn gave me a book entitled "on vital reserves." it tells how to obtain a nutritive equilibrium and how to develop a status known as "unshakability of the soul." how this will help me reduce my blood pressure, or make a good picture with jack, i don't know. a viennese neurologist is quoted at length in the book but i am sure any theories a viennese neurologist might have developed can be of more use to him if he is still in vienna than they will be to me in radio or pictures.

portland and i envy you and b on the boat and also doc and madelyn on the loose. i have been working on dialogue for the picture, getting fitted for wardrobe, inventing excuses to avoid dinners, etc. portland has been trying to keep busy with one or two girls she likes. when i start to work next week she will have to put on another friend, or two, or spend more time around the house. i am hoping for the best with the picture and if this one doesn't turn out well i have promised myself that i shall abandon this movie craft for all times.

F

f.a.
el royale apts.
450 n. rossmore ave
los angeles, cal.

old orchard beach
maine
july 22nd
1941

dear alton . . .

if it isn't too much trouble i would like to see the series of columns you wrote on vaudeville. we can't get the telegram here. the morning new york papers are on sale but since the afternoon editions can't arrive here until the following day none of the stands order them.

you should run across many colorful stories. all of the older performers have their pet yarns and it isn't much trouble to get them to talk. to me, the n.v.a. and the tattered ego of the old performers is pitiful. actors, especially those who were in vaudeville, seem to have a childish conception of what goes on in the world about them. if you mention the johnstown flood to a vaudeville actor he will say "oh yes, i remember it. that was the week we were next-to-closing in toledo." most actors' lives are bounded on the north by their entrance music and on the south by their exits. few of them ever end up with anything and the majority would rather sit around and tell how they turned down 600 to play the orpheum circuit, back in 1924, than to scurry around and stir up a job that might keep them going. i think the only thing that enables many of them to keep going is a sense of humor. no matter what happens they seem to be able to laugh it off and blame their quandaries on other people or conditions. the actor's attitude can about be summed up in a story no doubt you have heard. the vaudeville actor's wife had died and he ranted and cried around campbell's as the body reposed there awaiting burial. after the funeral a friend met the bereaved actor on broadway. the friend said "i saw you up at campbell's. you were wonderful." the ham said, "you should have caught me at the grave." to me that dismisses the attitude and the philosophy of the average vaudeville actor to perfection.

portland says to advise bertie that the sheila hubbard cookbook has been found. the kitchen here has turned out to be a calorie laboratory. portland rummages through the recipes, brews and potions are concocted, and promptly at six i don my guinea-pig skin and squat at the table wondering what gastronomic orgy is in store. my days are spent on the beach. kids have a new racket this summer. few have autograph books. most of them come with clam and oyster shells to be autographed. vallee played here last night. as usual, rudy packed the dance-hall and received his annual welcome. i didn't go out to see him. i've gotten so i can't enjoy a radio actor without the commercials and just rudy and his dramatic lowlights aren't enough for me.

nothing else semi-exciting. hope all goes well in the stern. best for now. will advise if i have any traffic with doc.

F

old orchard beach
august 25th
1941

dear mr. cook . . .

    i am a friend of rockwell's. i wrote you some weeks back re a vaudeville series you are concocting. since then i have had no word from you. i have been wondering whether you have had your hand caught in a compass or whether you have burned your fingers down to stubs stuffing down the tobacco in your pipe in nor'easters.

    you will be glad to learn that our annual pilgrimage to the rockwell estate came off as per schedule. doc was a little the worse for wear. a friend of his died and doc and madelyn attended the widow during the cremation ritual and later returned to boothbay to strew the ashes over the bounding main. doc provided a detailed account of the happenings at the crematory and reported that the widow ate an enormous steak, with french-fried potatoes, while they waited around for the body to be reduced to ashes. madelyn helped the widow to assemble the husband's clothes to give to the undertaker and reports that the widow insisted upon including the deceased's jock-strap in with his apparel.

    the rockwell fishing club, a small smelly group dedicated to wanton waste of bait and the conservation of deep sea mammalia, convened amid billow and for the fourth consecutive year nothing was caught. two days before our futile trek, there had been another expedition in which doc's guest had one bite, one catch and a fifty pound cod for his trouble. doc had the cod-skin drying out on his dock. it is large enough to enable him to add a zipper and own a sporty overnight bag. if you see a tired-looking chap headed belvederewards, carrying a cod-skin satchel you might as well hail him . . . it will be doc.

    i am waiting around for the hermit of pine point to visit me. the hermit wrote and asked for a prompt reply. he said his time was limited. he is the first hermit i have ever heard of who was in a hurry.

hope you both made the most of your vacation. i haven't accomplished much. i started to work on plots and other matter and then the agency advised that there would have to be some changes. i don't know what to try to lay out for the future now until after we know what is wanted.

will be here until september 6th or 7th. portland sends her love to tugboat annie and the ancient mariner. it won't be long now.

F

the belmont
west harwich, mass.
july 3rd, 1950

alton—

this is the first chance i have had to answer your letter. it has been so damn foggy here we haven't been able to find our room and have been spending most of the time roaming the halls. the sun has been out only for a brief appearance in three days. either the rainmaker has lost control or god is getting even with people who expect to make a living fleecing tourists. if the room gets any damper i am going to get a couple of loaves of bread and start making some homemade penicillin.

re my television future. it is strange that you should write about the alley. we had a great discussion about the alley at a meeting last week. some were for it and some were against it. one argument against it was that we shouldn't go into the new medium and give people the impression that we were merely putting the old radio devices before the cameras. another one was that all of the n.y. shows are going to be done in theatres. this means that everything will be photographed on the stage. there will be no opportunity to get effects of a walk down a street. the cameras will be all in front or from side angles. i wanted to eliminate the audience and try to do as you suggest with a decrepit alley or street but i was told that that thinking is for the future. at the moment the network and the client both want a revue type of show, with audience and everything else that will make the medium a bore in a hurry.

the director, choreographer and other department heads will not meet until the first of august which gives me ample time to have my suggestions in hand for the assemble date. when i get all of their reactions i will call you. i would like to function as simply as possible and the alley would certainly simplify the writing and thinking. my fate, however, is in the laps of the executives and i can only hope if not for the best at least for the next-best. forgot to mention last week. if the strike at the world-telegram continues and you need any financial help—let me know. we will be here until july 31st.

portland sends her best to bertie and jr.

regards—fred allen

H. ALLEN SMITH

The introduction or preface referred to in the following letters is the one Allen wrote for H. Allen Smith's first best-selling book of humor, *Low Man on a Totem Pole*. After Smith wrote the book and after Fred had contributed its introduction, neither of them could think of an appropriate title for it. Fred suggested among many others *The Two Sams—Flot and Jet*. Finally an editor at Doubleday, Doran & Company, the publishers, noticed a line in Fred's introduction about a low man on a totem pole and Smith wearily agreed to call his collection of reminiscences by that name. The two Allens had become close friends a year earlier, in 1939, when the author, then a New York *World-Telegram* reporter, had interviewed the radio comedian. H. Allen describes F. Allen as the only one of the many celebrities he interviewed during his newspaper years whom he wanted to keep on seeing as a friend after the interview was written and printed.

november eighth
1940

dear h. allen . . .

i finally found out what that h stands for. at least i thought i had found out. working in code i came to the conclusion that the h was for hernia. wednesday, however, i met mrs. cook and she advised me that you had been spared the hospital ordeal and that the two lumps were nothing but the after-effects of some bubblegum that had backfired, or something.

re the introduction. since you won't need it until next month, i can probably assemble some smithiana and turn it over to you. if it is suitable between us we should be able to fix up the grammar and if my name won't be a liability in merchandising the tome you are welcome to use it for any advertising purposes. when the book comes out, assuming that my preface is used (first assuming that it is written) i can even get a bit out of it on the program some week.

what with going on information please and turning up as the writer of a fragmentary contribution to a doubleday, doran publication i will soon be moving in the fadiman set. assuming that the fadiman set moves.

if you want to talk about the "who" treatise i can meet you next tuesday, at 3 p.m., in my atelier (which until recently i thought was one of two things that spurted from a deer's parietal area). if you are free we can discuss the "who" effort and the introduction. i will scare up some brilliant mots you can use. smith! the first man to put book-ends at each side of a psycopathic ward. smith! the first numismatist to collect his coins the hard way xraying gum slot to take to his studio. smith! the first writer to ever look to gravity to assure him that he will go down in history.

regards to mrs. smith and the sundry tiny smiths who roam your atelier. a word like that will bear repeating. sincerely . . .

f. allen (smith)

november 21st
1940

dear h.a. . . .

have been thinking at odd moments about the introduction, or preface if you will, to your book. i say i have been thinking at odd moments. at even moments i have been attempting to get out the programs, truck with the mail, appease panhandlers and look for some gentleman on variety who said that i was verbose and made the information please broadcast dull entertainment. it isn't bad enough to waste an evening, appear gratis, but i have to get panned on top of it.

i may have to go to the hospital for one day next week and as soon as that is over i will get started on my literary chore. will try to finish it semi-quickly. if it isn't right you will still have time to get a learned conspirator to lend a hand. i marked down a few audition titles. they may suggest something. wacks museum sounds good but the word wacks might be confusing. these may give you an idea to work on . . . album of unfamiliar people . . . you, the people . . . the sixth column . . . notes from the diary of a family tree surgeon . . . the human race . . . people on parade . . . rhapsody in riff-raff . . . unsocial register . . . you and you and you . . . nocturne in neurosis . . . complexes and cameos . . . to hell with it. let me know about the letter when you have time regards.

F. Allen
180 west 58th

p.s. i am enclosing a recently written verse

(enclosure)

The Executive
by
James Whitcomb Allen

The Executive is
A busy man
Who sits around
On his frustrated can

He presses his buzzer
He jiggles his phone
And barks his commands
In stentorian tone

His every word
Is a slogan . . . a phrase
He checks . . . He ties in
Buttons-up . . . and okays

He mother-hens it
He thinks in the groove
He knows his competitor's
Every move

He runs with the ball
Hits the nail on the head
And passes all dividends
To keep out of the red

He huddles in conference
With vice-minor officials
And addresses these menials
By their initials

It's "Yes, C.L."
And "T.H. is set"
F.O.B. . . . C.O.D.
The whole alphabet

Yes, the busy Executive
Knows no lull, Sir
His stomach's a composite
Duodenal ulcer

He fumes in his office
As big as the Roxy
At the stockholders' meetings
He's Mr. Proxy

On Wall Street, he's known
To each brokerage house
As a bull, or a bear
And sometimes . . . a louse

Each summer, he cruises
About on his boat
And wails "The New Deal
Is getting my goat"

With his bisodol, aspirin
Phenol . . . and pills
The Executive copes with
His executive ills

For Man must toil
And Man must work
And the Executive is
A dynamic jerk

Hail! Neurotic Napoleon
Long may you live
Amok on your buttocks
Bold Ex-ecutive!

december
14th
1940

h.a.

am enclosing the enclosed.*
after noting its length i would suggest that you use what you
have for the preface and make this the book.
as you know this is not my racket.
the trouble i have is that there are so few minutes available that
i cannot sit down at any one sitting and work out a mode of
attack.
whatever is done has to be done in dribs and drabs. when a thing
is done in a drib it is usually drab.
you can look this over.
you can do anything you want with it.
if you want to rewrite, cut, shrink, eliminate, etc. i, not being
george bernard shaw, will have no objections.
if the idea is entirely off the beam you have my permission to
throw the whole brochure away and approach gilbert seldes, or
another craftsman who understands the business, to turn out
something more suitable.

you can let me know what you think after you have waded
through smith . . . in the aggregate.
the picture opens tuesday night at the paramount.
after the paramount press boys have safely seen the egg into the
incubator and depart for the coast and after i get wednesday's
show on the air i shall have a little more time. if you feel that
this matter can be used in one form, or another, i can meet you
thursday, or friday, and discuss it. if i am mentioned in the book
i can use that as a basis for some radio banter so the preface
doesn't really matter on that score.

* The preface for Smith's book, *Low Man on a Totem Pole.*

trust that all of the smiths have been talked out of santa claus and that you have found a title for the tome.

see you soon.

f. allen
180 west 58th

december
27th
1940

dear guy de smith . . .

now that you are about to assume the mantle of authorship you should get one of those nance names. percy bysshe smith wouldn't be bad. james russell smith. henry wadsworth smith. with a little thought i am sure you can scare up a name that will add some dignity to the book's jacket and raise hell with the postman out your way when mail under your nom de plume starts pouring in.

why don't you steal roosevelt's opening remark for your title "my friends"? you just can't put out a book with no title. who the hell will know what to ask for? people can't walk in to brentano's and say "give me that book with no name, that bastard work of h. allen smith's." you might have a dotted line at the top of each book and let the buyers fill in their own titles. a lot of people always think a book should be called something else. you could list the author as h. allen smith and . . . when the purchaser has given your book his title he can also add his name as co-author. this would please the vanity of many booklovers and cause no end of confusion when each one started to sue you for a share of the royalties on the one book bought.

doubleday and the other guy must have a gallup poll on the book market, or something, and will bring out your completed work at a propitious time. i have met several publishers. they have all bewildered me. most of them survive through manipulating the work of others while they themselves concentrate on drinking or social contacts. as a class they are too precious for me.

i am always afraid that i will lean against a publisher and chip or break him. you can't very well champ at the bit. things are only important to each of us as individuals. to you the book is important. to doubleday and doran it is number #702. to me the radio show is important. to many a bum in the studio audience it means but an hour in a warm room and a fair chance to pan- handle me later. science wastes so much time trying to split the atom. it would be better if the small nugget of sincerity that exists in our world was split so that there might be enough to go around.

the older you get the more people you seem to know in the obituary pages. my aunt is 84 and has outlived almost two generations. she doesn't know anyone but god anymore. my doc- tor says that he never feels sorry for people who die. their troubles are over. he mourns for those who are left, relatives and friends whose status is affected through the passing of one of their group.

you at least relaxed on xmas day. we worked. too many cooks will spoil a quart. if alton was over last week you know this by now. we are going to have xmas dinner at alton's after the first of the year. it will be on a friday evening. if you are available you might stop in and catch two catholics eating flesh meat on friday.

do you think there would be a large market for a book about thorne smith? if you are going to do a hell of a lot of work it ought to be on something that will have dough possibilities. i imagine his life was antic-laden but unless turnabout and his other books were popular classics of their day i question the market for his biography. kindly have the figures at our next meeting. those bastards can't waste your time from now on. who is your agent? get him on the phone! is the advance in pulp money? you have got to be on your toes. some publisher may approach you to do the life of stonewall jackson and try to give you an advance in confederate money. what do you pay your agent? it wouldn't take much to wean me away from the radio business. perhaps after the government finishes with radio i will get 20 years in leavenworth.

hoping this finds you the same, etc. will ask alton to let you know the xmas dinner date. i think it will be jan. 10th if it is okay with bertie. will fade out with the pierre laval theme song "the last time i saw paris."

f.a.
180 west 58th

april 1st
1941

dear low . . .

scrivened fun has a far better chance than oral fun. that, to me, is radio's greatest problem for our type of show. instead of pointing everything for a certain class of listener at home all of the humor has to be lowered and played in a bass clef motif to get an audible reaction from the majority of the juks who make a racket of broadcast-going. with scrivened fun . . . there it is . . . you can read it, weigh it, work it out and finally enjoy it. oral fun is heard once by the hearee and its reaction can be marred by a thousand and one things rampant as the oral jibes are being dispensed.

mons. moran's reaction to "low man" augers well. if the doubleday doran people are limbering up socially i know where you can rent a windsor tie to show those crums what an author looks like. a blond goatee wouldn't look bad sort of hanging limp over the knot in the windsor tie either. if you want to become eccentric in six easy lessons let me know. i have some old pictures of a rake who pimped for the floradora sextet some years back. you would make a hit in his inverness with the satin outside especially with all of the neon around town to play on your cape as you did the town.

"omar—the preface writer"

may third
1941

loch . . .

this is the scot preamble to "low man" . . . used here as a salutation. i told you the damn book would cause a hernia to sprout in the peaceful loins of your ideal existence. come fame . . . you are a marked man. no longer will you be able to stand back and adjust your myopia to scan the clod and the exponent of non compos mentis. you will be under scrutiny from now on. lou sobol will chronicle your every move, ed sullivan will invite you to appear on his summer radio program . . . for free . . . josef bryan, 111 will tail you for a sat e post piece. your name will be added to all of the sucker and chump lists. real estate men will try to sell you an estate. house and garden will want a subscription. that sonofabitz who operates "who's who" will make your life a hot-foot. better to be named in "who's thro" and know that you can prowl around a nonentity than to be lionized and known from coast to coast as "low man on the scrotum pole." christ, smith! you've done it!

next friday, at 5.30, will be okay for me. if we make it later it will get confused with dinner and probably gum up the evening in the event that you have something to do. i don't know what i will be doing an hour from now, let alone friday, but 5.30 is angelus time. i always hear bells ringing at that hour. if one of the bells proves to be the doorbell i shall lift my head and open the door. if it is you and the d.d. man you may enter.

the letter might be all right if i wrote that i was soliciting preface work . . . or if i was always starting things i couldn't finish and must confine my literary efforts to introduction writing. i could ask the trade to keep an eye out for men like hemingway and steinbeck who might be in a position to write a book to follow my introduction after it had been written. we can talk about it when you show.

i am just about to write an amos and andy bit. with all of the voices i don't know what the hell is going to happen. i am supposed to go on their program next thursday. god knows what will happen then either.

amos and andy are really the cleverest team in radio today. their dialogue holds up better than any of the other shows which is really something when you realize that for over ten years they have been grinding out five shows each week. their voice changes, and the fading in and out of the characters as they come and go, are uncanny. most people cannot appreciate the skill involved which is to be expected. most people knee deep in the little messes they call their lives cannot appreciate much of anything.

"preface peter"

old orchard beach
maine
august 15th
1941

low man . . .

your breezy letter arrived yesterday. as i opened the envelope a gust from it tore loose and slammed every door in this beaver-board castle. this haunt is rather flimsy and we have to go outside to belch since even a zephyr will rattle the foundation and cause any open door to bang and make the interior a vacuum. finally, with the gale released from your scroll i managed to tack and reach a chair where each paragraph was carefully perused.

i saw you billed on one program but we couldn't tune the station in up here. radio is a problem. the set picks up storms within a 200 mile radius and apart from the portland station, which is part of the red network, we are radio poor. if you sound like willkie on the air you may be able to make transcriptions for him or double for wendell in doubtful areas during the next presidential election. it would be something if you did get a spot on a radio show. doing one bit on the show wouldn't require too much time for preparation and even if matson's asking price was shaded it would still be a living wage.

knowing phil brown i am not surprised at his lascivious observations. he is executive not only without portfolio, he is also without desk. he always seems to be roaming the halls at n.b.c. and i, along with thousands of others, have no idea as to his status with the organization. he may be bait for the tours. as brown's pratt disappears through various doors in the building the guides may shout "there goes a friend of kate smith's" or "quick! there goes singing sam." if you know what mr. brown does there in all fairness you should tell him. i am sure that he is in constant doubt as to his duties.

i have accomplished practically nothing here. relatives have been entertained and frequent visits to a medico in biddeford show, according to the medico, that my blood pressure is higher than it was when they sent me to the hospital. i haven't much faith in practising medical men hereabouts. one doctor here had two operations last week. one was a circumcision and the other was a tonsil case. for some reason the boy whose tonsils were to be removed couldn't come to the hospital. the doctor became confused and removed the other boy's tonsils. later in the day the patient's mother called the doctor and asked why no dressing had been put on the boy's member. the doctor said "when i went to give him ether i didn't like the boy's breathing and thought it best to take out his tonsils first." this bird taking my blood pressure may be using a speedometer for all i know.

no news is rampant here. we had a fire and the waxworks burned down. the woman who owned the concession fainted but the firemen couldn't spare enough water to bring her to. when she revived the place was a mound of slippery ashes. twenty or more pinball machines were destroyed which i know will upset you. when a pinball machine is exposed to fire all of the bulbs and mechanism lumps up against the backboard and when the remnants cool off the machine looks like a racked omelet on a charred piece of wood. the bay mare on the merry-go-round is pregnant. a bull termite, oversexed no doubt, is being sought as the culprit. the man who passes the collection plate at our church has short arms and people have to scale their offerings into the basket. the old hermit is putting all of his clam earnings into food. he has

21 pounds of coffee and a case of evaporated milk hidden away in his lousy shack against a bleak winter.

we expect to be here until labor day. then after a short stay in boston i shall return to salvage what is left of the program. we have a new director, who formerly worked for eddie cantor, and he has hired press men, advance men, authors and god knows what. i won't know what we have on tap until i return. this year will probably wash me up anyway and with the tax load and other headaches it will perhaps be just as well. formal regards pending.

f. allen
3 odena ave

monday
night

low man . . .

am writing from my quarters, "nephitis manor." the carrier pigeon bearing your letter was disemboweled by a buzzard who has been lurking over 58th street since the shootings on friday last. apparently, the carrion canary is a catholic for it disdained the human flesh that littered the sidewalk on friday. an atheist buzzard would have made short work of the man who shot himself through the head and the officer who was drilled through the rump (as some papers put it). fortunately, for me the vulture only consumed your pigeon down to the beak. your letter, locked in the pigeon's beak was delivered to me this a.m.

we are going to interview crossley on may 14th. we'll find out about the ratings. they don't mean anything to me. it is simply the trouble they cause in the agency and sponsor's office when they go down. i guess the cosmopolitan man has the right idea but you have to be a yuck to cater to yucks. you can't go through life writing with your tongue in your cheek. half of the world will think you chew tobacco and the other half will think you have bitten off the end of somebody's goiter. you have a much better chance with written humor than with oral humor. all hu-

mor is a matter of opinion. the thing to do is decide where you
can get the most and then adjust yourself to the level demanded
by that publication or the medium involved.

well, to hell with it. my brother had company last sunday.
the man and his wife had to leave early. he couldn't figure out
why until his wife told him that the other fellows wife told her
that she had just had an operation . . . the incision was itching
and she had to get home and scratch it. why she couldn't excuse
herself and scratch her scar in my brother's house . . . i don't
know. that is the life. i would be better off knowing the people
my brother knows. half of the people i know are scratching themselves while they are cuffing me for liquor, rent, etc.

f.a.

october 20th
1941

dear low . . .

i met ben serkowich in an italian restaurant two weeks ago.
he told me that you had gone to the nude, or dude ranch with
jimmy street. i don't know street but the hibernation sounded suspicious. ben said you were going to work like dogs on the play
but apparently all you consummated were the intermissions. bac-
chus is certainly making a game attempt to gather you in again.
i trust that you will fend him off. the grape is a globule unlike
trousers. the grape does not improve with pressing. i can't drink
any more. i brought some brandy over to alton's that last time.
it tasted as though sloan had merged with hennessy and had a
beverage miscarriage. it was sort of a three star liniment. i was
sick for two days, didn't know what i was doing, and wrote a hell
of a script. it is too much trouble to get in that condition to
write each week. with my essential hypertension i am supposed
to report to the doctor every two weeks for blood pressure check-
ups. i can have no salt and a mere peek at a snapshot of lot's
wife sends my pressure up. hope you kept a diary at the ranch. i
might get some sketch plots out of it.

hope i can see some of your columns when they get going. now, look what you're in for. ten years. i knew that book would kink your life. as soon as you wrote a tome along comes gypsy rose lee to lower the tone of the craft so actually you haven't progressed socially. six grand isn't bad, considering the times, etc. i imagine if you ever have time to write another the sales will profit through the friends low man made you. then again, it is responsible for getting you off the paper and who knows where you will end up now? runyon is a producer at rko. i wonder if his ulcer knows where runyon is? if it does there will be colonic hell to pay shortly. if you are coming over to the city some afternoon let me know. my days have been screwed up with guest stars and college guests but i am generally here tuesdays, thursdays and fridays after three. tomorrow, tuesday, i am meeting miss madeleine carroll at three. last week, friday at three i met miss boland. i am moving in better circles . . . my eyes have told me so.

thanx for the wire. good luck with the column. see you soon. the ex-preface writer . . .

f.a.

nov. 20th
1941

h.a.

thanx a lot for your billet. it wasn't expected and can not be termed a billet-over-doux. the modernistic house sounds swell but i wouldn't know what the hell to do with it. you, at least, have matered the intricasies of the kerosene burner and the sluggish spark plug but i can't drive a car and i haven't enough ingenuity to master the art of getting cellophane off of bread. if we had a place like that i am sure that portland and i would be found there dead of malnutrition as soon as the snow thawed and the natives came up in the spring to see how we were doing.

your house is wonderful. i can't imagine a more ideal setup for you and nell. if i had enough confidence in my writing ability i would screw this lout-baiting racket and retire with my thoughts. i would be damn lonesome, i imagine. i don't see why nell is bothering to redecorate. the interior looks perfect to me but don't forget that i spent twenty years traveling around the country sleeping in flea-bags and actors' inns.

one consolation you should relish is knowing that when it gets a little colder you won't have to worry about the puppy not being housebroken. on zero days you can push him outside the door. when he makes water it will freeze instantly. you can break it off and throw the urine icycle into the hedge. during the warmer months you might invent a way, with your new-found mechanical skill, to connect the furniture to the frigidair. you could then have all of the chairs ice-cold and when the puppy raises his leg against the ditto of a chair his urine would freeze instantly and you could break it off indoors and hurry to a window with the albumen popsicle.

we dropped abel off at his street. the following monday i had a note reminding me that the deadline was approaching for my cuff story for variety. this year, i have too many things on hand and will have to sit out the anniversary edition. i have advised abel. it may break up a great touring friendship.

thanx for the modern library tip. i am going over tomorrow to see about brann, the iconoclast, and the knickerbocker history. when the winter gets going, if you meet all trains, i may come up some day to see how all goes. thanx for last saturday. best to nell.

f. allen
180 west 58th

december 19th
1942

h.a.—

i saw the television show thursday night and watching you on the mccaffrey show and ours you have developed an ease that should make anything you want to do in radio a simple project.

on several occasions i have argued with john steinbeck. i claim that when a writer becomes successful, generally without giving it too much thought, he assumes another style of living. with the introduction of luxury into his life he withdraws from his old friends, haunts and the contacts that enabled him to find material that made him successful in the first place. john says it isn't true but i don't think you can come out of the stork club with your belly full and caviar rolling down your vest and rush home and write a "grapes of wrath." john says you can, so i must be wrong. i think it would be swell for you to do something in radio or break up the convenient routine you have had for the past few years. if the book business is going through a dull period you won't lose anything and you will probably get a big kick out of some activity for a change.

f. allen

january 22
1942

sir:
    i am in receipt of your protocol and the enclosed panegyric having to do with atlas, charles, as we who work around the directory printing office call him. my intentions to acknowledge receipt of your portfolio were thwarted as a result of my contact with miss dotty lamour, of the cinema.

    miss lamour reported for rehearsal on monday and read the little mirth muffin we had cooked up for her as though it were a billet-doux from a sweetheart with whom she has just severed relations. i returned to my outer sanctum, (schuster was using the inner one) peeled my typewriter and emerged wednesday at 1.40 a.m. with the gaudy trivia miss lamour and i committed last evening. my contact with paramount's sultry siren ended with the score . . . lamour . . . o. allen . . . 3 (days behind with mail, touches, etc.)

    when the totem pole did not appear in the telegram (i even searched the help wanted columns thinking it might have been reduced to fine print to catch the magnifying glass trade) i thought that perhaps you were down with the vapours. i asked alton. hence, the inquiry as to your physical status and the request for a sample of your urine. i cannot understand the attitudes of messrs. howard and wood. if the last minute war news is crowding other items out of the paper, that is one thing, but if those pock-marked bastards intimate that there exists another motive for not using "the pole" . . . they have me to deal with.

i have made a new arrangement with my newsboy. i have stopped buying the damned world telegram in bulk. alton is my friend and i read his column each day. pegler is a stranger but he writes with a harpoon dipped in venom and i feel that he is entitled to the support of all readers who enjoy briefs written with harpoon. the new deal i have worked out with the newsboy functions, as follows; the world telegram runs about thirty-four pages daily. i buy one page, the one containing alton's column, each day. at the end of the month i have purchased some thirty pages and accordingly pay the newslad three cents. when the "pole" ran daily i bought the telegram six days each week. messrs. howard and wood, who formerly received about 72¢ monthly, from this ex-subscriber, now get 3¢. if i can get dr. townsend to start a "totem pole" movement we will bring those ink-barons to their knees.

trust that all is going well down by the inkwell. formal regards to mme. smith and your son. your daughter, who listens to cantor, can get her well-wishes from her thyroid idol.
from . . .
a brother member of the so-called human race . . .

f.a.

may
fifth
1942

dear "cornsilk" . . .

despite the fact that you played that "cob-rayon" selection over and over again i can't even remember how the damn thing goes. it proves that this is an oscar levant tune. i could hum "dancing cheek to cheek" the first time i heard it. after i had only heard "dardanella" twice i blew two cold sores off my upper lip whistling the melody but that damn "cornsilk" i must have heard forty times in one night and i still don't know how it turns out melodically. either your ear for music has a hernia in the lobe or you are far ahead of this generation musically when you pick "cornsilk" for your hit parade. i would rather not hear "cornsilk" sung even by ray sinatra . . . and you know who he is? god forbid.

it has taken me days to answer your letter. the draft is playing hob with my writers. one fellow is in touch with the draftboard. he has enlisted in the navy and he is taking a course at the air-corps school nights. he will probably end up in the cavalry. the other fellow was put in four a on account of his eyes. he can't see the punctuation when that sky-writer spells out i.j.fox in the welkin. recently he was called back and reclassified. he is now in 1.a. if he takes off his glasses he won't even see the war if they lead him to it.

i am still going nuts around here. dr. carver, the tuskegee wonder-worker sent me 75 pounds of peanuts last week. dr. carver neglected to roast the damn things or i might have become an elephant tommy manville. what one does with 75 pounds of green peanuts, i don't know.

trust all goes well down by the shift-key. if i ever get organized perhaps we can report at music-lover cook's sanctum one night for another go at "cornsilk."

formal regards to the long-suffering nell and the two children who have a beast for a father. more anon.

f.a.

july
second
1942

dear h.a.

there has been so little news of you, of late, that i thought that perhaps you had changed your name to mark twain to insure a freedom from pests and extemporaneous well-wishers who delight in testing a successful man for claustrophia and frigging up his days and nights to keep the man of letters from getting the muse behind the door and accomplishing his foul purpose. i assume that you have things under control and that nell has you in the same state.

perhaps we can see you later this month. i don't know how long i shall be at the clinic. nor do i know what will happen when i get out of there. i have had so many doctors' digits poked up my rectal orifice that i should start wearing a glove sarong instead of drawers. last sunday, before the man in the control room could wave his finger at wallington to start the program my rump waved down and wallington was off.

mr. joel, of dial, had a look at the fallstaff poems and agreed that they would hardly be something posterity would be interested in. the poems, as part of the news reel, sound okay for a once over lightly hearing but held up to the light fallstaff's rhymes cannot hold a candle to an early xray of percy bysshe shelley's chest.

f.a.

september
18th
1942

dear "friend of zero mostel's" . . .

this is the first chance i have had to get at the mail. we returned to the haunts of the "little flower" last week but an aunt passed away up home and my brother was in the hospital. i had to journey to boston to attend the funeral. when i saw the open grave it was a great temptation. peace at last. the end of everything. a chance to relax until resurection day.

i have been having quite a time in recent weeks. when i returned from the clinic i reported to a medico here and started to take a potassium treatment for high blood pressure. potassium is powerful and acts differently on systems. i don't think many doctors are too familiar with the drug and i doubt if the doctor who started me on the treatment had had any previous experience with it. i went along for seven weeks getting blood tests and varying the dosage. finally, my system became saturated and i broke out in a lavender rash, my nose closed up and my throat got as dry as a bedouin's instep. i didn't sleep for ten nights. the doctor became alarmed and i have spent the past two weeks trying to get the potassium out of my system. i have been drinking kalak water and taking capsules and appear to be shedding the drug at a rapid rate. i will be fortunate if the doctor can get me back to where i was with only the high blood pressure. my entire summer has been given over to medicine and i know now what a guinea pig goes through.

since i have been through the potassium siege my mind seems to falter. i don't know whether i am through as a personality, or not. perhaps you can get me on your air-warden staff. i look well in a helmet. i can't sleep. i spent the entire summer in an eternal blackout at the beach. i can see in the dark and have just about enough wind left to operate a small whistle if the pea isn't too heavy.

f. allen

october
17th
1942

h.a.

double r i g a n spells harrigan. you have the initials to start a song revival if you care to contact the merry macs or the andrews sisters and get the melody distorted to insure its success. annie laurie made the grade with the jitterbug element and there is no reason why "harrigan, that's me" should not be revived.

if you do not see fit to keep away from the air raid squad leader who had the spiked grape juice punch at his house you are headed for perdition. it won't be long before this cretin will have you down behind the barn pasting those decalcomania pastels on your forearm. i realize that to you jackson heights is "our town" but you have an ex-good name to protect. you don't want people pointing at nelle and the kids and saying "there goes the family of the man who has decalcomania etchings on his long palmaris."

i don't see anything glaring wrong with the copy of my letters that you want to use in "life in a putty knife factory." personally i don't care. all i have to fear is the reaction of the client, the dealers and a few stray zealots. i have marked a few things. on page 7 . . . i think if wooden leg was changed to glass eye the joke wouldn't suffer. our ex-sponsor did have an artificial limb and since i know the book will get around among the advertising element i wouldn't want to have this gentleman offended. glass eye to me is funnier. if it wasn't sacrilegious it could be a priest with a "stained glass-eye." but it is so it can't be.

page 8 . . . the expression used by vaudeville actors is "the manager came running back." for some reason when an act was changed on the bill or a joke was cut out the manager always came running back. he never walked or crept. he ran.

page 9 . . . i think louse would do as well as "son of a bitch." it sounds kind of strained and if the texas company man cuts out any mention of the song "praise the lord and pass the ammunition" because it might offend people in the bible belt god knows what his reaction would be to "son of a bitch" even in a letter.

page 13 . . . inserting "in my estimation" qualifies the statement and also eliminates one "really." also, page 13, i think the point is "i should start wearing a glove for a sarong." i think the drawers mention is superfluous, even short drawers.

as i say, i don't give a damn about anything in the book or letters, etc. as long as i can avoid repercussions that might crop up later and cause some bother in our artistic circles. the entire chapter reads funny to me. if i get chased off the air i will start writing and perhaps have peace of mind for the first time in ten years.

there are a couple of gags you might use in the book. the description of an advertising agency . . . an advertising agency is eighty-five percent confusion and fifteen percent commission.

a radio producer . . . is an ulcer with a stop-watch.

the head of the advertising agency who never looked up at a conference. when he was in college he played quarterback on the football team. every time he looked up he saw nothing but a lot of asses. that is why he never looked up during a conference. it made him think he was a quarterback again.

i didn't tell godfrey about "low man." he found the book down in washington. he got such a kick out of the whole thing that he devoted most of his program one morning to the book. too bad it didn't come sooner. apparently brother godfrey makes up his show as he goes along. he read a times article i wrote on his program one morning. last week, he read a letter i sent him. i wouldn't be surprised if he spends a week reading the various chapters of "low man." he, incidentally, is a very nice fellow.

will return chapter ten via mail on monday. i haven't a large envelope around here. i have to interview roy rogers. will get the envelope later and mail the stuff back monday morning. have been busy but will try and find another time we can visit alton. i stood out the last time. most people on your street had their dogs smelling trees. i had you. fortunately no one appeared or i might have had to slip a leash on you to make it look good.

see you sooner or later. i still feel lousy from all of the medication and pressure remedies. regards to nelle and the kids if they are speaking to you. more anon.

F.A.

nov. 9th
1942

h.a.

the program is still a pain in the iliofemoral ligament. the orson welles show was the only one i have liked. it is hard to take guests each week and make the thing jell. the time is short, ideas cannot be worked out and we generally end up with a few gags and an anemic sketch that stems from some activity that concerns the guest. orson was a lot of fun. i had never met him before but the impression i had conjured up of the genius was all dissipated. he is a jolly man about glass and in our dealings was regular in every respect. i would not hesitate to propose him for membership in the woodman of the world, grange number 7, boothbay harbor, if he cared about joining this worthy order.

i hesitate to make any suggestions about the index and preface of the book. it is no doubt too late now. i think too many liberties taken with accepted practises hurt more than they help. if the book has guts, which i am sure it has for this book has to live and how the hell can it live without guts? if it has guts i think that any didoes in print might tend to make the setup appear gaggy. those things, like jokes about the sponsor in our business, are enjoyed by a few people who are privy to the workings of a trade but the great mass of people, those who listen to fibber mcgee and bob hope, resent any trifling with custom or tradition.

have had 10 phone calls since typing the last line. also, two callers. i give up. regards to nell. hope all goes well. (a fallstaff rhyme). may see you soon.

f.a.

jan.

2

1943

h . . . (as on page 516 funk & wagnalls practical standard dictionary)

a . . . (as in the third bar of brahm's immortal "touche made with a chambermaid")

i have so much mail unanswered around here this joint is beginning to look like sub-station 7, of the post office department. sub-station 7 is located at floral park and is the foulest, most-littered hole this side of the famous hole noir of calcutta. i have either got to get around with a gun and kill all of the people who write to me or i have got to ply my pratt to the wicker and spend a week answering mail. i am seriously considering the bottle again. if you think i have a future as a toper will you let me know. also, could you give me a few letters to some reliable bartenders to enable me to get a start drinking. i know it is difficult to get off on the right foot drinking and a letter from an old newspaperman to a bartender sometimes helps a nouveau drunkard get under way.

you will be glad to learn that the president sent me a personal note on the coffee bean. frank put in a couple of gags which auger well for his future if he wants to write for red skelton when he leaves the white house.

more anon. regards from a man who passed perry charles on the street yesterday. i didn't get the chap's name.

f. allen

sept. 12/43

dear h.a.

have been intending to write you for some time. some added pavement was needed on the road to hell and my good intentions were used for this purpose. portland and i gave the welkin a workout over at alton cook's last monday. we learned that jackson heights had been de-smithed. it seemed strange to roam the streets of "commuters' gulch," as i in a witless moment once christened jackson heights, and not hear the foul strains of "cornsilk" soiling the breeze. the entire neighborhood seemed strangely still. the bartender in that jungle tavern near alton's dozed over the cash register, stray dogs scurried through the vacant lots with their tails and their genitals between their legs, the pinball machines were draped, little children peeked between venetian blinds and sliced their glances evincing no desire to leave their houses to play, salvation army lasses stood about the corners with muted tambourines, air-raid wardens wet the peas in their whistles so that they might blow silently come the drill and a stagnant lull permeated the dunes. de-smithed, jackson heights had become a ghost town, its vitals had been removed.

some weeks ago, i wrote harry tugend and asked him to look you up when you arrived in hollywood. the lone ranger has his horse for company but a new writer locked in his cubicle at a picture studio is a lonesome sonofabitch and i thought harry, knowing that racket, might be of service if you had any immediate problems. since he has been "upped" to a producer's berth, i haven't heard from brother tugend. he may have his pratt caught in a swivel or he may be in conference this month or he may have gotten in front of the demille unit on its way to the commissary and been trampled to death. several writers and producers have met their ends in this gruesome manner and i hope when mr. demille and his entourage are on the loose that you will take cover.

portland and i are leaving for hollywood this coming week. i am supposed to work on a story and later make a picture. there are a few minor problems. the man from the black market is holding up the celluloid, the cameraman can't get a priority on a tripod, he has been working at republic with his camera strapped to the back of a dwarf, and we have a mexican director who speaks no english. as soon as the producer finds a mexican interpreter, the cameraman finds a tripod, the black market man comes across with the film and the screen play has been completed we will go into production. these problems, as hollywood goes, are minor ones and you might say we are as good as "under way," a technical expression used by many executives in your profession.

hope that you have an eddie bracken story, or a bob hope farce, on the fire and that assorted situations, quips, jibes and mots are flowing from your pen like gore from an open wound. trust that nell is getting accustomed to wearing a sarong around her midriff and that you have found a way to keep your beret from slipping down over your eyes when you nod to mr. desylva as he passes you on his way to see the rushes. perhaps you can introduce me to preston sturges. he always wears a muffler on the set. they say he has to wear the muffler because he has no neck. good luck . . .

f. allen
180 west 58 st

may 20th
1944

dear h.a.

as you know "man-hog day" was observed several sundays ago. i had beaters go up through maine and stalk doc rockwell out of his lair. the doc was duly provided with a quota of remarks and some jibes at the smiling lithuanian and appeared on the texaco star theatre as is his annual custom. as long as i have a program "man-hog day" will be observed and rockwell fans, who are thinning out not unlike the ranks of the g.a.r., will have an opportunity to hear their idol.

from your remarks about the book it would seem that you are on the horns of a duenna at the moment. these periods of despair are common to all creative artists. i am told that there were moments when the man who used to write the lord's prayer on the head of a pin went into a bitter funk and berrated the lord for the inadequacies of his supplication and scoffed at himself for not being able to write the prayer on the pin's point. i cannot tell you how to remedy your attitude towards the book but if you can catch hypertension i am a whiz on blood pressure.

hope nell is well. i am involved with a gentleman named skirball who has suddenly appeared with morrie ryskind and a new version of the picture we didn't make last fall. my writers leave with the winged victory cast this week. i don't know what the hell is going on. perhaps we can gather at alton's some evening and exchange troubles. open a grief swap shop.

f. allen

GULLS' PRIVY
(the allen summer home)

old orchard beach
maine
july 10th
1945

dear allen . . .

sorry i didn't have a chance to see you before we left the city. i called nell one day and you were down in a swamp with a pest-control tank strapped to your spine jousting with mosquitoes, gnats, gadflies and other forms of mt. kisco annoyances.

before leaving new york i spent two weeks in the hospital with the mumps. i was supposed to speak at a school dinner, in boston. i sat down to think about the good old days at school and must have overdone my reminiscing. the next a.m. i awoke with a head that looked like a secondhand basketball and the doctor rushed me to the hospital to play host to some 200,000 units of penicillin. the school dinner was postponed. when i finally escaped from the hospital i still had to write a speech and go to boston and commit it.

from boston we came to maine. i went out in the sun the first day and the next day i had 103 fever and have been in bed again for two weeks. the local doctor pulled me through and once again i am rampant but weakly. i think the doctor was a veterinarian. he was telling me about a baby he delivered and happened to mention that he went around in back of the woman to receive the infant.

am enclosing a letter from the new yorker for which you are responsible. portland and i were in st. patrick's cathedral one sunday. in the pew ahead of us a sailor was attending the mass. with him he had brought another sailor who had no interest in the ceremony. during the mass the guest sailor sat in the corner of the pew reading a book. the gospel, the sermon and the collection didn't bother him. he sat all through the mass reading his book. when the services were over the other sailor poked him and said "okay, let's go." the literary sailor closed his book and i saw it was "life in a putty knife factory." i thought it was funny. i told it to several people and they reacted well so i figured the new yorker might use it and a mention of the book wouldn't hurt. i sent the story to wolcott gibbs and the enclosed letter resulted. it didn't click. that is the first time i have ever bothered with the new yorker and i am afraid it will be the last.

f. allen
3 odena ave

hollywood
august 20th
1945

dear h.a. . .

a short report on my activities. not that anyone is interested. you may, however, be walking up or down broadway some day minding what is left of your business and some strange sonofabitch may come up to you and say "whatever became of that horse preface writer allen?" if you are equipped with a few facts you can astound the bastard by telling him.

have been working for four weeks with morrie ryskind. the screenplay is eighty percent finished. we are having a conference with the director and mr. skirball tomorrow and after that we will know better what lies ahead. the story is much better than it was thanks to mr. ryskind who knows the picture business. we still have several problems. skirball wants to get bing, geo. raft, john charles thomas and sinatra for some bits. if he can get them we have a couple of scenes that should be funny. if he can't get them and we end up with slim summerville, crispan martin, a friend of caeser romero's and perry como we will be sunk. the picture is supposed to start after labor day. i expect to be home late in october and skirball expects to be in bankruptcy about that time.

haven't seen chuck daggett. skirball moved his offices to the california lot and the picture will be made there. the california lot is across from lucey's backyard and opposite paramount on the side of melrose. harry sherman has made all of his hopalong cassidys there and if a couple of horses play the love interest in our picture you will know that horses work cheaper than actors and horses mr. sherman has in abundance. most of the dressing rooms on this lot are stalls. since skirball has moved i can't get on the international lot which is why i haven't looked up brother daggett.

perry charles has had all of his teeth pulled out and is breaking in a plastic smile on his friends. he can't eat very much and has been living by sucking the butter off asparagus. he is going to a night school that has a class where a person with false teeth can learn to eat solid food. perry's homework last night was a hamburger.

i still think it stinks here but the same people are going through the same routines. the sun is still out and panama and frank are still working on duffy's tavern. if you want me to throw a stone through y. frank freeman's window . . . say the word.

f. allen
beverly wilshire hotel
beverly hills, cal.

sunday

h-a-

portland has been ill for the past week. i wanted to wait until she was germ-free and in her right mind before writing you about your invitation. i really should demand some proof that you are in your right mind. why you would want the two of us on your land boring you and nelle demands some explanation. it is all right for you and nelle to bore each other to death and it is okay for you to expect some of the rustic inhabitants of that wealth-infested area to stop by and bore you on short notice. everybody who pays taxes in a town has a right to bore, or attempt to bore, folks as far as he can throw his drab. but what you need sending down to the city for a couple of people to come up to your place to distill tedium—it is all approximately too much for me.

i don't know much about mr. godfrey since dame fortune has been hustling for him. some hatchet-faced fellow came to see me in hollywood about a piece time was doing on arthur. i gave a short discourse on the machine age in comedy and this stiff twisted it around to sound as though i was mad about arthur's success. the next time time comes around to see me they can go stick their henry up in their luce.

f.a.
180 west 58

feb. 26
1946

h.a.

surprised to receive your letter. i thought you were snowed in with st. bernards baying around the estate. there is a rumor that alcoholics anonymous is putting out a st. bernard to cope with snowed-in writers. this new model st. bernard has carrot juice in his cask. when the creek stops rising and you can get through to the outside world (mt. kisco) you should be ready to outdo thoreau with graphic accounts of nature's marvels as you have witnessed them at first hand.

i am acquainted with the disc jockey you mentioned. he is a mental runt with a mouth too big for his face, and the things he will ever have to express, and he has guts enough to re-embowel all of the men who have been disemboweled since time began. some months ago, he sent me a note reading "i have been saying some nice things about you. when can you appear on my program for an interview?" i ignored the whole thing. this season, he sent me four pages of stale gags to use with frank sinatra. i confiscated the jokes. he is perhaps sore at me. i don't pay any attention to little festering fellows of his ilk. i have enough trouble trying to get the shows together without discussing them after they are done. we have a writing budget of $2600 weekly and i am still in the house doing most of the work. i write the whole opening, the alley and the fallstaff poem myself and most weeks the guest spot has to be done over. most radio writers get away with murder and if a comedian expects to survive and avoid the trite he had better be prepared to do either most of the writing or the selection of subject matter himself. yet a lot of scavengers survive in radio. why—i can't say.

portland had a kidney stone but it got away. president truman's daughter, i hear, is named after mary margaret mcbride. there must have been a radio in that haberdashery. happy snow-piling.

F.A.

august
3rd
1946

dear h.a.

the weather has been terrible here. in three weeks we have had no more than five sunny days. i might have been better off staying home with one of those liggett sunlamps. i saw a guy at the dancehall here with a tuxedo and moccasins. there is also a gull here with a hernia. the gull can't lift anything and it comes around every a.m. for me to raise a fish to its beak. otherwise, things are dull. best to nell. trust that all goes well up your hill. regards.

fred allen.
old orchard
beach . . .
maine

4.

SHOW BIZ PEOPLE

GROUCHO MARX

sept. 1
1951

dear groucho—

i know that you must derive much more pleasure dashing off a note to some old bag you hope to tree on your next trip east than you do writing to goody or to me. there is an old legend written on the wall of the men's room at the martha washington hotel. it reads—it is better to marry a young girl and satisfy her curiosity than to marry a widow and disappoint her. when you write ace you know you are going to get an answer. when you write me you know that the letter will never show up in court with a request for a breach of something settlement.

goody sailed last week on the queen mary. several days later i read that the queen mary had the roughest august crossing in its history. if his dramamine didn't work we may have lost a citizen. goody will probably stay over there. portland and i are flying over sept. 9th. the last i heard at nbc was that they were trying to book bee lillie, gracie fields and the andrew sisters on the first show from london. that will be some novelty. you hear all of those people on the air over here year after year. if they would book british talent never heard here the venture would have novelty at least. if the show stinks goody can always blame the labor government.

closing out my affairs before we leave some clippings fell out of a grouchbag i was airing. am enclosing them to bring you up to date with affairs hereabouts. there is an autographed copy of a nick kenny poem. (an original) a standout line quoted from a recent warner brothers film. ("I don't like the looks of this") a sad tale of a tv actor, mogi the lion, who couldn't get any tv jobs and was on his furry bottom around here before the spca stepped in. a joke clipped from a maine weekly up rockwell's way. an account of what happened to a chap who wanted to marry margaret truman to get a job singing in a sunday school. also a fan letter i received last spring asking for my under weight pamphlet. these items should kill a few minutes if things get dull around your estate.

will make notes in england and france and if anything worthwhile comes up i will ask goody to join me in a full report to you.

meantime, hope that all goes medium rare. say hello to harry tugend and irving brecher and to the late mr. hutton.

banzai—

fred allen
180 west 58

april
30th
1951

dear groucho—

i spoke to goody this a.m. (through channels—he was with some tv actors at nbc) and we will arrange a meal next week at your convenience.

while i was at nbc i dropped several hints to goody and the writers, that you would not be averse to getting a few laughs on the tallulah show come sunday.

they have margaret truman and when i left they were trying to hook macarthur. if they get the general we may end up with all of the straight lines in the script. if macarthur refuses to do straight for truman i am sure that goody won't be able to talk him into standing around while you and i get a few snickers. they will probably flood the studio and have mac wade through the audience up to the stage.

i should warn you that this is the last show and from the writer's collective attitude i take it that they are not going to take any nonsense from any of us on the show. they have been tacit all season and i sense that a wrong word may stampede the writing staff and cause them to beat one of the guests to death with selma diamond. i merely mention this so that you may be on guard.

mr. salpeter recently trapped me into investing in one of his ventures with the usual results. if you have any money i suggest that you leave it home. i believe mr. s is planning another venture.

portland joins me in best wishes. we will look forward to seeing you. regards.

fred allen

june 12

dear groucho—

i have just returned from boston. it is the only sane thing to do if you find yourself up there. in the boston paper i saw two headlines. groucho marx in hospital for minor surgery. (some under age ailment, i assume.) the other headline read "eden coming to boston for operation." i thought that after your new york trip you and your wife, eden, were both exhausted. i later learned that anthony eden was coming to the lahey clinic. some surgeon in london has evidently operated on anthony with a mad leech or cupped him with an unsanitary candle-snuffer in an emergency.

now that i know which eden is in an oxygen percolator the concern is about you. since i have been practically out of work for two seasons i have been able to get a little publicity collapsing and being taken to the hospital or giving out announcements that my blood pressure is worse and i will have to stop working. now that you are getting into my sick racket i am a dead duck. i will either have to go to work or get some new exciting disease.

i hope you have no trouble and that you will soon be out of there. i thought, at first, that you had run out of contestants on the show and had gone into the cedars of lebanon to case the nurse and patient potential for next season.

sid perelman and i went up to boston to appear at the brandeis university festival program. i was sid's straightman and we presented an entire evening that explained the development of the comic performer down through the ages. the show was sloppy but the reaction was fine. it was a leonard bernstein deal. he hustled sid and sid sucked me into the project.

i have a new book, "encyclopedia of aberrations." there are

some definitions of "head bangers"—"philoneism" etc. there must be a million head bangers in show business. if i can't work later i think i will try to get a job in a psychopathic ward as the head banger pro for novice head bangers i might be of some help. there is one definition in the book. an "afradisiac" is an afra member who chases dames. portland joins me in best wishes. we hope that everything is exaggerated and that you will robust in short order. regards—

fred allen

june 14
1952

groucho—

last saturday, one of the hillcrest country club members quoted the amount he hoped to get for his membership. i have been trying to get out of another club for some time. if this member cannot get the money he wants he may be interested in an exchange. i will swap him my honorary membership in the frank sinatra fan club (352 east 69th st. branch) for his hillcrest membership. if he isn't interested see if you can get any nibbles around the table some noon.

since i have been back i have had no word from messrs. goodson and todman. they have eight shows and are auditioning a new one with garry moore this coming week. they have either forgotten about mine, they are so busy, or they may be dickering with conrad nagel.

portland joins me in best wishes. we trust that all goes well by night and by day.

f. allen 180 w 58

july 14th
1949

dear groucho—

your letter arrived here on cape cod yesterday. i am down here taking a four week refresher course in talking through my nose. since rudy went hollywood i am about the only practicing nose orator left. (doc rockwell is out of print or in public domain —i forget which.) the great problem that confronts the man who talks through his nose is the hyphenated word. saying the word quickly, one part can come down each nostril. the catch is how to handle the hyphen. it takes quick thinking to say bird-cage through the nose and decide instantly which way you will tip the hyphen to have it tumble out of the nostril you have chosen. this is merely one of the facets of the nose oratory course i am taking here. if you are interested i will go into detail when i see you.

your report on the reaction to my life interview doesn't surprise me. i am afraid that it doesn't take too much to arouse a torrent of opinions at the hillcrest round table. berle's opinion doesn't bother me. it must be someone else's that he is using secondhand. berle is the moron's messiah—a mere chant of the mediocre—a sorry mime who mistakes gusto and thyroid condition for talent and ability. he has been around for twenty years and has never been first in anything. if he is first in television, either our standards have disappeared or there is something wrong with television.

i am sorry that i cannot accept your invitation to appear at la jolla. some years ago, i appeared at the chase theatre in washington. in the back of the orchestra there was a large mirror. i found out the opening matinee that i could look out over the heads of the audience and see myself in the mirror as i performed. for fourteen shows i watched myself. i realized that i could not act. if i had shot off my mouth i would have been out of show business years ago. i kept quiet and have been able to make a living without having my secret exposed. i am sure a week at la jolla, as the star of your play, would prove my undoing and possibly break up your friendship and association with norman. i like the play. i read it twice allowing ten minutes between acts for intermission. you really should play the part. if it doesn't go then you will have a right to suspect that something is awry.

thanx a lot for your letter and your offer. for assorted reasons i have to stay here until after september. medical treatment and family problems are involved. otherwise, i might be your bait.

trust that you have that area under control. say "hello" to mr. tugend should you see him as you are out raking your money some day.

best wishes—

fred allen
the belmont
west harwich, mass.

march
31st
1949

dear groucho—

have been waiting to write you. i may need that writer who is willing to walk from hollywood to submit some material. there is a bad stretch of road coming out of olathe, kansas. i don't want the writer to get bogged down in that area and arrive with a set of "hello, muck—hello mire" gags. as soon as roy acuff advises me that the road is okay i will confirm the pedestrian punster's deal.

i do not think that you are the asp that has bestowed the kiss of death on vaudeville, the picture industry and radio. vaudeville committed suicide, the picture business ran out of adjectives and radio was thrown to the cretin. at the present time, your radio show is the only one that is mentioned by critics and listeners who, because they have dirty windows and cannot see the aerials on their neighbors roofs, do not know about television and still listen to radio. if you want to give television the buss of rigor mortis you had better hurry. after the last couple of berle shows, guys in this section have been dragging television sets out into the yards and burying them.

today, crossing 54th street, my eyes must have been reminiscing for suddenly they focused into view a man from the past—max gordon. max and millie are going to europe late in april. i think max is going to put on "the man who came to dinner" in some of the marshall plan countries. he said that you would be here before they sailed and i suggested that if you were agreeable perhaps we could have a bon voyage dinner and evening with max and millie. i don't know when you will be here but you can mull it over and decide later.

the paper claims that "the homosexuals in capital are estimated at 5000." it looks as though garner was the only nance to ever leave washington. you may have read that arthur godfrey has a new plane. when godfrey isn't on the air he is in it. i still haven't seen ace to give him your regards. i also have some old regards from irving breecher to give ace. fortunately, i am not a card player. if i had to wait this long to see an ace i would be the talk of the friars. be of good cheer.

F A

october
13th
1950

dear groucho—

you realize, i hope, that it is a hell of a lot of trouble to put on a so-called tv show just to get you to write me a letter. i don't want to be in television. i met goody ace the other day and said that i never heard from you. now you have made a liar out of me by proxy.

our revue type of show is the wrong approach. we have to work in a theatre with an audience. the cameras can go no place and the intimacy that is so important in the medium is totally lacking. i hope, after a few shows, to shed the audience and attempt to do something with more scope.

you are fortunate that your show lends itself so well to the alleged new tv medium. portland and i saw your first one. the film is good and it is a pleasure to be able to enjoy some good dialogue without the old tired devices that the tv comedy shows here seem to be using. thanx for your letter and regards.

f. allen

BOB WELCH

The late Bob Welch was a masterly creator of comedy on radio, where he served on the staffs of the Allen, Eddie Cantor, Jack Benny, and Bob Hope shows and originated the Henry Aldrich series. Later he was the producer of several successful Hope movies.

august 15
1949

b.w.—

enclosed you will find a blade of grass. this grass is from the other fellow's yard. take it. step out of your office and go into your yard. pluck a blade of your grass. compare the two. then you will know whose grass is greener.

tell mr. robert hope i received his note. his stationery is very funny. comparing the letterhead with the written content reminds me of the old hollywood retort— "it's all trailer and no show."

regards to all from rexall and

f. allen

december
25th
1949

dear mr. welch—
i do not want any money.
i do not want to tell you how to run the picture business.
i do not want you to use your influence to get me an introduction to louella.

i do not want you to get me mr. ginsberg's autograph.

i do not want you to put me in one of your hit pictures and make me another bob hope.

i do not want you to get me a swimming pool wholesale.

i do not want a pass to go through the mammoth paramount studios.

i do not want to know your unlisted phone number.

the reason i am writing you is because i have one lousy xmas stamp left over which i want to stick on the back of this letter.

yoicks away, mr. welch.

fred allen

october 1st
1950

mr. welch—

i spent last evening with alton cook. he went into great detail about the great improvement in the quality of the hope films since you have been associated with them. as the evening wore on alton became a bit garbled and his personal tribute to your ability became more and more indistinct. i could tell, however, that he holds you personally in high esteem and up until the time alton started talking like a tobacco auctioneer i kept abreast of his encomiums.

hope you have received good news from your medical brother. you must remember, when you are tempted to give your all for dear old paramount, that there is only one welch. when there isn't enough to go around you must always keep enough welch for yourself and your little brood.

i am enclosing an interesting note from professor galiardo. breathe-rite-dynamics may be the answer to your problems. if you can get the front office to breathe rite, like martinelli and many others, they may achieve success. gatti-casazza was breathing rite but suddenly stopped for some reason. he does not mention why in his letter—also enclosed.

knowing that you are always in the market for material i

am sending a note from "ovady julber." with the name ovady julber on your next screen epic you can imagine how your loyal booster alton cook will react. some bastard, i will mention no names there are so many of them, mentioned in writer's digest magazine that i was looking for a play. i have been swamped with letters from writers of ovady julber's ilk and have spent most of this past week returning manuscripts.

continue your good work, b.w. your new house looks fine and tempy and all of your tinker set appear ditto. remember "there will always be a paramount" but there will not always be a welch unless you breathe rite and put the industry in its place as your scheme of things goes.

portland joins me in good wishes to tempy and to you. do not bother to answer. if i can get a few guest dates set after january 1st we will come out for a few weeks. see you then.

fred allen
180 west 58

august 22
1952

r.w.

since brother stalin has sounded the tocsin to call the boys together to alter a few views, i am sending out the word to all "allen" followers. men! your chief is not indestructible! our new five year plan will be to get the chief through to december 1957.

i agree with you that the picture business is rather a snide caper. i enclose an ad published recently by the plaza theatre in lamar, missouri. a sterling comedian spends a lifetime winning his way past the popcorn through into the hearts of his public. he becomes the biggest money-maker on the paramount lot. his name is known to every human being who crawls every clime of this hectic marble and to every bird that has ever looked in through the window of any army plane carrying actors to korea. the comedian has a right to feel secure, atop his notices and the twined shoulders of barney dean and doc schurr, that every man, woman and child knows his name. then this ad appears. the work of his lifetime is undone. one bastardly printer, in lamar, missouri, doesn't know that mr. hope's first name is bob.*

"we're not married," is rumored has been doing very well. i hope my next episode release turns out well. the o. henry collection. i would hate to be out of work and have people panning the hell out of me simultaneously.

your comment on tv is sage. this is a word i never use except when you venture a comment. the baseball game you didn't see with all of the fighting is easily explained. the medium is so costly that the sponsors are running the cameras. that is why you see only the commercial with rarely a fleeting glance of the actor or player. i think that this coming season will find mass audience available at 18 million sets and that this sticky mob will have some audible comment on its fare.

i had a real bad time, bob (not bog—you have made *your* name) but the doctor feels that if i quit for three months, or so, i will be able to ascend my pinnacle. portland joins me in best to tempy and to "old atom" as i like to call you.

                                                    fred allen

                                                    jan.
                                                    28
                                                    1955

"eagle-eye"
feathered sir:
    i am sorry to acknowledge receipt of the inventory of your recent jousts with organized medicine and its practitioners and the report on the various organs that have been snatched from your person while you have been rendered dormant.

    as an old vegetarian and as a veteran of seven intravenous vegetable feedings, when carrots were inserted into my veins to supply sustenance, i know what you have been through. i think

* The ad referred to Hope as Bog Hope.

that your main trouble out there has been that you have been stringing along with the old-style medicine man. what we need is new thought today. men who do new things with patients. i recently talked to a chiropractor who told me that he had been called in on a serious heart case. i said "what did you do?" the chiropractor said "i hugged the patient as hard as i could." i might add that it was a male patient. the patient survived and screwed out of the house as soon as he was able to escape. this same chiropractor uses another method. no matter what your ailment is when he arrives at the house he has the patient engage in a game of leapfrog. while the patient is in a frog position the chiropractor calls in a friend of his who is the house surgeon at a pet store. invariably the case is diagnosed properly and the patient is restored to society.

personally, i have been seeing a dr. theodore r. van dellen. dr. van dellen writes for the daily news. am enclosing one of the doctor's theories. it sounds logical. if you have that pooped feeling —find what's pooping you. dr. van dellen goes to the other source of the trouble. you may be over-pooped. there are a couple of other cures in this piece—heartburn—thyroid deficiency. let me know. i can get to the doctor through channels.

glad to know that you like "treadmill." you could have done the book if you had thought about it. i haven't heard from chet yet but pat and the others who worked around the program all reported that they enjoyed regurgitating old memories and recalling some of the odd crises. i am supposed to start on an autobiography. i am on "what's my line" to keep alive artistically and to enable me to have the entire week to write. if i can't make any progress come june then i will abandon the whole thing and slink back on the treadmill again.

bill morrow was here last week but i didn't see him. i didn't know he was here until the sunday he did the colgate show. then i had to go down to "what's my line" and i couldn't even stop in at the theatre to see bill before he got away. bill wrote three shows for bing plugging my book. he was certainly very nice about it and bing, too.

let me know how joe besser's hemorrhoids come out on "medic." hope you are able to get around and throw a writer or two at mr. hope if you meet him at the springs. portland joins me in best wishes to tempy and to you.

fred allen

HARRY TUGEND

Tugend was Allen's first assistant writer on his early radio shows and later moved on to become a film writer and producer in Hollywood.

july first
1938

dear harry:

your letter this a.m. i finished the season with some 800 fan letters unanswered and am going to try and bounce them off before we pack. i have put the fans in the corner, for the nonce and i hope the nonce shows up, until i can get a word mushed through to you.

your new house must be the next to the last word. i wouldn't dare say the last word while you are under contract to darryl for consequences too great even to be conceived by the scenic department might ensue. walter told me the house looked beautiful from the outside, in the process of construction, and i know that jean has overpowered the interior decorator and worked billy rose magic on the inside. i feel sure that her will power has kept the next tugend entry in the human race from arriving to interfere with your gala opening. how do you open a house there in beverly? do you have a mike on the lawn? do you have those bastardly wagons with the lights shining on the front door? and do you have louella parsons cluttering up the entire house on the first night with stars she is trying to hide until such a time as she can use them on hollywood hotel? do you have this . . . or do you just get a key on a carrier pigeon, that flies back to the bank in case, and walk through the door with your immediate family and staff of servants?

houses always cost more than you plan but if it is what you want it is worth the candle. if it isn't what you want, and you have saved money, you start kicking yourself in the pratt and then you don't need chairs so you save one way and waste another and if you like it you save a pain in the tokus. (tokus is a word used by the natives here in new york. you have no doubt lost all contact with these quaint folk and their peculiar jargon. anolick is another word used around a lot. it means anything from insurance to income tax hubbub.)

nothing has been signed for the radio. tiny made us a swell offer to come to hollywood for one of their shows but i don't think we should stay there. portland's father has had two strokes and has been bad all spring. both of my aunts are sick, one in the hospital, and my brother just escaped from a hospital. i know if we made plans to stay there for a time something would be sure to happen in one of the families and then we would have to come back here for a readjustment of one home or the other.

if i stay here another season it will work out the same and if i am any good in the picture perhaps i can make some sort of a deal that would warrant checking out of here for a prolonged stay. you had everything to gain going out there but there are a million things around here for me and since i don't look like tyrone or mr. ameche and since i don't drink and can never get to look like w. c. fields i don't see how i can ever hope to be more than a baggier-eyed ned sparks and since i don't particularly like him in pictures i am apt to see myself again on the screen and turn against myself . . . that would make it unanimous.

i hope nunnally is well again. i don't think anyone can produce and write and rewrite himself. a writer who has become a producer should know what the story needs and get it from other writers working on it. i guess it is like everything else when you get in a spot like that; you want to do everything the same as though you were writing it and passing it over to a producer.

directors, i can't understand either. you see a fellow's name on a great job and two months later you see some turkey with the wishbones sticking out in the lobby and find that the same director hatched it. i guess they have good and bad days but the bad ones are more expensive.

jimmy fidler raved about new faces. i happened to look in the paper tonight and it got two and a half stars with a tepid review. the hit of the picture is dave freedman's broker's scene that lahr did in the follies. the marx brothers picture has several good scenes in it. as usual they crucify the love interest and story but the night i saw it at the capitol the audience screamed . . . that's screamed not scrammed . . . every minute they were in view. they can do gag routines that other comedians couldn't use since groucho is accepted doing long rambling things. i think he is great, though, and i go for anything they do . . . but then again who the hell am i?

i wrote jack a long letter about radio. i thought if i could tell him a little of what i know about it it might help him get off on the right foot but, as you know, the weeks come around all too fast and once you get under way you've got plenty to worry about. b & b offered me the colgate show on columbia against ours for next year but i wouldn't walk out on joe unless their proposition was out of the question. i haven't heard from jack so he probably has his own troubles what with someone gone and showboat starting next thursday. after dave and boasberg it is silly to worry about radio. it is only dangerous if you are conscientious. a guy like berle will not only go on forever but will be the major bowes of tomorrow when he gets old. guts never wear out if they are in your head . . . it's only when you're silly enough to keep them in your stomach that they show signs of wear and tear. hope, you say, has a slap-belly. tom revere has a double-chin, one for the repeat show, and there you are. i feel lousy.

i was going to write you a letter but you will have to be satisfied with just this prologue. criminals are giving themselves up to hearst papers. midgets will be giving themselves up to readers digest. just when you get the goose hanging high the guy wants his rope back. forgot to mention! flash! i submitted your idea about launcelot shovelwell one week with his vitalis activities and n.b.c. turned it down colder than the sheet on an eskimo's bed. you picture authors can't pull that stuff in radio. . . .

best for now and portland sends her love to jean.

F.A.

JAMES MASON

august
25th
1951

dear james—

i haven't bothered to write you for some time. i know that in hollywood a person is always busy and there are enough problems to keep him engaged without adding mail-answering to his burdens.

making pictures, flushing silverfish out of the drapes and furniture, hiding about the grounds so that film friends cannot find you to get at your scotch or your pool, doing the grounds with sickle and mower, attending previews, showing films at home, reading lousy stories brought around by agents and w. wanger, coping with the baby and sundry other activities make for a bulging day in your community. we often think of you and pam, or pam and you if there is a billing sensitivity in the family, scurrying around with the baby at your heels attending to the many chores listed above.

portland sent pam a card recently to tell her that we had heard and enjoyed you both on the screen directors' guild radio program and also to advise that we had seen the pictures of the baby in mccall's magazine. from the baby's appearance in the candid shots she is thriving.

we had hoped to come to the coast next month but we were summoned to go to london and paris to do two radio shows with tallulah bankhead. we fly to london on september 9th. tallulah will probably swim the channel while she is in england to get a bit of extra publicity for her radio appearance.

when we return i am supposed to work on odd weeks with sister bankhead and to narrate some tv shows occasionally. george kaufman and abe burrows were planning to write a play for which they wanted me. if any or all of these enterprises come apart we may come to california later this fall. we are now about to leave a watering place called sea girt. it is in new jersey and is a cross between brighton and bournemouth i would say. the trunk has gone, our vacation is over and i have been answering all of the mail left over. when portland mentioned that she had sent pam a card it reminded me that i had not been in touch with you for some time.

hope your recent pictures turned out well and that life, as it is acted and portrayed by the denizens of beverly hills, still holds its charm for you both.

portland joins me in best wishes and hope that the goose is hanging at an altitude that augers well for the future.

fred allen
180 west 58th

JACK MULCAHY

A Hollywood film company publicist, Mulcahy supplied Allen with guest stars from movieland and arranged publicity campaigns for the occasional pictures from Twentieth Century-Fox that featured Fred. One such movie, mentioned here, was *Sally, Irene and Mary* in which Allen appeared with Alice Faye and Tony Martin.

april 12th

dear jack . . .

this is the first chance i have had to answer your letter. have been busier than a horse-fly at a polo game and last week sunk to professional depths never before sounded by even a radio comedian. i had to apologize to the town of pottsville, pa. we used some broken down gag which some demented jerk in philadelphia misheard. he, having nothing to do, wrote the chamber of commerce at pottsville and then the trouble started. after an exchange of letters it was decided that i should apologize to pottsville.

i have been further disgraced too by your firm, mr. mulcahy. a friend of mine sent me a picture of a theatre at woonsocket, rhode island. the picture sally, irene and lousy was billed and apparently it had set the block afire. ladders were up against the front of the joint and the billing on the marquee was "alice faye, tony martin and the black doll." gad! if i have to appear in blackface billing i will go back to apologizing to pottsville. i sent the picture to harry tugend who will be glad to prove these assertions and also let you look at the picture for a small charge.

you complain about the ice-woman on my show having her material written for her. naturally, she sounded "ready." what do you expect? a woman is hustling around on an ice wagon all her life and probably has never even read anything out loud before and suddenly finds herself in toscanini's studio before an audience of 1300 morons. what do you want, garbo with tongs? we have been very lucky with the people. we pick them out of barrels and crannies and up to now they all at least have been able to read and you know what they are saying which is more than you know on cantor's program.

the "town hall" idea might make a good picture but i have no time to go into anything like that. sometime later, when i get bounced out of radio city, i may have time to think about it but by then there will be no demand for it so why even think of it. the ritz brothers arrived last week. this is a long way to run from a preview. i hope their picture comes out well for they are very popular with the fans and we mustn't let the fans down.

re surley temple and your request to publicize her and her movie on our show. our first broadcast is at nine p.m. eastern time. while the publicity angle would be excellent i would be afraid to expose the child to one of these jokel audiences we get in the studio. jimmy dunn was up last year and they nearly mobbed him. they still thought he was a picture personality. if they'll chase jimmy dunn they'll trample little surly and then where will you and i be with darryl, even if we do scrape the remains of his ace box-office bet off the shoes of the people? i read that the baby was going to make another picture before june. you can do anything you want, if you do come here, and i will take care of our end. i just wanted to acquaint you with the studio situation. let me know what you think and if it ever comes off i can probably get you and your party one of the client's glass enclosed rooms where you hear the program and look out through the glass feeling like something to eat in the automat. we finish around the last wednesday in june.

jimmy durante is here and he left an anchovy at our italian restaurant with his initials on it.

best for now . . . i've got over 600 other letters to answer around here.

f.a.

november 25th

dear jack . . .

thanx a lot for your letter which arrived via carrier-robin on yesterday. there are priorities on pigeons now. all mail is delivered by robins. mayor laguardia wanted to keep the blue mailman uniform alive and tried to operate bluejays on the airmail beats. the bluejays were rounded up but there were only enough jays for 57th street. the mayor called in the audubon society and the audubon boys had two million robin eggs, in an egg bank, in the cellar of the society's building. every fat man was called in. huge nests were built and for several weeks every fat man caught in new york was drafted for the hatching. the birds were all hatched and today mayor laguardia has these robins delivering the mail. when you see something with a red breast at the window you know it is either a robin with a letter or linda darnell in technicolor.

i spoke to walter batchelor about louella parsons and no doubt he has gotten in touch with you ere this. there seems to be a guest star shortage here and the same people are going on all of the programs. we try to get them first or line up other people who may make up in entertainment what they lack in publicity value. am sure if walter has a date open and arrangements can be made with miss parsons that your suggestion will culminate in a triumphant venture some weeks hence.

we are still grinding away. with the guests it is tougher than ever for me but i guess i'll weather the season. give sammy benson, your wardrobe impresario, our best wishes. i know sammy is doing a heck of a job with those mothballs. in his last two pictures i have distinctly smelled camphor when don ameche came on the screen. ray sebastian is doing a swell job with the makeup, too. john carradine is beginning to look as though a buzzard has replaced his tapeworm and is slowly eating all of the meat off of john under his skin. if you come east with miss parsons we'll see you. hope all goes well at 20th. the product seems to have had a great life in recent months. hope it continues.

f.a.

november 11th

dear jack . . .

thanx a lot for the variety. that program is on against us and i have never been able to hear it. have heard many reports that the first part was weak but that the dramatic section held up very well. to me, most of the guest star shows are about the same. the same guests appear on all of the shows, doing the same type of condensed plays and bits plus a little talk about "the grand fun" had making "mr. moto gets a hotfoot" or some other masterpiece.

radio shows get results mostly in smaller towns. to give them some appeal the content of the program should be as simple as possible and exploit a few likeable people who won't wear a person out over the long pull. most of the shows use the same type of matter, mostly patterned after jack benny's layout. that is why i try to keep our stuff more topical and go after more things. at least our headache sounds different even though it isn't as good, according to the radio critics, as the charlie mccarthy or benny shows. according to the latest ratings it also isn't as good as burns and allen and allen and jolson.

despite the crossley i will bet the part i played in sally, irene and mary against ten pounds off the front of ben silvey that we have a more loyal listening audience around the country than most of the others. the only proof is in the sales reaction. our company, despite business conditions, is ahead of last year's business for the first three quarters. most of the actors think in terms of their crossley ratings. we are in our seventh year and all i know is that if the company is selling the product the program can keep going.

what the heck i am boring you with this for . . . i don't know. but it always makes me laugh when those big publicity spreads come out about the lineup of talent and the money some agency is going to spend on a show. when they round up a million dollars worth of talent they bring in two, or three, crew writers to turn out the scripts. the result is that an actor who is worth a fortune to a picture company becomes a bum on the air in a few months. i hope that darryl will not let mr. moto go on the air for mr. moto's own good.

sorry to hear that darryl is smoking so much. all of those producers and directors will be dropping off with tobacco heart unless he can find some way to swallow the smoke at conferences and exhale it every few weeks at previews. i am still in a daze around here, jack. walter is back on the coast. we may come out next summer. i won't know until after the first of the year. this grind is too tough. if i only looked like tyrone power i might get set over at universal . . . if anyone is set at universal. hope all goes well. regards to harry and king of the moths . . . sammy benson.

f.a.

may 22nd

dear jack . . .

your letter okay. there has been a rumor around here that mr. benny was appearing on your lot in women's clothes, testing for charlie's aunt. i don't know what darryl is doing, trying to make an old shirley temple out of mr. b. i don't see why you can't write rochester into the picture. you can make him a little hattie mcdaniel. i didn't see the play here, nor did i see syd chaplin play the picture version of charlie's aunt so i am not familiar with the task mr. b has undertaken.

after that last turkey i got mixed up in with mr. b. i don't want any part of your synthetic industry, mr. mulcahy. you can have that big candid camera racket. you can also have all of those beaverboard people who keep giving each other parties at ciro's. someone ought to go in ciro's some saturday night and wax all of those people and then start running the place as another madame tussauds.

i may be nuts but i would rather keep grinding out programs, as tough as it is, than to be out there doing good. mr. b likes it and he is welcome to it. most of the actors end up behind the six ball. even when eight ball time comes for an actor the agent takes his cut and gets behind the two ball. when an actor dies and is buried most of the agents have it in their contracts that they have the flower rights to the grave for ten years with options. by the time an actor gets ready to die he hasn't enough friends left out there to act as pallbearers. at most funerals the six men you see motivating the casket are from central casting.

when charley's aunt gets out around the country mr. b will probably start getting mother's day cards and fan mail from orphans claiming they are his illegitimate children. i hope he doesn't fatten up on the commissary food at 20th and finish playing the picture looking as though his is pregnant.

f.a.

may 29th

dear jack . . .

received your letter this a.m. i saw quote in the reporter. personally, i don't care about it. the only bad thing is the gravity that is accorded the bunk in gossip columns by most of the people out there. to call the last picture a turkey might upset mark sandrich, y. frank and mr. b.

the pallbearer lines and the impersonal stuff i don't care who prints but matters that can be misconstrued by some of the touchy chaps in your profession can lead to a lot of bother and lead to hard feelings as you know how things finally get magnified in certain circles.

i have never met that west coast columnist named stein. he had the audacity to print that portland and i were living in a flophouse, or something, while we were in hollywood. i never even bother to correct anything those finks write for to pay any attention to anything they say or quote only gives importance to their semi-libelous trivia.

in the future i shall be more careful what i write. if those yucks have to fill their columns they can scurry around and find items the hard way.

we had some trouble with the earl derr biggers estate but it has died down. we killed charlie chan on a program a couple of months ago and the lawyers or mrs. biggers hopped on us good. we have been plugging all of darryl's pictures when we get a chance and i guess the office didn't check on the charlie chan reference. the name didn't mean anything to us. we could have used any name but being 20th-minded i put in chan and started the whole mess. legally, they have no claims and some day someone will go into court with one of these shakedown cases and after one decision has been handed down all of the jerk nuisance letters, etc. will be stopped at the source.

you have my permission to tell stein what we think of him.

sincerely . . .

f.a.

1943

dear jack . . .

we are having all sorts of air raid precautions drummed into our ears. the mayor bought a siren for the city. the big day was wednesday. the mayor went over to the other end of the brooklyn bridge to see if he could hear the siren. everyone in town had his window open. the thing finally blew at four o'clock and it sounded like slim summerville belching. now we are going to have 500 sirens to be used for raid warnings. and so it goes.

i like louella parsons but when she follows winchell with all of his excited barking of trivia louella seems much quieter than she is. with a setup to fit her voice and personality i think louella could do a very interesting hollywood gossip show in her own style. heretofore, she has always invited comparison through using the same technique as those other hysterical commentators. those guys yell their brains out and when you sift out the news the item is either that mickey rooney took the check at some nutberger stand or lana turner opened a second front while weaning her baby.

if we come out will look you up. hope and benny are entertaining the boys in north africa. as soon as they arrived the drive on sicily started. it looks as though the sicilian invasion was nothing but the troops walking out on hope and benny.

f.a.

jan. 28th
1938

dear jack . . .

thanx for the encouraging words anent our movie. when i hadn't heard anything about it i naturally thought that perhaps mr. zanuck was trying to get the photographs off the celluloid and turn the second hand film over to sol to be used for something for jane withers.

had a letter from harry who told me that they are making additional scenes and no doubt when the epic is finished we will have another "happy landing" sans ice. i hope so!

everyone around here is fast going nuts. benny goodman opened this week at the paramount and the line formed at five a.m. several thousand kids were out in the street doing the big apple, shagging and doing the suzy q. police were called and finally they opened the theatre and let the yowling mob in at seven-thirty. goodman has built up a covey of flog-happy kids around here and if his followers get any more in number or any louder decibally . . . if there is such a word . . . i am sure that the city will ask mr. goodman to do a pied piper and lead his public down to the edge of the east river. the stage show starts so early now that goodman is adding a coffee percolater to the drummer's equipment.

you are right about our public missing gags on the coast broadcast. the trouble is that we start at midnight and the class of people we get in the place i wouldn't be seen with . . . except professionally. most of them look as though somebody had turned over a pool table and they crept out of the pockets. they will only react to the stupidest material and since we at least try to get something half decent week after week we are generally up against it when we flaunt our verbal wares before our patrons at this late hour.

darryl zanuck has so many yes-men following him around the studio i have often thought that he ought to put his hand out when he makes a sharp turn. someday, he will turn off and the mob will keep on walking and continue out the gate at the other end of the lot. if they ever get off the lot several of them will have a difficult time getting back in.

read that bill seiter is starting on another one so charlie hall will no doubt be around testing the accoustics on the various stages to make sure that he will be heard in every nook and cranny, once production is under way, for i know that charlie expects to win the academy "quiet, please!" for 1938.

hoping this finds you the same in your department. thanks again for your words, sir! and best for now . . .
P.S. Regards—Kosher—to Harry Brand.

f.a.

march third

dear jack . . .

by the time you get this the louella special will be over. i am taking care of it with the fellow at columbia studios and we can shake off all of the excitement. i have four minutes written, the salary is "no," and we don't need a lot of executives buzzing their buzzers and writing memos to each other. i had a whole rain routine but since it turned into a flood and today's paper says 35 have died i will have to do the opening over tonight and send it over for censoring tomorrow.

thanks for the trailer contacts. i missed it at the roxy but called mr. benjamin at the office and he said he will dig it out and let me see it whenever i am over that way. after seeing the picture i doubt if i shall bother him further about the trailer. i thought . . . confidentially . . . that it was pretty weak. the thing had been cut up into something that looked as though jack benny had directed me to get even. so much of the story was gone that the relationship that exists between the characters is never properly explained and as the picture goes along it cuts from song to gag and the story cannot weather the treatment and come out believeable. there must be a reason why it came out this way. if i am lousy i am willing to admit it but i could hardly contaminate the cast and the celluloid as well.

mr. zanuck once said he wanted to make a "town hall" picture but i still go 16 and 18 hours a day, jack, and i seldom have a minute to sit down.

if you hear the hollywood hotel show let me know how it sounded to you. meantime, thanks for all letters and it might be well to keep my undercover opinion of the picture sub rosa. if anyone asks you how i liked it all you have to say is that i asked you to send me the wishbone when they were through running it around the country.

portland sends her best and we both hope that all goes well. best for now!

f.a.

may sixth

dear jack . . .

your letter arrived this a.m. it is too bad to have you waste an airmail stamp on it. darryl was coming this way and i'm sure that he would have been glad to drop it off at my stale quarters for you. some of the boys saw darryl at the stork club one night last week and said that he spent the evening in serious conversation with some chap at his table. bert lahr danced by a couple of times in case darryl had an old option in his pocket but bert ended up winded and still here on broadway, in dubarry was a lady.

we have had quite a hollywood session here. mark sandrich and an impromptu gang have been here for the benny opening at the paramount and also to discuss my forthcoming epic with mr. benny. the boys left for the coast yesterday and jack left this afternoon. i don't know when we will leave. mr. sandrich said he will let us know this coming week and if he wants me before we finish our season we will probably leave here june sixth and do the last three shows out there. i don't care either way. our program, for this company, finishes in june. we have a lot of offers for half hour programs but we are trying to stick with an hour show to keep the attraction together. if we are successful i will be back on the air in the fall. if not may end up as number two moth-man in your wardrobe department or perhaps a map authority looking for countries in which charlie chan plots can be laid.

i am all-in again, as usual, but hope to snap out of it shortly. i have nothing but headaches seven days a week and with the writing and other matters that pile up i can't relax or get any rest. i should have stayed in boston and become a fireman. portland sends her regards and we will be looking for you when you arrive.

regards to harry, ben silvey and anyone you can find who remembers sally, irene and what's her name. i saw michael whalen in the jimmy fiddler unit. hoping this finds you the same. . . .

f.a.

october 15th

jack—

thanx a lot for your letter and your report on our first tv show. it is a tough medium, jack, and a lot of the critics around here jumped on the show before we even have a chance to learn how to work in the new form.

i think when we have had a chance to do three or four of these shows we will find a way to cope with the bloody thing and come up with shows a lot better. most of the comedy shows around here eat up their time with vaudeville acts. we tried to write a little revue and if we didn't have to have four commercials within fifty minutes we would have had a much faster and more entertaining hour.

doing only one show a month makes a little more trouble. writers and actors want to get paid every week. nobody wants to wait around all month to work one week. we have to grab what we can when we start to rehearse which doesn't give us the best of it.

quite a few of our friends in hollywood sent us their opinions of the show. harry tugend and groucho saw it and both sent me some suggestions that were good. i didn't see the kinescope version you saw so i don't know whether the show we did was cut or altered in any way.

tv at first hurt the picture business but i think when the sets have been in homes a few months that television will have a place and the theatre and pictures will also have their audiences. the quality of the tv shows, with the exception of some of the dramatic shows, is generally low and as all of the comedians repeat their devices and the same acts show up on all of the revue type shows i am sure that people will start going out of their houses for other forms of entertainment.

hope all goes well with you in your refined racket. i don't think we will be out your way this winter. if you come east—let us know. meantime, best wishes to gwen and all mulcahys far and wide. . . .

ABE BURROWS

The little man in uniform described in the following letter is Frank Loesser, who later composed the music for Burrows' Broadway hit, *Guys and Dolls*. Before he became a successful theatrical director and author, Burrows was a radio comedy writer.

feb. 26th 1945

dear mr. burrows . . .

the other day, i happened to pass the ascap offices just as a little man in an army uniform was being thrown out into the street. when i had seen gene buck's back vanish into the darkness and heard the double-bolt on the ascap office door slip into place, i turned my attention to the little man in the army uniform, who was picking himself up from the sidewalk. after i had helped the little fellow dust off his uniform and pick up several decca records and 300 copies of a new song called "roger young" he told me his name was hank besser or frank lesser. the name escapes me at the moment. he also told me that he had met me in hollywood. since i had once met a veritable mob of people in the nbc studio, after a repeat show of "people are funny," i thought the little chap might be a friend of art linkletter's. i questioned him and the name linkletter meant nothing to him. as i helped him tie a stout chord around the 300 copies of "roger young," the little man said "if my memory isn't up to some shennigan i recall meeting you at the home of a man named wurrows or zurrows out in holly-wood."

naturally, the names of wurrows and zurrows meant nothing to me and i pressed the tiny one for further details. after humming a complete verse and two choruses of "roger young" to himself, the little man dismantled his frown and said "i have it. the name wasn't wurrows, it was burrows. i met you at burrow's house. his first name is lafe or gabe, some odd name." when i insisted that lafe burrows sounded like a friend of zeke manner's and that i had no hill billy acquaintances in hollywood, the little man said "you know burrows. he is known as the delicatessen dwight fiske, the last of the meistersingers, the singing sam of the psalm. burrows is the man who goes around to the houses of poor people. if they haven't got food he goes to the piano and sings "shortenin bread" and "one meat ball." burrows is the man who broke into a piano store on hollywood boulevard with an octupus under his coat and played on seven pianos simultaneously until he was ejected by a nightwatchman. surely you know burrows," said the little man.

with this, the uniformed gnome took a firm grip on his decca records bundled the 300 copies of "roger young" under his arm and walked briskly up broadway. the incident puzzled me. i didn't feel like eating dinner. i nibbled at a sturgeon sandwich. that night, i knew no rest. i tossed and turned. i kept seeing little green grasses in my sleep. where had i seen this little man before? who was lafe zurrows? the next morning my nerves were on edge. i could know no peace until the mystery was solved. i looked up a friend of mine, a famous broadway revue writer and actor, a chap named adolph green. i told him the story of the little man in uniform with the 300 copies of "roger young." adolph green is well-known in hollywood. he is privy to the secrets of hollywood withholds from the masses. after a moment's deep thought adolph said "i think i know the party you want. around hollywood he is called the bald balladeer. his right name is abe burrows. you will find him at this address." i thanked mr. green who turned into a ticket speculator's office and proceeded to dump scores of ducats for "on the town" into the speculator's lap.

that is why i am writing to you, mr. burrows. are you the man who once played seven pianos with an octupus under your coat? if you are—did i meet the man with 300 copies of "roger young" at your house? if you are not the derma duchin forget the whole confused business.

i have been trying to write you a letter since last november. finally, portland and i had to come to atlantic city so that i might have a chance to overtake the mail. today, it is raining harder than you have ever seen it rain in any sequence in a picture directed by fritz lang. sea-gulls are hiding in doorways afraid to brave the storm. one solitary wheelchair on the boardwalk has pontoons on it and the man pushing the chair is using the australian crawl. it is a perfect day to answer letters mr. burrows. if i had received a letter from you i would answer it today. there are three men living in our hotel. they are inseparable. one is a well-dressed elderly man. the other two men wear overalls around the lobby. i asked who those men were, who seem to be always together and i learned that the well-dressed elderly man has a hearing device and the electricians' union made him put on two union men to operate it. the two men in the overalls are union electricians.

how is hollywood? we had a preview of "it's in the bag" two weeks ago. the trade papers gave it good notices but the picture is pretty weak. this is the one man's opinion and i am the one man. how did ed's picture turn out? i wrote hy a couple of weeks ago. i have a million offers. the morris office thinks i should do a radio show in the fall. are you going to stay out there? why don't you get a job at mgm or paramount and take it easy with the quill for a season? frank expects to go to the coast, i think. we see them quite often. he refuses to go to bed at night. lynn is fine. i have been doing more work for nothing than i used to do for money. two or three more guest shots will complete my season. you have only 18 more shows to go. broadway is loaded with hits.

trust that all goes well in technicolor. give our best to ruth. if you want anything mailed on from lindy's . . . let me know.

best wishes, regards, etc . . .

fred allen
180 west 58th st.
new york city

march 17th

dear abe—

the reason we haven't seen each other lately is because i have been looking for you every sunday at the actors' chapel in st. malachy's.

i know that you have been watching rabbi burstein's house waiting to catch me going in. portland and i are invited for his seder dinner but we won't be in town. you might have trapped me if we could have made it.

am going to hollywood next week. have started on autobiography and hope to talk to some old vaudeville actors out there. perhaps we may see you when we return next month. portland and i saw "silk socks" this week. we thought it was excellent. stand by for the show—life is an intermission.

some men hail i. eisenhower   F.
others hail hardy babe,
but we hail a.s. burrows
to us he's just "our abe."
   F. allen

5.

YOUNGSTERS

march
3
1956.

dear
jane

—
i
am
a
sleeve
in
another
one
of
your
uncle
fred
allen's
shirts
—
i
happened
to
see
your
letter
on
uncle
fred's
desk
and
wanted
to

write
you
a
letter
—
it
is
hard
for
a
sleeve
to
write
especially
when
it
has
no
arm
in
it
and
no
hand
and
fingers
on
the
end
of
the
hand
—
that
is
why
i

cannot
write
you
because
i
am
only
an
empty
sleeve
lying
on
uncle
fred's
typewriter
but
like
your
sleeve
i
have
a
monogram
too
—
good-bye
—
the
sleeve

DAVID RATTRAY

september
8th
1946

dear dave . . .

have just returned from maine and found your newsy letter awaiting me.

am happy to know that the taffy arrived all right and that you enjoyed consuming it.

about that man, mr. mansir, who smoked the cornsilk you brought him, now that corn is going out of season, it will soon be impossible to find silk for him to use in his pipe. why don't you try bringing him some milkweed? if he starts smoking milkweed the weed will burn off and his pipe will fill up with hot milk. when he draws the hot milk down the cool stem of the pipe it will solidify and it will be a lot of fun watching him inhale and blowing cheese out of his nose. if you try him with the milkweed, let me know how it works out.

it must be a lot of fun making model planes. you had better be careful though. i read about a boy who wanted to make a jet plane. it pulled the jet off of the gasjet in his mother's house. it left a big hole in the wall and gas started escaping. when the house was filled with gas somebody lit a match and the boy's mother left suddenly through a window and passed two douglas planes going in the same direction. the jet the boy used on his model plane didn't work. it taught him a lesson. now he has a model plane that won't fly and a big hole in the side of his house. his mother is mad, too, as it cost her three dollars to get back from where she landed.

give ev my best wishes. we hope you are well.

f

EVERETT RATTRAY

february
7th
1944

dear everett . . .

portland and i received your letter this morning. you didn't
have to bother thanking us for the book. portland picked it out.
she noticed a little space between two books on your father's book-
shelves and she really bought the book to plug up that crevice.
if you want to read the book before you used it for that purpose
i am sure portland wouldn't mind. if you enjoy the book, too, i
know she will be happy when i tell her.

i guess you are too busy poking around the barn, and trying
to fly your kite in that high wind you get at east hampton, to
bother much with your mail. you had better be careful with those
old shells. you can't drive a nail very far into a shell and expect
to be in the barn for long. if you have closed the barn door you
may rise unexpectedly, hammer in hand, through the roof.

at the end of your letter you say "i guess i will stop writing.
i am coming to the bottom of the page." it is always best to stop
a letter when you arrive at the bottom of the page. i know a boy
who never stopped his letters in time. he would keep on writing
past the bottom of the page and write down one leg of the
table until he finished. then when he mailed his letter he had
to saw a piece out of the table and cut off the leg of the table,
too, and send it along in a large paper bag instead of an envelope.
another time, this boy was writing on a desk he didn't stop again
but wrote down the front of the desk and along the floor for
nearly two feet. when he mailed that letter he had to tear off the
front of the desk and pry up two feet of the floor. this left a
big hole in the floor. his father and mother both fell through the
hole and since the boy lived on a houseboat and his father and
mother couldn't swim the boy became an orphan. this is why

it is always better to finish a letter when you come to the bottom of the page.

give dave and your mother and father our best wishes. we will see you when you come to the city. meantime, best wishes. . . .

fred allen

DAVID RATTRAY

hollywood
november
18th
1943

mr. david rattray
att. secretary in
charge of mr. d.
rattray's personal
correspondence:

dear mr. rattray . . .

i am in receipt of your gold star school exercise and i want to compliment you on this achievement. i took your paper around to shirley temple to show her the type of work brilliant scholars are doing in the eastern schools. i am sure that miss temple will be spurred to new mental heights when she realizes that you are setting such high standards down there in east hampton.

you must be pretty busy, tending pal, seeing barbara, dickering with ev for a chance to go gunning and preparing for your theatrical debut at the cubs' show. i would like to be there when you and arthur kinsler immortalize the dragon. if you are inside the dragon you won't get the credit for the sterling performance i know you are going to give. i think the only solution is to either have two little dragons, instead of one big one, and let st. george make a doubleheader out of the dragon slaying or you and arthur should put a cellophane stomach in your big dragon. with the cellophane stomach, when the show is over and you and arthur have given a great show as the dragon, the people will start applauding not knowing who is in the dragon. at the climax of the applause, which you will sense, you can give arthur a kick in the leg. this will be his cue. the dragon will rear back and the audience can look through the cellophane belly of the dragon and see you and arthur. otherwise, some other kids may go around saying that they were in the dragon. if you can't prove anything it looks as though all you will get out of the show is a stuffy evening inside the dragon.

while you are out of the dragon some day will you tell your father that we are returning to new york on november 23rd. tell him not to send the star to hollywood since we will not be here. also, advise him that i have mailed him dr. fink's book on "nervous tension."

when i get back to new york i shall get in touch with you. we are starting the radio program december 12th which may be news to some people who are spending a lot of time in dragons these days. portland wants to be remembered to you and ev and pal and you might mention my name to mr. and mrs. rattray, your father and mother.

sincerely . . .

fred allen

december
25th
1945.

dear dave . . .

i received the xmas package you sent and was happy to receive the book and the candy.

most people are inconsiderate at xmas time. they either send a book or candy. with only a book it is pretty monotonous just sitting there reading, your eyes are enjoying themselves but your mouth is quiet and your tongue and your throat, along with your ears, aren't getting in on the fun. it is the same with just candy. you sit there munching away. your tongue and your teeth and your neck are all having a good time, but your eyes are hanging around doing nothing. just reading a book, or just eating candy, isn't much fun.

but you, with that uncanny gift you have for sending the proper, managed the ideal xmas gift. a book and candy. now i can sit here with my book open and my bag of candy open, my eyes, jaws, teeth, throat, digestive juices all going a mile a minute and i am eating noisily to let my ears get in on it, too.

thanx a lot for your present. i am enclosing two envelopes. one for you and one for ev. i would consult your mother before you make any decisions as to what should be done with the envelope's contents.

happy new year, mr. rattray.

fred allen
180 west 58th

september
4th
1943

dear mr. rattray . . .

i am in receipt of your letter acknowledging the arrival of the five dollars. i think you had better pay some immediate attention to your arithmetic. if you had $2.19 and ev had $2.25 there is a six cent difference there. ev apparently owes you three cents which would bring your total to $2.22 and shrink his holdings to the same amount. i don't know who figured out the division of the money but if i were you i would go down to mr. osborne, at the bank, with your figures and ask for a new deal.

you will kindly advise your mother, mrs. jeannette rattray, and your father, mr. arnold rattray, that the express package arrived in good condition. we now have enough clams and canned vegetables to last us through the winter. portland and i are thinking of getting a cow. we can keep the cow in a closet and every morning we can open the closet and get fresh milk. during the balance of the day we can turn the radio on and if the cow likes music and starts dancing a little we will have butter for the rest of the year. if we keep the cow in a closet we can use the cow's horns to hang things on and when we go to hollywood we can tie mothballs on the cow so the moths won't eat her coat off while we are away.

i would caution you against being fooled by false friends who hide in the barn and imitate cats. the next time you hear a cat in the barn pay no attention to it. this will discourage the cat impersonators and if it happens to be a real cat it will be meowing the next day and you will know it isn't fooling. i knew a boy who heard a rooster crowing on top of a barn. he climbed up the side of the barn to see what the rooster wanted and when he got up there it was an old man hiding behind a weather vane. the old man was crowing to fool the boy. well, sir, the boy came down from the top of the barn and hid the ladder and as far as i know the old man is still up on top of the barn and he is pretty cold during the winter. i hope you won't get fooled again or some day that old man will crow hoping you will climb up to the top of the barn and that he will be able to climb down the ladder when you are not looking.

you will hear from me again, mr. rattray. when i get out to hollywood, if i am not too busy, i will write you. meantime, best wishes to all.

f. allen

EVERETT RATTRAY

september
12th
1945

mr. everett rattray
east hampton, n.y.

dear sir;

i am in receipt of your letter listing the various items you purchased with the money you shared with mr. david rattray, also of east hampton.

naming your train the "fred allen" express is rather risky business. as you recall, all last summer, i didn't stop at east hampton—i went right on through to montauk. through force of habit. i would suggest that you and mr. david rattray build a stout fence around your house to prevent the train from getting away when your backs are turned.

your graphic account of the battle of apples was very exciting. if your forces scored all of the hits you claim the immediate vicinity must have been knee-deep in applesauce. if you had been exchanging watermelon barrages you might have finished with enough water in the neighborhood to float your grandfather's boat. this would involve swearing your grandfather into service with his harpoon and changing your army over into a branch of the navy. all in all if you were able to retire your apple corps "according to plan" i would consider the engagement a rattray victory. i would like to see the report turned in by the queen of rattrayland before considering the incident closed. you still have plenty of apples but italy with mussolini gone has lost its lemon.

sincerely . . .

fred allen

GERALD HAMEL

(Cheering note to a young summer camper.)

july
27th
1947

dear
gerry
:
an
old
seagull
that
spent
some
time
near
your
camp
flew
over
our
beach
today
.
when
the
gull
saw
me
he
sat

down
and
told
me
that
you
had
not
been
getting
much
mail
at
camp
.
the
gull
said
you
would
appreciate
a
letter
.
i
am
sending
you
the
letter
"b"
it
is
a
good
letter

.

you
can
read
it
quickly
and
you
don't
have
to
open
an
envelope
to
find
it

.

if
you
prefer
another
letter
let
me
know

.

sincerely

.

fred
allen

.

.

.

.

VIRGINIA LIBBY

(Note to a friend's daughter who has announced her marriage.)

august 27th

virginia—

to put it mildly—portland and i were a mite gasted in the flabber regions upon the receipt of your wedding announcement.

we both rushed to our mirrors to check on the white hairs that the scalp so subtly inserts among the darker strands to caution us that time has passed.

news of your wedding can only mean that you have grown up and that we have grown older.

if you had only remained an old maid we would never have thought about the years and we would have remembered you and ourselves as we were when last we met.

we plan to take this up with your father and we hope to see you both on september seventeenth.

with best wishes—

Fred Allen

6.

THE RADIO TREADMILL

ARNOLD RATTRAY

dear mr. r. . . .

many thanx for calling o. o. mcintyre's column about my alleged tightness to my attention. odd comes to my defense in the last few lines but it isn't at all necessary.

i do eat at a drug store in the morning. an orange is an orange in a drug store and since all i have is orange juice and coffee i can get bad coffee at a drug store easier than i can at home and i don't have to dry the cup and saucer, nor the little orange juice glass, when i leave the drug store luncheonette. i defy mr. mcintyre to prove that i eat dinner at a drug store and i defy him to catch me quaffing bi-carbonate regardless of where i eat.

i run an apartment without servants. all i do in the apartment is go to bed and work on radio programs. i do not need a servant to help me get into bed . . . since i do not drink . . . and i am well able to get out of bed the following morning without the aid of some fat male or buxom female hireling. a servant cannot help me write the radio shows. i have hired many writers and even they couldn't help a great deal so we must acknowledge that, regardless of mr. mcintyre's attitude, a servant for collaboration is unnecessary. i'll be damned if i am going to hire a servant to please mr. mcintyre and then just have the lackey sitting around the apartment watching me go to bed, get out of bed and write radio scripts.

i often help portland with the dishes . . . otherwise there wouldn't be a dish left on the premises. my crockery washing and drying comes under the heading of self-defense and i see no harm in trying to salvage butter-plates, saucers and other china that might come in handy should a guest squeeze through the door before i can squash him on the threshold.

my enormous pay is also a figment of mr. mcintyre's unsteady conjecture. ten people share the weekly stipend . . . there is agent's commission . . . and countless obligations, some inherent, others transient, that auger ill for my financial stability in later life. what is left i share with two state and one federal income tax departments and what remains is small recompense for an eighteen hour day and the multiple headaches that go with the daily routine of the radio comedian . . . especially when we consider that the popularity of the comedian rests on the whims of the masses who taste his wares mentally for nothing . . . and again when we realize that the comedian is supposed to spend his waking hours in cellophane so that all may peek in to ridicule him personally and to pick his life apart for the edification of those this sort of thing edifies.

well . . . to hell with it! odd has been swell to us and these items roll off my mind along with any worthwhile knowledge i may have picked up years ago.

tattered regards to mrs. r. and hopes that all goes well. regards to val.

fred allen

FRANK SULLIVAN

The noted Saratoga Springs humorist and contributor to *The New Yorker* received these notes from Allen in the fall of 1938 "when I tried being a writer for Fred and was no good at it."

december 8
1938

dear frank . . .

this has been an exceptional week . . . even for me. while i was in boston the office decided to put on jack benny in our tomorrow's show without telling me, mr. bristol, our sponsor, dug up a druggist who collects old photographs for me to interview and the courtroom sketch we wrote is ten minutes too long. on top of that the man i was supposed to interview, the one who sends thought waves to his dog, showed up with a stick with which he beats the dog to get his thought waves across and the dog's barks overlap his answers to my questions . . . and so it goes.

things are gradually getting back to sub-normal however. mr. benny will not be on the program. the druggist will appear shortly for a rehearsal. i suppose if we don't put him on the show he will hide all of the ipana and sal hepatica in his store. the man with the dog has been cut to nothing and the show, unlike the 6th avenue el, will go on.

i, too, am sorry our mutual experiment didn't work out. this is my seventh year of this drudgery. unless we find some way of lightening the burden i will have to look for something easier, like checking the altitude on tiddlywink chips for the american aeronautical old age group. if i get something easier next season maybe we can try again. thanks for everything.

fa

december 29
1938

dear frank . . .

wish you could have been with us this week to see the peak in radio confusion. mr. tomaso guzzi, our bootblack guest star, disappeared on wednesday. prowl cars were sent out. mr. guzzi's agent ran through mott street hiring boys on bicycles to pedal along the bowery in search of mr. guzzi. we waited until five thirty. no signs of mr. guzzi were forthcoming so i contrived the bit with uncle james harkins that was foistered on our listeners last night. mr. guzzi's agent, who has an office in an ash can on eighth avenue, received a call from four maffia representatives who said that for a nominal sum they could guarantee mr. guzzi's appearance on our show next week. i am afraid we have another musica case on our hands with mr. tomaso guzzi so i am forgetting him and starting work tonight on an interview for next week with a canary doctor. there is something assuring about a canary osteopath. a man who will leave a warm bed during the wee small hours of the a.m. to rush to the cage side of a canary in the throes of angina troubles will certainly show up at the microphone next week. you will be happy to know that we, the chambermaids of radio, continue to make our bedlam although we have scant time to lie in it. best wishes.

F

DON QUINN*

april 12th
1940

dear mons quinn . . .

i have been having a hell of a time preparing an answer to your not-too-recent scroll. everything i write, including personal mail, has to go to the client, the advertising agency and a miss mink, at n.b.c. i wrote you several letters but by the time the sponsor, legal department and agency men had suggested cuts and "musts" there was nothing left to mail you but your address, which i assume you know, and a few harmless conjunctions. all of the buts were stricken from the missives since the word "but" has a derriere connotation throughout the south. an executive from the dixie network was called in to render this cut.

you speak of "slices" and "sleepless nights." you are out there where executives are comparatively harmless and decisions are passed on to you in a quivering voice. you should try writing in radio city for a few weeks. here, an executive is only a buzzer-cry from conference. here, no more than ten radio comedians are permitted to assemble or herd. the vice-president, or the "man from miss mcrory's office" only has ten fingers. lest a comedian escape unimpaled ten are allowed to congregate. that assured a finger for all. the two little men who generally "get the thumb" are fortunate fellows indeed.

we are flying the banner around here even on days when there is no wind. i refuse to believe that the all-american brow

* Creator of the famed Fibber Magee and Molly radio show.

is so low that it can be mistaken for puberty-silk. i am sure that you are on the right track. your magee and molly show is very popular in the east and up in maine where we go each summer. the natives all swear by fibber. i mean the right kind of people whose loyalty to a program will prompt them to support the product that fornishes their entertainment. other shows may have an hysterical following for a short time but the yowling cretins who echo catchlines and whistle at the conclusion of broadcasts will certainly ignore the commercial propaganda and rarely feel that they should be obligated to buy, or try, the product. most of these people live in trailers and i doubt that floor-wax would fit into their scheme of things.

i guess all we can do is write and trust. i was going to say hope but why plug a competitor. none of us in radio are going anyplace. you put your mind on a treadmill in the fall and remove it, winded, in june. it can't last. save your money. join the townsend plan! now! don't be caught like an indian high priest with your cants down! trust in crossley and the lord will provide. keep up the good work—there is too much bad work rampant in radio today.

thanx for your note. best wishes . . .

fred allen

AL MAISTER

june 20th
1941

dear al . . .

i am in receipt of various columns you have sent me. i can't seem to get any action for my correspondents these days. by the time i finish working on one program and get it on the air, i have to start on another show. when that is finished i repeat the procedure. add thirty-nine of these dilemmas and you have a radio season. there is no time for mail, outside activities, the welding of friendships or the forming of bad habits.

miles o'smiles holds up well. i don't know whether the writing comes easier to you, or not. it seems, in the reading of the column, that you are writing with less effort. the material appears to flow along and reads as though you had the words up your sleeve and were just turning them loose. of course, if you are home banging your hand against the door to get ideas you can get credit for camouflaging your efforts and keeping the strain from showing through your lines.

you ought to spend a few months in radio. with the sponsor, agency, network and strange people roaming around the studios cutting out your jokes and telling you what is wrong with the program, you would be ready for a fitting for either a coffin or a straitjacket. today, it seems to me, about ten percent of the people in america are trying to do something and the other ninety percent are either ballyhooing, picketing or condemning the minorities' activities.

well, it's all in fun. paths of glory lead but to the grave. you will find, if you live long enough, sir, that paths of ignominy, paths of profligacy, and paths of skullduggery lead to the same incision in terra firma. in other words, we who attempt to write and amuse the masses joust with futility. you may have heard of the golf player who saved his money and bought a cemetery. the first day, he took over, he walked around the grounds and saw an undertaker lowering a casket into a hole in the ground. as the golf player passed he said to the undertaker, "don't forget to replace the divot." thanx for all of your columns and good luck.

fred allen

LETTER TO A FAN MAGAZINE

Dear Alyce . . .

Judging from the number of Radio and Movie Fan magazines rampant, on the news-stands today, I take it that the mythical "Average Reader" is mildly interested in the private life of his, or her, favorite ether or celluloid star.

Thanks to the activities of the high-powered press agent, no stone has been left unturned in the drive to lay bare the innermost secrets, hereditary taints, and present foibles of the person unfortunate enough to be in the Public Eye at the moment. When we consider the scores of monthly publications, and the hundreds of articles printed, it is surprising that the actor, or actress, finds time to ply his, or her, art. If the artist involved is lousy . . . the word "art" doesn't go. It would seem that the day must be an endless succession of flashlights and grillings and the nights turned into a series of flights between night clubs to be on hand when the Master of Ceremonies "innerduces" the celebrities.

Portland and I have been talking it over and wondering if anybody would be interested in a couple of people who are minding their own business. We have been hanging around on the outskirts of fame, and popularity, in the Theatre and Radio for the past few years but we have been loath to set the World on fire. One of the reasons we have put off kindling the Universe is because we don't feel that we have reached the age mentally where we can be trusted with matches.

I know, if we ever do become famous, our Xrays will be printed in the Fan Magazines and I suppose I'll have to mail out my wisdom teeth, which I have been saving and listing as assets in my Income Tax, to the World's Fair. Our every move will be known to the Man In The Street and the intimate phases of our home life will be pool room chit chat. IF . . . we ever become famous!

Today, however, there is a world-wide lull in our fan interest. Who knows what we are doing Today? To enable you to scoop Radio Burp and Microphone Hullabaloo here is a detailed Account of how we spend the time between sun-up and night lunch. This is news!

7 a.m. We're generally still asleep.

8 a.m. Subconsciously, we feel for the White Collar Man who, at this hour, is dusting off his desk. We feel for him . . . but he is never there.

9 a.m. The alarm goes off but it is generally next door so we seldom pay any attention to it.

10 a.m. Australian Opera Singer starts vocalizing upstairs. In Australia, it is three p.m. the next day and the opera singer has neglected to change his larynx to Daylight Saving Time. It's our tough luck and after the third fugue we decide to get up. The customary ablutions follow and we are ready for the dawn of a new day.

10:15 a.m. Fifteen minutes of leap-frog which is fast replacing the Daily Dozen in the better bedrooms.

10:30 a.m. Portland retires to the kitchenette where she spends a good half-hour preparing a bad breakfast. This generally consists of half a watermelon, which is served with tiddley-wink chips. Watermelon tiddley-winks is a game we invented ourselves . . . the idea being to snap the seeds into a large bowl in the center of the table using the chip as a motive for the seeds to get about their business. The seeds are later dried and dropped, with a metallic clink, into the cups of doubtful blindmen who are not flying the Blue Eagle. Following the watermelon, a single half-grapefruit is served but neither of us touch it. Long experience has taught us that the "squirt is quicker than the eye." Rather than diminish our purchasing power, however, grapefruit is still served. We have Peter-Peter, not the pumpkin-eater, but a set of unemployed Siamese Twins who come to the apartment each morning for the sole purpose of consuming the spurting citris fruit. Twins invariably confuse a grapefruit. The juice takes aim but, in the general optical confusion it never fails to dash between Peter-Peter's head and spatter on the wall. The laughter that follows Peter-Peter's liquid victory always brings tears to our eyes so we might just as well eat the grapefruit in the first place. We have sworn our allegiance though and as long as there is a depression, and a grapefruit left, Peter-Peter is sure of his . . . or their . . . job or jobs. Breakfast is hurriedly concluded with eggs, toast, a phone call and coffee . . . in the order named.

11 a.m. Finds Portland busy mailing the breakfast dishes to a correspondence School maid at Rutland, Vermont. The

maid, a Mrs. Pratt, studied housekeeping through the mail and sensing a possibility in postal scullery work, opened a mail chambermaid business that nets her a tidy income per annum. For a small fee, and postage, you can mail her your dirty dishes, carpets to be beaten, and waste baskets to be emptied. Several of Mrs. Pratt's clients even send her their unmade beds via express. The dishes are washed at the Rutland General Delivery window, where Mrs. Pratt brings her portable sink each morning. When they're dried, the dishes are mailed back to your return address which should be plainly marked on the package. Mrs. Pratt makes the beds at the American Express Office and as soon as the second pillow is tapped into shape the bed is off to the client. So much for Mrs. Pratt.

12. Noon. While I am busy answering the morning mail, Portland goes window shopping at a motorboat agency. As a rule there is only the one motorboat in the window which simplifies her task and after a few "oh's" and "ah's" at the propellor and paint job she is on her way home.

1 p.m. Usually, Portland spends the entire afternoon hitting herself on the head with a croquet mallet so that she will be in the mood to give dumb answers should anyone ask her a question later in the day. I sit around with an old joke book trying to find original funny things to say on the radio programs. When we tire of our separate pastimes, we reverse the activities. Portland takes the joke book and I pound myself on the head with the mallet. The time passes pleasantly but we are both happy to stop when it is time for dinner.

6 p.m. If we have been invited . . . we generally go out to dinner. If not, we both stay home for a tasty Chiropodist's Buffet which consists of . . . pig's feet and pressed corn. After bi-carbonate and swizzlestick have been served for dessert, we are free for the evening. Sometimes I make up as Mr. Farley and Portland disguises herself as a little old lady who has lost a registered letter and we play Post Office. Other nights, we go around giving our autographs away to people who are convalescing or perhaps we'll spend the entire evening jumping in ambulances with bags of fruit for people who have had accidents

and can't depend on their friends to bring apples and bananas to the hospital. We eat the fruit in the ambulance which saves messing up the hospital ward later in the week. By midnight, we are both tired out, as a result of this wholesome sport, and glad to get to bed and be tucked in by Peter-Peter. We have twin beds and with the Siamese Twin chambermaids we are both tucked in simultaneously and are able to pop off to sleep without having to keep getting up to tuck one another in.

So you see, Alyce, our lives, at the moment, are unlike the busy, glamorous, existences of most of the popular Hill Billies and successful Radio Singers you read so much about in your favorite Fan Magazine. Of course, if we ever get famous the World will want to know what we are doing every minute of the day. This may prove embarrassing reading so I would suggest that you read this and ignore us from now on.

Sincerely . . . fred allen

BILL ROUSSEAU*

august 18, 1937

dear bill;

a recent issue of the new york times carried a few disturbing lines to the effect that a william p. rousseau had permitted his engagement to be announced.

since i am poet laureate of young & rubicam's the following ode was concocted on the spur of the exciting news. it is called—

. . . fiesta . . .

the office force danced—and shouted with glee
memo pads flew in the air;
buzzers were buzzed—a conference was called
and chet swivelled round in his chair.

* * *

* Then a member of the Young & Rubicam radio department.

mr. rubicam danced a stiff highland fling
don stauffer jumped over a client;
bill stubler scaled his inkwell into a fan
george mcgarrett dialed O-something bryant.

* * *

fred wile, all agog, razzed our friend dinty doyle
alton cook got the bird from bill thomas;
joe moran tore his hair and said kiss my—packard
and packard wired back "it's a promise."

* * *

general foods rang—but von zell thumbed his phone
a vice-president cried "i'm all wet";
"we the people" tried hard to speak
this was no time to plug calumet.

* * *

an office boy foofed at the jello account
shouting "down with all over-production";
a contact man goosed a stenographer stout
who said "shorthand?—or is it seduction?"

* * *

out on the coast—things were going to pot
weaver was twiddling his cate;
tom harrington, thin,—was yelling "ed wynn"
johnny green ran around mumbling "notes."

* * *

the din became worse—there were catcalls and shouts
even crossley was gnashing his polls;
when ed grimm looked out, through a crack in his door
and sang "yippee" for benton and bowles.

* * *

two-eighty-five was a bedlam for fair
the roar sounded strangely like lions;
a typist, quite handsome, looked over a transom
and said "god! is this ruthrauff and ryan's."

* * *

a cop on the beat yelled to mr laroche
"hey! what's this?—is somebody pullin a knife";
a memo fluttered down to the limb of the law
it read "rousseau is taking a wife."

* * *

congratulations!

portland and fred allen

STEVE BIRCH

may
first
1943

dear steve . . .

it is six a.m. i have just finished cutting the program and patching it up with gags. as i sit here slumped over the corona i don't know of a better time to envy a person in florida. it has been so cold here that the sun comes out chapped and as dawn is breaking reluctantly it would seem that we are in for another brisk day. i trust that you have both cheeks under control and that you are getting in some good, high-class sitting down there. i further trust that the weather is good, for without sun florida is nothing but a mecca for grapefruit and denizens of the swamp.

you will be glad to learn, if you haven't heard it, that the program is dragging on as usual. last week, our guest mr. lugosi had a dialect and couldn't read long speeches. yesterday, our guest akim tamiroff showed up with laryngitis. if he can't talk on sunday we will probably hide that talking bird in tamiroff's shirt and do the best we can. next week, we have booked frank sinatra, the current singing sensation of new york. life gave him a big spread this week and we may as well dedicate one program to his unwashed majesty, the jitterbug. women faint when he accidentally sings on key.

am enclosing a card that will enable you to do a favor for a friend, or two. the national educational alliance wants you to list the names of four friends who might be interested in taking a streamlined course in plane geometry or calculus. i am sure you know a host of people who are eager to drop what they are doing and get back into algebra and long division. as this card explains the alliance cannot promise to enroll your friends immediately but i am sure that if you attach a quarter to the card and mail same your influence will be felt and your friends will receive their courses at an early date.

i hope you and mrs. birch are enjoying yourselves and that you will soon return to our harried fold tanned and ready to cope with mr. shimmick the man who formerly deleted our jokes on sundays. john l. lewis has called out the miners. i guess he is trying to stop people from getting coal and put an end to mr. roosevelt's fireside chats.

portland sends her best wishes to you both and we hope that you will have a pleasant stay in florida.

sincerely . . .

fred allen
180 west 58

MAGGY O'FLAHERTY

(She wrote an article "There's Room for You in Radio.")

august
31st
1945

dear maggy . . .

i don't know why you have to get involved with coronet. if the agency is not paying you a living wage you should write the plb. this is the peace labor board that is taking over all of the problems left unsolved by the war labor board. you are entitled to a salary that will enable you to survive without having to worry about sidelines and writing chores for coronet.

the easiest way to get into radio is to become a quiz contestant. when it is your turn and you come to the microphone whip out a revolver, kill the master of ceremonies and take over the quiz program yourself. a lot of listeners will be grateful to you for killing the m.c. and good will is important if you hope to survive in radio.

i got into radio the hard way. back in 1912 i didn't know that radio was going to be invented. i started preparing for the inevitable. i spent twenty years playing in vaudeville and broadway shows. the inevitable turned out to be radio and when it came i was ready for it.

if you do not want to spend twenty or thirty years in the theatre getting ready to go into radio you can cut down a few years through becoming a quiz kid and growing up in the business.

another good and easy way to get into radio is to be born the son of a sponsor.

your title is rather vague. i should think that whatever type of work you do would determine how you would get into radio. a writer certainly couldn't get into radio auditioning as a singer. and a singer couldn't very well get into radio submitting a script.

i think it is going to be easier to get into radio in the future. many schools and colleges now have radio courses for potential writers and actors and eventually i believe that the networks will provide opportunities to the more talented graduates to enable them to get a start in the business. radio uses so much material and outmodes ideas so quickly that there will always be a market for the wares of qualified youngsters who can bring new ideas and fresh personalities to the microphone.

comedians have the greatest problems in radio. all comedy and humor is a matter of opinion and every advertising agency executive, every vice-president in the network employ, every man with any authority in the sponsor's firm and every listener is an authority on what is funny. i keep trying to do what i think is funny and let the opinions fall where they may.

best wishes . . .

fred allen
180 west 58th st.
new york city

BILL MORROW*

march 13th
1948

dear will . . .

i am in receipt of your scroll advising me that mr. crosby has informed you that it will be "eastward ho!" come april 19th.

an exchange of shows seems to be in order. re the script for your program—why can't we do as we did last year—read the fine print on the back of several johnson & johnson kidney plasters. with mr. crosby twittering at spaced intervals it seemed to work okay. if you insist on going to the bother of contriving a script— that will be all right, too. you can advise me when you sample mr. crosby's mood after he has seen his nine old friends of abner doubleday's romp around the diamond at pittsburg.

re our show—for appearance sake—it might be well if mr. crosby could be prevailed upon to attend a rehearsal. the actual broadcast isn't too important but since our mr. reber of our sponsor's advertising agency will be back with his new wife, by then, he may want to bring her to a rehearsal to obtain the guest's autograph.

i am available—preferably on a monday or tuesday if you are still transcribing—or on any date if you are live. (this, of course, includes mr. crosby. advise if he is obsolete.) *send me an okay for a date on our tableau.* we are set until april 4th.

mr. welch and i haven't corresponded since he became a producer. i may remove all reference to mr. welch from my memoirs.

* Then writer and producer of Bing Crosby's radio show.

your shows have been swell—jack's with tom brenneman especially hot—portland joins me in gala wishes to you and your employer.

f. allen

T. J. SMITH*

july first
1939

captain gregg . . .

"tonowando sologodam how-how."

i know you will recognize this native polynesian greeting. it means, as we know "what can you expect from a pygmy . . . but a litter."

this is the litter which will acknowledge your recent note on harvard club stationery. the mailman who was a yale man spat upon your missive . . . or mayhaps he was a cornell man who drooled . . . whatever the cause your scroll arrived semi-moistened but we tied it to an andiron and fanned it with an ikon until the watermark on the paper perked and then portland and i fell to reading it.

it made mighty fine reading . . . as the man said as he recounted once having seen the lord's prayer etched atop a pin-head; the pin-head, incidentally, was no one we know.

i am enclosing an intimate snap of us to tack on your wall at the harvard club. i would send you a bore's head but decapitation is so messy what with the light cretonne covers on the furniture.

met mr. van nostrand in an italian bistro tonight. i nodded and made suttee on an anti-pasto which conveniently made its appearance at the next table.

portland and i hope that you will have a pleasant summer

* Member of Young & Rubicam radio department.

beating the contestants to the answers as "what's my name" is
being played.

     sincerely . . .

            "20 seconds over" allen

            old orchard beach
            maine
            july 13th
            1939

t. j. smith-minor . . .
sir:

    advise captain gregg that his combination walking-stick, pool
cue, divining rod and jiffy-adjustable, air-conditioned, collapsible
openwork divan arrived in a-1 condition.

    you can't beat abercrombie & fitch for service, as the package
was opened, a small but alert gnome popped out, demonstrated
the contrivance, inquired the way to route #1 and left.

    assure captain gregg that his unusual gift will come in
mighty handy. outdoors, it will be used to poke the embers at
weinie roasts, to flail gnarled bunches of kelp, to whack reckless
clams on the thyroid as they are caught with their necks out and to
lance the beaverboard knapsacks of good humor men.

    advise captain gregg that, as per his last minute instructions,
i am checking on his ancestry. the captain knows nothing of his
father and mother. his first recollections concerning his discovery
that he had been shanghaied into the human race are noted in
his diary. his first entry reads . . . "may 27, 1852. awoke in a
waterfront bagnio off the coast of casco bay, maine. the hole
reeked of shandy-gaff and the slattern behind the bar paid me
small heed. i gave her a receipt . . . and left."

    the world knows captain gregg from that day on. ah! but
what of the years before 1852? the captain will never be happy
until the intimate facts concerning his birth, his early life and the
identity of his unfortunate parents are disclosed. in his last letter,
written on snug harbor stationery, the captain writes "go to it,

lad." and that is just what i am doing. no stone will be left un-turned, no scallop will be left unopened up maine-way until i can report the true facts to our captain.

i sent your mr. van nostrand word yesterday. the rumor that the captain's mother was a mermaid, who had been raped by a fragment of male ambergris, proved to be without foundation. i am checking with an old fellow here now. he claims to be a blub-ber grader. he used to grade the blubber when whaling thrived in the nineties. he says he recalls a young boy who used to sit in the water all day. crabs, barnacles, periwinkles and other sea-snailiana would attach itself to the boy's rump. as night fell the boy would return to the shore, light a small fire, and proceed to eat the small shell-fish that clung to his posteriors. the old man says that as he ate the boy would often burst into tears. one night the old man said to the youth "why do you cry as you munch away at your tiny crustaceans?" (the plural is no doubt crustacea but the old fellow was illiterate) the boy replied "how would you feel eating your old friends? these anthropods are at-tached to me."

whether this witty lad was captain gregg . . . time alone will tell. portland and i trust that you will have keen bermudaing. ask jack if there is anything i can do to further your interests re l'af-faire town hall for the fall. i spoke to tom but will be glad to write him later if jack thinks it would help.

avoir, smith-minor!

"cyclops"

december 25th
1939

dear captain gregg . . .

it seems odd to address you as captain gregg after calling you fatso for four years at oxford. but you have won your spurs, cap-tain gregg.

this is christmas day. to us, in radio, it is monday. about the studio we sense that it is not just an ordinary monday it is a monday apart from other mondays. the momentous event that occurred in bethlehem 1939 years ago plays no part in the strange pall that hovers over studio three 3 in the rca building today. the feeling of "all is well" and "peace to men of good will" is not inspired as a result of the ghostly incantations of the little dominie who is not there. the aura of concord and tranquility is present on this hallowed day because mrs. mcrorie, the pontius pilate or pilatess of the script world, is absent.

today hells, damns, buggers and hermaphrodites romp in the scripts. today, radio comedians rant and rave to their heart's content. today no names are cleared and the patronymics of the great are bandied about with abandon approximating impunity. today, the little man has his fling.

we in radio this day are thankful for many things. we are thankful that the guest star's spot looks semi-entertaining. we are thankful that but two of the news reel interviews have to be rewritten. we are thankful that the sketch looks as though it will play. we are thankful that we have this work. we are thankful that we are alone to be able to do the work we have to do.

we are thankful for the many presents we received and that brings us once again, to you captain gregg. we are thankful for the gulliver coffee cups. we often have new england midgets as house guests. new englanders are accustomed to having urine crockery placed under their beds at night. these jumbo cups will be known as the "double-duty" cups about our humble quarters. they will be used mornings for coffee and evenings for midget relief. we are thankful, too, for the colored cravat. it will look well on me as i journey forth to interview the seagull gelder or the other guest we contemplate for the coming week. we are indeed thankful to you captain gregg for your thoughtfulness and your generosity.

we trust that you enjoyed a dulcet xmas and that you are back, hard at it, ready to lose miss hunt's address again and ready to get for the silver theatre the crossley ordained for it by your mr. laroche.

a confused new year, captain gregg.
sincerely . . .

trueman goodbody

CHARLIE CANTOR*

december
20th
1942

dear charlie . . .

received your letter okay.

i will write a bit and also take care of the sketch material and have it cut and ready for laying on sunday morning.

our routine is the same. 11 a.m. at 53rd street. you should get a look at the present cast. teddy looks normal but everett sloan has a little red beard and looks like a poor man's christ. jack smart has a round henry the eighth beard and his head hangs out as though he is being born again. he has the dirtiest unkempt muff i have ever seen. we really don't need much alley material. as soon as everett and jack show we are sure of two bellies.

we have been off to a great start. the first week i used john anthony for a kidding bit and i guess i was the only one who thought the idea was funny. yesterday, we went over to the joint at 11 a.m. and word arrived that orson welles couldn't get out of bed until he paid the doctor, or something. we had to run around and get a whole show together during the afternoon. what it sounded like, i'll never know. melton, who was taking jan peerce's place at a met concert ran up between numbers and did a bit and we pulled an old sketch out of the privy. well, that's radio.

new york will probably look good to you after being out in that yokel section of the country.

trust that all goes well. see you shortly. regards . . .

f. allen

(formerly with minerva pious)

---

* Actor who worked on Allen's radio shows and later on the Duffy's Tavern show.

april
27th
1944

dear charlie . . .

it is about time i scared up an answer to your letter. things, as you may have surmised, have been a little hectic since you left. we have had patsy flick doing a jewish dialect that will bring back the columbia wheel and with the good weather the writers are out on the rifle range one morning and drilling in central park the next. how the programs get together i don't know. all i do know is that i always seem to be in the house, or at rehearsal or going to some fleabag to interview next week's guest.

my blood pressure stays up and i don't know how i can keep it down meeting writers on the fly, trying new writers and trying to cope with the new tenants in the alley. i guess it is better to be a fat gin player around the friars than it is to have a twenty-two crossley. i may find out shortly.

tell abe he hasn't written me. he may not know it. that is why i haven't answered him. i missed the show last tuesday but all of the others have been up to the burrows standard or is it the gardner standard. i hope ed is getting plenty of that sun he was raving about on his thin behind. if he ever bends over in a turkish bath people will think he's an hawaiian.

hope your picture outlook is brighter than mine. the script came last week and it looks as though i will be the new ned sparks in my next movie if i ever make it. i haven't got enough trouble—next week george jessel. georgie, the papers say, is coming east to speak at cantor's testimonial dinner. that is like going to salt lake to take a leak.

give my regards to brother kempner. min pious starts with us this week again. portland sends her best and we both trust that all goes well. i have nothing against god and i know that is his country but i still don't like it. tell abe portland sends her best to ruth. good luck.

from "the goy louse" . . . the failing chief . . .

180 west 58th

may
27th
1944

dear charlie . . .

i finally received a letter from abe burrows. he may have his hands full but the duffy's tavern shows are swell which either proves that he is a cousin of superman's or he does his writing first and then worries about his political obligations. the only trouble getting mixed up with causes is that the people who have plenty of time on their hands keep thinking up things for the busy people like abe to do. at the blow off, the fat guys are still sitting around getting someone else to do the work after the first champions of the cause have fallen by the wayside with ulcers or an offer from monogram.

read that you are going to have a summer show with ransom sherman. hope it is true unless new hampshire looks better to you than the dough. you really should have two or three good paying jobs and let the rest of the stuff ride. if i ever get organized again the first thing i will do is to see that there is enough dough for everybody. these days, in any brackets, the taxes are tough and it doesn't make sense trying to kill yourself when you can't even save enough to pay the doctor when you come apart.

mr. skirball is here with morrie ryskind working on the picture i was supposed to make last summer. if the story is fixed i may be out there this summer. i hope not. i am all in. nat hiken and bob weiskopf left wednesday for the service and i have five shows to get out with no writers. when i finish this mess i will be through and probably deaf from patsy flick yelling "green bims" and other greek expressions in my ears at close quarters.

tell abe i am using his old partner frank loesser on the show the week of june 11th. expect to repeat the oklahoma burlesque with frank listenin, if you fellows aren't doing your dress at 6.30 that night. will let you know what happens later. trust that all goes well.

regards.

f. allen   180 west 58

montauk
july
29th
1944

dear charlie . . .

your letter came last night. from the looks of the stationery i would say that you do not find many townsend club members stopping at the lake tarleton club. offhand, i would say it is one of those places where the waitress has a caddy follow her with the asparagus.

nat wrote me from the coast. he went out on the train with benoff, levey and some of the other gardner-duffy tavern staff. they were all surprised when they arrived to find that ed gardner's picture deal was off but nat said that ed was expecting to make a deal with some other company. if the boys have a story written he might be able to peddle it to universal or republic and get a good piece of money for it. i hope he gets some action as it seems a shame to move the whole crew out there to hollywood just for the ride.

we are trying to get a rest here. the place is very nice. few of the guests are under eighty. nobody bothers anybody. i guess they figure making friends is a waste of time. none of these people will live long enough to get to know another person very well. there is no fishing, no gas for golf, nothing but eating, sitting, swimming and sleeping.

let me know when you get back to n.y. i don't know what i can do yet. i am supposed to see some specialist up in boston, after labor day, and he will tell me what i can do. bob weiskopf goes in the army, august 5th and nat hiken is still walking around not knowing when he will be grabbed. if my pressure will only go down i may be able to go back to work later in the fall. if it doesn't it looks as though i am cooked for the present.

hope you will return well-rested with your pocketbook peeled.

formal regards to mrs. cator (cantor . . . this victory corona will never last for the duration).

will see you backstage at a freddy, or charlie, martin, broadcast.

Fred Allen

march
12th
1945

dear charlie . . .

i have just finished a letter to fallstaff whom you probably know as alan reed. he mentioned in his letter that you had played a little gin at hellcrest last week and while he didn't exactly say you were moulting he hinted that on that particular afternoon you were the pigeon. i know you do a hell of a parrot. i have proof that your parrot impersonation some years ago forced brad barker to bite his nails off down to his first finger joints. since you are so good as a parrot i hope it will not encourage you to insist on being the pigeon whenever a friend sees fit to produce a pack of cards. watch these bird impersonations. a friend of mine in vaudeville used to do crows, whippoor-wills, seagulls and chickens. he wasn't satisfied. he got a week at the palace and started to impersonate a peacock. after the third show his pratt spread out and he had lavender and an assortment of other beautifully colored spots on his rump. this could happen to you. if you start doing pigeons you will start snapping at the corn in the script before abe has a chance to cut some of it.

i wrote abe burrows from atlantic city a couple of weeks ago. i never expect to hear from him. the income tax people are lucky to get a short note from abe once a year so why should i complain? i told you that i thought our picture was only fair. if you get a chance to see it out there wish you would let me know what you think of it. i saw it downtown, at a preview in the loew theatre in the village, and there were a few good laughs but a lot of it seemed draggy to me.

you louse. i don't mind you enjoying that california house but when you start to brag about the lack of rain and the climate out there—you're overdoing it. you say it was 80 feb. 14th. how would you like to know, mr. cantor, that here, in new york, it was 110 down at libby's baths that day? you are sounding like a native in one season. it's too fast. wait a year, or so, and then you are entitled to write east and say "today is xmas. an avocado fell down the chimney today. my wife looked out the window just for a second and had a sunstroke." you know there is no place to live out there. don't write that propaganda to your relatives.

i am doing a guest shot with "the voice" wednesday night. later, i am on the hall of fame. i had to miss you the week you were on. i was doing a show at a hospital that sunday. have been busy writing and making transcriptions and it is a pleasure not to worry about the crossley or that sonofabitch at nbc who used to come to work on sundays just so that he could cut out jokes from our script. saw nat and bob last week. they are still with winged victory and the show is booked all through the summer so it looks as though they will be on the road for a long time yet.

have heard most of the tavern shows lately and they have been swell. too bad you didn't come east this winter. lindy is putting more sour cream on the herring and the new chef is putting twice as many onions in the fried eggs and onions.

port joins me in best wishes to mrs. c and the "kiddie." trust that the old gander is hanging high.

regards . . .

f.a.
180 west 58

may 6th
1945

dear charlie . . .

i wish you would write my address on the wall in your bedroom. your recent letter was sent to 100 west 58th. that is the windsor hotel and, as you will note on enclosed envelope front, the clerk has a large red stamp to cope with guests who live elsewhere. we used to live at the windsor and if you can't remember 180 west 58th, i can take a room down at the windsor weekends, or whenever you intend to write, to be there when your letters arrive. i think it would be simpler though to write my present address on john brown's back. you will see him every sunday on the greenwood show and that will remind you.

spent the last two weeks in the hospital. some well-wisher threw a louse on me and caused a gland infection. i caught up with all of my mail while i was confined and also heard a lot of radio shows i had never been exposed to before. incidentally, i heard fallstaff (in person) playing the western scamp on the greenwood show yesterday. i owe him a letter which i hope to bat out this afternoon.

abe burrows wrote me last week saying that he was quitting radio for the nonce. i think it will be good for abe. actors can get stomach trouble just reading those scripts week after week but god knows what can happen to the guys who have to take the blank paper every week and come up with the gags and plots. the tavern shows have kept up a wonderful standard and before abe blows his top i think a change will help him greatly. he is so clever that he can do better in pictures with less work which will assure him of a longer creative life. he said that you had two clever boys working on the shows and ed knows the writing and production ends as well as anyone in radio so the show could continue its merry way. it is one of the best programs on the air week after week and should last as long as you all want it to.

have just finished writing a routine for min. she wants to go overseas with a u.s.o. unit this summer but she had no material. i batted out about a nine minute monologue with a little idea. min tried it out at a canteen last week for the u.s.o. heads and they okayed it. she hopes to play a couple of other hospitals and camps before she goes and i am going to try to patch up any weak spots she finds after she has had a chance to do it in front of different audiences. with the occupation armies stuck over there indefinitely the u.s.o. is planning to send a lot of units and plays over this summer. abe lastfogel told me that hughie diamond, whom you must have known with the diamond brothers was killed in a plane accident overseas. it seems he took an unauthorized trip with some pilot and then the plane crashed. joe woods, may woods' brother, who was a keith agent years ago died last week. you must have known may woods as she was a big shot in the keith office when albee and murdock ran everything.

i expect to sign for a show next fall. there are a lot of offers around and i guess before the week is over we will decide on a deal. i will have to stay east on account of my brother's condition and there may be some problems getting under way again. as you know ninety percent of the comedy shows and good actors are out there on the coast with you. i am not going to worry about it until after the summer, though. radio is nothing but whatever dough you can get. the minute you do a show it is forgotten and nobody knows about the ulcers except the people who have them.

bob welch wrote me from pearl harbor last week. he doesn't seem to know how long he will be gone but he has some duties to perform on some of those pacific islands. say "hello" to pat weaver when you see him again. that outfit will probably have plenty of work ahead for the occupation armies. today, broadway is covered with paper and people are walking the streets celebrating mildly v-e day. when the japs are knocked off perhaps we can get back to normal.

jack benny wrote a very funny review of our picture and i wrote one of his. i think they will both be published in the june screen guide. jack's picture is in the strand for four weeks. i think ours opens at the globe late this month. the moral is . . . don't make an independent picture. we have had a lot of great notices and time gave the picture a full page two weeks ago but it really isn't good. jack's sequence is the best in the picture and the rest of it is hit and run. it burns me up as we had bill bendix and some other wonderful people and should have had a smash.

after the philco show the company offered me the "hall of

fame" as an hour or half hour for the rest of this season and next season. i turned it down. i will be a lot better starting off fresh in the fall and i can probably get a good hour on a good night which should help the rating. that rating will be the end of the radio business now that the companies have no products to sell.

well to hell with this . . . it is running as long as an old town hall script. hope that everything is tip-top. i saw john in the benny picture and he is excellent. when jack's picture and duffy's tavern come out perhaps you and john will be able to get some decent shots around the studios. that is a good racket if you can get in on the right foot.

portland joins me in good wishes to mrs. and the kiddie, we expect to go back to maine in june. as i go through new hampshire i will lean out of the train window and tell your friend at the golf club that you won't be there this summer.

best wishes . . .

F.A.

f. allen
180 west 58th
(to hell with that windsor
address)

ZEKE MANNERS

march
7th
1947.

dear zeke . . .

received your wire and later your letter arrived. i thought there was a publicity angle involved. i thought you might want me to walk down broadway at three a.m. some morning with a lantern and a sign on my back saying "i got up to listen to zeke manners." going on at your hour you make arthur godfrey look like a nighttime attraction. arthur gets up at 5:30 a.m. to get his ad libs up. you are up too early to even have a milkman for a straightman.

a few weeks ago, in variety, i read about a nightclub comic in cincinnati who was caught robbing a house on his way home from work. i figured then that if night spots were paying these kind of salaries an actor was better off in radio. now you come along getting up at 2 a.m. to work in radio. i hope you are getting decent money so that you will not have to start breaking into joints on your way to the studio.

if you get tired of that routine you can always come back east. with all of your old sponsors up the river you can do a new version of showboat. staying on the coast with those hours the best you can hope for is an occasional fan letter from elsie the cow. at abc i imagine they have a neon mike so that you can find it in the dark without turning on the studio lights and putting the network to extra expense.

you will be glad to know that nat has so many jokes left over from our show that he is putting on a package with milton berle starting next tuesday. if i start sounding like berle you will know that nat has enough jokes left over from his new package to give some to me. we are still going along with the same routine. the tax guy showed up this week and i discovered that last season i worked 31 or 39 weeks for nothing. what i need with all of the imgluck to get eight weeks salary, i will never tell you. it may be because i like to hang around with the writers. hope hooper gets up early enough to give you a good rating.

fred allen

BOB WELCH*

OFFICE OF THE MAYOR

MEMO FROM THE MAYOR: Date *October 31, 1941*

dear welch . . .

am in receipt of your communique under philadelphia post-
mark. it is too bad that you have to flee the city after each
cantor show. when you worked along with us it was safe to hide
for but part of thursday after we had been on the air. i know
you are out to shrink our crossley but we are washing our script
in lux, welch, and even with your swan account and the avail-
ability of samples, i am afraid it will take a bit of doing. however,
i wish you well, welch. good luck to you! and good luck to those
neurotic, stomachless gnomes who flutter about your premises,
those little men who are born to work for young & rubicam, tiny
bloodless creatures who give off the body odor of the leprechaun,
who have small glistening foreheads, who have but one arm jut-
ting out desk-high from their spectral bodies, and but two fingers
on the one hand to enable them to pinch a memo from mr. harrington's desk and flit with it to the sanctuary of the tinker bell,
of advertising, your mr. laroche. good luck to you and the merry
munchkins who inhabit your pixie world. good luck too, to the
thyroid elf who rules over your little flibbertigibbet kingdom.

while perusing the society column of alton cook's daily to
see if any of our swank listeners had departed park avenue for
their florida haunts, where the palms applaud as we take the air,
i am reliably informed, i stumbled over another item enclosed.
now that young & rubicam is behind china, where is china on
the crossley? if mrs. x is holding a benefit for china why should
the automat get the business? were horn and hardart, either of
them, chinamen? what is wrong with lum fung? lum fung is a
chinaman. why not help a chinaman here while helping chinamen at home? were the slots, at the automat, slanted on the night

* At that time, Welch was producing Eddie Cantor's radio show.

of the party for atmosphere? what was the hostess doing in a "black-and-beige ensemble?" why not a mandarin coat and chinese jodhpurs? just because mrs. x ran into valentina and said "do me something," is that any reason valentina had to "do her" this get-up yclept "Les sylphides?"

come, come, welch! let us face facts! what has china got that cantor hasn't got, except perhaps a mad russian? this is no time to be spreading bric-a-brac before a booted husband. what about a guest star for next week? what is eddie going to say to harry when the nasal lyrics of "hi, neighbor" have given way to dialogue? this is hardly a time for "masses of coral." the masses don't want lombard. the masses want CANTOR!

another social item comes to mind. mr. alton cook will be "at home" on friday evening november 7th. i believe he is going to invite you to his inner sanctum. i expect to be there. if toil permits, i would like to take up china's problem with you. we might get abbott and costello for the next automat benefit. formal regards to the patient little woman the world knows as your wife. thank you for acknowledging the taffy, mailed last september, within sixty days. avoir, welch!

the mayor

2

i am in receipt of your note written on mr. cantor's stationery. when mr. c counts up

13

in a rainbow and made a spring coat out of same, sang "blues in the night." with the milk-pail obligato. that was writing, welch. does the navy know what you are doing in the navy? vick knight has enlisted in the army. i think he leaves for the

8

testimonials. kate smith says, etc. when you look at that lark on kate you can appreciate what the pinesbridge buffet is doing in pelvic circles. william powell also says. as you know he has had his

12

on the air before this mystery can be solved. myrna loy eats bones and all, i guess, she admits there is never a morsel left. if you don't want to patronize the pinesbridge outfit you can smoke an old cantor script, the one in which mr. menjou, the man who put sleeves in

1

dear mr. welch.

4

the premises. the man with the eyes knows every grain of mustard seed about his premises, welch, and the sheet and envelope

6

the fact that they have recently been sprung from dannemora must be gratifying. if these felons are stir-crazy i trust they will cause no disturbance at our broadcast. a word to them might help.

10

this may account for the wishbones strewn about the pierre lobby last fall. basil rathbone, the man with the hacksaw profile has been mailing turkeys away to friends. how basil gets

3

at the end of the month and finds one sheet and one envelope missing there will be a bit of derring-do around

7

uncle jim looks like a warden,
you know and i might set your
friends off. if you are entertaining these folk, until the f.b.i.
catches up with them, how
about a "pinebridge buffet." am
enclosing some

11

the turkeys into an envelope is
known by only nigel bruce and
he can't tell you unless he is in
character as dr. watson. since
bruce is out of work, at the moment, you will have to wait
until bromo quinine gets back

5

are bound to be missed. re the
tickets. i shall mail you four
when i get them early next
week. i am pleased to learn that
you still have four friends and

9

stomach taken out twice. once
for a long-shot in a dr. kildare
picture and once to have his
bowels lined. you will also note
that countess defroceville has
been using smoked turkeys at
her affairs

14

coast in a week, or so. it looks as
though i shall work with a stop-
watch strapped to my script from
then on. give my regards to chet.
i hear he jumped up at a recent conference and tore a big
gap in his jodhpurs. i thought
he was still wearing the big
mink mandarin coat at conferences but i have been out of
your circles so long i don't know
what is de riguer. regards to jack
and tj.   f.a.

october sixth 1942

dear mr. welch . . .

mr. shimmick, the columbia tycoon, deleted the word "rabe-
lasian" from the script last sunday and another line of mr. laughton's where he said "my hobby is stuffing field mice" and i
answered "do you mount them?" and mr. laughton retorted
"hardly, old boy." this gem was stricken from the banter and there
were other cuts. we couldn't say "just plain charlie" in the serial
burlesque and we couldn't kill grandpa david because there is a
papa david in "life can be beautiful." you can see what i am
going through, mr. welch, and i hope if you and bill made it with

the jehovah witness brigade, that you will tell the major about me.

your description of mr. morrow's apartment is intriguing. what the hell is he doing with mounds of waste paper strewn about his quarters? is he operating a one-man salvage drive? does he intend in later life to sit in his apartment overlooking hollywood and blow spitballs in the general direction of young and rubicam's? or is he just dirty?

heard your first show sunday and thought it was swell. it moved along great and you certainly got plenty of matter in a thirty minute script. charlie cantor claimed that you appeared personally with that hysterical conference laugh we all identify with young and rubicam. i maintain that mr. morrow hired a clever mimic to take you off. let us know if you have joined afra. i might have something for you later. if you do know when you are coming and bill would like to do that guest star bit you can let me know and we can do it any week after you get here. sorry to hear that your wife, tempy, is going on the road with "guest in the house." you are going to look like a chump hanging around stage doors at your age. say "hello" to mr. benny if you ever get in to see him personally. hope all goes well. if percy kilbride needs a stand-in let me know. if you see ida send my regards to eddie. more anon. when you finish with this letter roll it up and throw it under bill's bed where it won't be noticed. regards to sam hearn. avoir, welch!

"Mr. Five By Five"

july 25

b.w.—

i have returned the don barclay water color under separate cover. don did a hell of a job and when the day comes that you leave paramount and you are going down vine street with my caricature under your arm who knows—some art lover may stop you and your fortune may be made. if you don't split this money with don barclay you are a louse and that will make it unanimous out there. money isn't everything welch. even when twins die the two of them can't take it with them.

tell robert hope that i took the two snapshots of him down to the town here and through showing them to small boys and fans who saw him in "sorrowful jones" i played to $407, three clam shells and two buck teeth that fell out of a small boy who bumped into my center-pole as he was leaving the tent. if he can play to these grosses with his stills why go to all of that trouble with cameras, stand-ins and sydney lanfield.

as a producer you have recently presented mr. hope in a re-write of "little miss marker." if you are thinking about a remake of "trader horn" kindly check with enclosed photo. i don't want to screw bob out of a job, and take the pastrami out of the mouths of al melnick's children, but if you are considering "trader horn"— i have the suit. these seersuckers are scarce and mr. ginsberg may be interested in the money he can save through using me, with *my own suit,* rather than bob hope who will have to buy ward-robe.

i don't want to knock mr. hope's sex appeal but enclosed note will show you the effect i am having on delinquent maids in adams, mass. i am also sending a column from the cape cod paper. i am the only man who has cut his throat with his tongue. i am answering berle and ed sullivan the hard way—through a small town paper. give this "trader horn" remake some thought, b.w. mr. hope cannot make all of the pictures. if we make a deal i will see that alton cook makes a retraction on that "sorrowful jones" notice and i will further see that he receives a mickey the next time i am his host.

i will close with the official closing lines of the secretary of the moline conservation club—"may the whistling wings of the wildfowl at dawn awaken your soul—and the thrill of a smashing strike and tight line be with you."

regards to eddie and tempy and all—

fred allen

HELEN STRAUSS*

september sixth

dear helen . . .

sorry that you are not coming here the tenth. i had advised mr. brand, the studio publicity head, that you would be here on that date, and that you would tell him what you could use.

i have been working from seven a.m. until post-twilight for many days and you will excuse me if i don't see eye to eye with some of the publicity departments novel exploitation ideas. i do not intend to ask the fox studio to tie a banner on the back of the train when i go back to new york. after a hectic summer i don't want to be annoyed with any radio editors crawling out of corn-fields enroute to ask a series of nonsensical questions so that they may publish their interviews in the privy center daily journal.

publicity is fine and i appreciate the sleepless nights spent by the members of your staff as a result of their ceaseless efforts to publicize your radio attractions. the only thing that helps a radio program is a radio program. standing on my head on top of the empire state building may cause a flurry among a few jersey pigeons and such an action might make a gaping tourist gasp but if the material in the weekly show isn't good the pigeons will ex-press themselves on your loudspeaker if they can get into the house . . . and the gaper will turn off the dial and rush out for a bit of night-gaping.

it is pleasing to learn that the office was impressed by the clever handling of the gracie allen return to your city. without much ado, last winter, we saw to it that many of her listeners were won over to "town hall tonight." if a banner on the back of a train will sell more sal hepatica than better jokes at the microphone then i shall gladly devote the rest of my contracted

* Publicity director of Benton and Bowles, when that advertising agency repre-sented Allen's radio sponsor.

time to tying banners on trains for it is far easier than wringing jokes out of what is left of my brain.

we made some ipana pictures yesterday for the studio publicity department. all other special pictures were awaiting your arrival on the tenth, there have been countless stills made of all scenes taken in the picture and now, that you won't be here, if there is anything you want the office here to do i shall be glad to advise them before i finish.

i hope to be through here around the 19th and shall leave for new york as soon as possible. portland and i expect to bring a friend of ours back . . . a girl who had an unexpected appendectomy performed on monday . . . and since she will be too weak to travel alone i am willing to forego the debatable pleasure of meeting radio editors enroute in order that she may arrive with a maximum amount of health restored.

the presidential idea is an excellent one but i am tired and i prefer to concentrate on the program and let the newspaper breaks fall where they may. the picture company will exploit the picture and if you want to write harry brand . . . 20th century studios here . . . he will be glad to do anything within reason to cooperate.

if there is any specific tie-up you want me to mention to him i shall function.

sincerely . . .

F. Allen
1416 n. havenhurst drive
hollywood, cal.

AL DURANTE*

THE BELMONT
West Harwich, Mass.

august
12th
1949

mr. durante—

   i appreciate your recent master stroke of publicity work which landed me on the cover of tv guide. recently i made the front page of the duxbury, mass., clipper through not going to duxbury to visit neal o'hara. now, through not appearing in tv, i have made the front page of the new industry's leading weekly.

   i may have something here. by not going places and not doing things i have been getting more publicity than i ever did when i was in the public's eye—as the fellow says. if i can find a way to survive not working and not traveling, with you at the helm of my press frigate i may reach new heights in items and matter printed. if you think that i have anything here—let me know. i will get right to work on not doing things. you and i will soon be on easy street which, at the moment, only boasts one resident—mr. d. golenpaul.

   a number of people on the beach here have told me that they liked dan's first program. if they have written in dan must have a lot of messages on clam shells and on the backs of guests who were checking out of hotels and leaving in the general direction of wor. it sounded good to hear information please again. it is still the top show of that type and i hope that dan can sell it this season.

   am enclosing a notice from a recent paper. a young man of 20, in good health died quietly as he sat before a television set in his home. he was probably bored to death. if this continues

* Then publicity director for J. Walter Thompson agency.

mr. durante, your bosses at j. walter thompson may be snatched out of their offices some day and charged with murder.

also, enclosing invitation to swim behind the national guard camp targets. i wrote the lieutenant that i had enough lead in my lower anatomy without giving some guardsman, who remembered me from radio, a chance to augment my lead content. we are returning aug. 20th. will call you that week.

regards.

f. allen

THE BELMONT
West Harwich, Mass.

july
29th
1948

dear al . . .

nothing exciting here. guests are so old there is a sign in the lobby "guests sitting on the veranda will move once an hour." it keeps the buzzards from circling over the hotel.

trust all goes apace in your cranny.

regards . . .

fred allen

EVELYN JOHNSON

december 29th
1939

dear miss j . . .

thanx
a
lot for my xmas present. it was not necessary
for you to go to any trouble or expense on my
account.

i
appreciate
your interest in the program and am happy to
send you the tickets when they are available.
please do not feel obligated in any way and
on
weeks
the program doesn't come up to your expectations
don't feel too badly about it. enough of us,
around the program, are upset when things don't
come
off
and we do not feel that strangers should share
our grief.
sincerely . . .   f   a
                                                         r   l
                                                         e   l
                                                         d   e
                                                          . n

PAT WEAVER

In the Thirties, when Allen's Town Hall show was sponsored by Sal
Hepatica ("The Smile of Health") and Ipana toothpaste ("The Smile
of Beauty"), the program was supervised by Sylvester L. (Pat)
Weaver, Jr., who was then manager of the radio department at the
Young & Rubicam advertising agency. The following letters, most of
them undated, were written during that period, Allen's happiest days
in broadcasting. Weaver moved on in 1938 to the American Tobacco
Company and later became president of the National Broadcasting
Company.

old orchard beach
maine—
august 18th
1936

dear helio . . . (am saving the gebelus for the next letter)

your letter arrived via woodchuck this morning and i am answering pronto, via ferret, so that you may have a last note of encouragement before you take off on your alleged vacation.

portland and i have kept our eyes glued to the sea expecting to see you luff past in your trim sloop one of these days but either you haven't luffed past or you have been too quick for us. you might have gotten by me on monday last. i couldn't glue both eyes to the horizon on that day. i slept with my eyes open sunday night and woke up with owl dung in one eye on monday and naturally when we went down to the beach to open our day's vigil my one eye was almost useless. you know how owl droppings sting. i was in agony. i could see out of the eye but everything seemed to have feathers on it and had you passed, on that day, i wouldn't have recognized you.

we thought we had you sighted one day. a man passed using an old ipana commercial for a jib but upon close inspection it proved to be a catboat trying to get away from a school of dogfish. another day, we saw a small sailboat skimming along when there was obviously no breeze. i thought it could be you but raising the glasses again i recognized a clerk from mr. brentano's who was sailing along holding a copy of that best seller, "gone with the wind" up in the stern. i guess you haven't passed along our coast or we would have seen you all right.

we haven't been able to hear many of the jello shows. we heard the first two and they started off fine but since we generally go out on sunday for dinner it isn't always possible to return at seven. i know you have your nose to the client though and it is probably damn uncomfortable for him and no doubt it takes his mind off of a weak script in the event that you find yourself confronted with one occasionally.

i have heard all of the "town hall" shows and think they

have been great. i don't know anything about the gallup check, or those other mythical pulse feelers, so popular with some of the agencies but the colonel's material is fresh and up to the minute and i think it has been excellent.* there won't be much left to burlesque when we return and i suggest you spend part of your vacation getting twists on some of the burlesques the program has used recently. perhaps we could twist stoop and budd and make them come out jones and hare and then we would be on easy street . . . or 47th street . . . for the better part of the winter.

i have been intending to write carlos. i have a knock! knock! joke using the word fornication, for the opening program, and i thought that perhaps carlos could get our n.b.c. censor, miss mc c, in the mood for the first blow of our '36–'37 campaign. i don't know how harry can keep his vacation straight with that checker-board arrangement. he has been swell on the shows. that one dig-nified character, with kelp between his teeth, that he has done several times with the boys sounds very funny over the air and i hope that it is not an exclusive improvisation copyrighted by the colonel. you and i can turn this character into another "smiling ed mcconnell" if harry will take direction. have written p. t. meade wishing him well and hoping that fred astaire will head the next edition of mary astor's diary even if he doesn't top the crossley after the first twenty minutes of his show have made radio history.

i have checked on most of the programs but there isn't much to learn from our competitors. they have no structure, or form, and most of the production is slip-shod but perhaps that is the new style. if we let the show alone in time we will stand out as being the only comedy program not written by dave freedman which should mean something. one thing we might do. instead of putting the winning amateur into the roxy, we might put him into the window of the druggist who has won the display contest for that week. that would save twenty seconds at the end and cutting down on jack smart would earn us a vote of thanks from many firms who have weighing machines near the studio.

* Colonel Stoopnagle was Allen's summer replacement on the Town Hall radio program that year.

jack has made a test for pictures and expects to go to hollywood. walter is still out there and i turned down a picture for mr. zanuck a few days back. it is to start around september 15th and he wanted me out there right away to start to work on the comedy scenes. i figure there will be trouble enough around studio 8 h late in september without having the entire 20th century-fox outfit on my neck simultaneously.

portland and i both hope that you will have an hilariously effervescent two weeks and that you will return to 285 madison avenue loaded with ideas and ready for a strenuous season at the conference tables and waste buckets.

i don't see why you should go to bermuda. you can grab off a good two weeks sleep down in the sound effects room and barry can give you boat whistles, surf sounds and tropical gales and you will emerge more rested and in far better trim than you will if you succumb to the temptations one finds in bermuda and other like ports. portland sends her best and give my regards to stoop, budd, harry et al. (this is latin for "say hello! to al goodman")

bon voyage . . .

F A

september tenth

dear 765 . . .

the enclosed message has been received here via carrier snail. agent k9 has been leading a dog's life on the salary we have been paying him and we cannot afford to "pull a bone," as the saying goes, in k9's presence. the message translated into code reads; "weldin-clapper-4-6-9 lower colon-paw paw 2-5-dash-mccrory-quasi-butterworth" i suggest that you act along these lines until further notice.

a double-check and a shepherd plaid made of the entire state of maine reveals listeners ears filled with wax. present indications indicate trend to tropical settings for fall program. a mrs. dank-fuzz, of biddeford said to our agent, "either them goddam radio programs will go to the tropics or i will by the great horn-crotched tophet." another listener, mildew thud, one of the leading pine needle sharpeners of this state, when asked what he thought about a tropical setting for the "town hall," replied; "i can go back to the civil war and by jesus, i will!" still another maine resident, a crossley virgin, said, "grant took richmond. if he hadn't let him go richmond could never have made the flight." you can see from these bona fide comments that if the "town hall" is to survive the setting must be changed to either "the cave of the winds," a colorado locale where we could get guests stars on their way out to california to appear on the small chateau, or we will have to stick by our spears and launch our first show in a jungle cave and pray that our listeners will not detect the difference.

we are leaving here on saturday and i shall be in new york next week ready for immediate conferences with frank buck, the malay consul and other advisory heads on jungle data. suggest guest starring head hunters weekly and having peter van steeden black up and install twenty-eight piece tom-tom ensemble.

am enclosing ad for new ostrex tonic tablets. suggest you present same at next executive meeting. the program department, always in need of instant vigor, could be supplied with these tablets, containing the raw oyster invigorators, and in months containing the much abused R young and rubicam would have the satisfaction of knowing that the program department was chock-full of ostrex and running from script to script leaving little streams of iodine in the executive's wake.

i expect to be in your city around the 18th ready to start research for authentic tropical data to insure town hall success for coming year. the agency shows will rank first alphabetically what with astaire, allen, benny, baker, butterworth. if you can get things started there will be no stopping the firm.

see you next week??????????   —FA 7—

tuesday night

p.w.

your endurance memo received in good form. i would beware of that obese fellow, tinker hesse. his only purpose in plying
you with spirits is to get you sagging around the navel so that
when people laugh at his bulging abdomen he can turn around
and say "eh! you think i sag, do you, well, wait till weaver gets
here." he fattened chase up so that he couldn't get out of mr. la
roche's office in the event that the boys' option was to be taken
up at a slight decrease. with fat clients mr. hesse is playing safe.
the scene as i see it plays something like this.

scene; mr. laroche's office. as curtain goes up chet is singing . . .

(CURTAIN)

chet. . . . .(SINGS) Boola Boola boola boola boola boola for simone simone!

(KNOCK AT DOOR)

chet. . . . .come in! come in! whoever you are!

(DOOR OPENS)

(ENTER HIPPO, CHASE AND A FAN FROM SOUTH NORWALK)

hippo. . . .hello, boys!

chet. . . . .they came in with you, mr. hesse. do you have to wait
until you get to my office to greet your friends?

hippo. . . .yes. i can't greet them in my office. my partner snores
so loud my friends can't hear what i'm saying. they think i
am saying "have a drink."

chet. . . . .yes, i will. what vintage bi-carb did you bring?

chase. . . .neither of you have any guts. it takes guts to go on the
radio that's why budd and i are on the radio and you laroche
and hesse are making money.

chet. . . . .who said you were on the radio stoopnagle, not crossley i'll wager.

fan. . . . . .(from south norwalk) . . . excuse me.

chet. . . . .who are you? russo?

fan. . . . . .no. i'm just a man from south norwalk. they told me
if i wanted to see a radio program to follow stoopnagle when

he got on the train. they said he'd lead me to a broadcast.

chet. . . . .that person was a visionary, not a sponsor or an advertising man.

fan. . . . . .where do i get tickets for town hall tonight.

chet. . . . .that's what i'd like to know.

fan. . . . . .i'm getting out of here.

chet. . . . .you're lucky. i wish i could.

hippo. . . .ha! ha! ha!

chase. . . .what are you laughing at hippo? i haven't said anything yet.

hippo. . . .you might colonel. i'm playing it safe.

chet. . . . .if this man stoopnagle had anything funny to say why didn't he say it when he was on minute tapioca?

hippo. . . .he was coming to it, mr. laroche, when something came up.

chase. . . .he means the option, mr. laroche.

chet. . . . .call me chet, colonel. the exterminator man just left he'd be upset if la roche was mentioned around the office.

chase. . . .thank you. now about our option.

hippo. . . .the boys won't take it for that.

chet. . . . .for what?

hippo. . . .for what you're going to offer them.

chase. . . .yes, i'm getting out of here.

(COLONEL STARTS TO LEAVE BUT GETS STUCK IN THE DOOR)

chase. . . .help! hippo! i'm stuck! get me out!

hippo. . . .i'm an agent. i can only get actors into these offices. i can't get you out.

chet. . . . .good! now, boys! about your option you will have to see the elevator man.

hippo. . . .the elevator man!

chet. . . . .yes, he's taking it up!

chase. . . .but i can't stay stuck in this door people will think i'm a vice-president.

chet. . . . .aren't you?

hippo. . . .no! this is colonel stoopnagle of we the people.

chet. . . . .oh yes. we're keeping you on for another thirteen weeks, fellows. but at a slight reduction in salary.

chase. . . .oh no you don't.

chet. . . . .okay, then young & rubicam will move to radio city and leave you stuck with the lease here.

hippo. . . .you will have to unbend, colonel.

chase. . . .yes. we'll take it, mr. la roche. now tell me how do i get out, i'm stuck tight.

chet. . . . .think of your crossley, colonel, you will feel small enough to crawl out.

(CURTAIN)

that is how mr. hesse operates, p.w. his plan is to get you fattened up to the point where you can't get out of your office and he will always know where to find you when it comes time to take up the options of his clients. beware!

the goose has come down a little for this week. the sketch doesn't look too hot and the cuts were "titillate" and "john l. lewis." nothing is written for prof. quigley yet. will listen to the packard show tonight. hope all goes well and that you are whipping it into shape. sent the wires. best to tom and ev and anyone who remembers the prennial favorite . . . you can fool around with that prennial. . . . f.a.

THE BAY VIEW HOUSE
Sidney A. Staples, Prop.
Bay View, Maine

MEMO

To: WEAVER

Re: ALLEN ON VACATION

P.W.   As you loll back in your tycoon nest, spinning filmy strands of red tape, i know that while you hum and buzz as though normal and you nod and yawn in conference in a manner that catches the eye of the older cob tycoons, you are not the weaver of old. there is something on your mind, weaver. something that one finds in the mind of every budding tycoon once one has located the mind.

(LAUGHTER & APPLAUSE)

you are worried weaver and not without cause! while you, chet, bill, don, ed, carlos and friar rubicam sit around the conference table snapping at the bubbles as they reach the top of the community bi-carbonate bowl, the links of a chain inter-office weight tinkle in your thoughts and to a man who has devoted one ear and the better part of his life to a concentrated survey of tycoons this tinkling is audible, you fellows have reached the top of the pile! still you are not happy! you have set the packard show. you have arranged with all of the mosquitoes who have lighted on butterworth in the past to light on him again and return the blood. you have signed benny for three years. you have wrought havoc with mr. von zell. from a writer of mystery skits, an a-one announcer, a quiet family man and all round good fellow you have turned him into a harried buffoon who has to worry about his laughs and whether he can trust another to fling the applause card on high at a crucial moment. you have taken rousseau and transformed him from a buxom playboy into a neurotic finger-pointer and stop-watch toter. you have worried phil baker until he has ordered a toupee with a streak of gray in it for next season. yes! you tycoons have done many things and yet you are not at ease. why, weaver?

I'LL TELL YOU WHY!

you are worried about the tycoon of tomorrow. who will step into your shoes? where are the new men who will have the stuff that will enable them to carry on as you fellows have carried on in the past? they are in the offing, weaver. yes, in the offing, you will say, but where? the tycoon of the morrow is rampant in the smaller town, he is not on the dartmouth campus. he is active in a buried strata of little business but if you will stoop to scrape off the top soil he is there.

knowing that you, weaver, will never enjoy a second of executive peace until you have found a tycoon to take your place, i call to your attention the gentleman whose picture i enclose. mr. a. randall crapo is the man, weaver! hitch your wagon to a crapo, weaver, and you can lean back and have plenty to say in conference. think! fancy all inter-office memos coming through marked crapo! crapo is going places in radio, weaver! comes the trend! i have signed crapo to a personal contract and can deliver him the minute you say the word. do not hesitate! he who hesitates will be talking into the station break!

you will be glad to know that i am relaxing. i am so relaxed that my skin has slipped down to the point where i am considering an offer to rent my navel to a man who is operating a miniature golf course here. he wants to use it for the tenth hole.

we have a nice room with a flashlight. rooms without flashlights are cheaper but with the light it is much easier to find the privy which is only a mile or so down the road and rather difficult to locate at night.

let me know if you are leaving for the coast on the first. there is talk again that the picture will be postponed until october first but walter is still in new york and i am expecting a call from the coast later today. i will advise what happens later.

nothing exciting, p.w. will continue to take options on mr. a. randall crapo until such a time as you tie in and see eye to eye with me on that all important question, WHO WILL STEP INTO WEAVER'S SHOES?

—Faljek Prink—

august sixth

MEMO:
URGENT! RUSH! TEAR UP BEFORE READING! THROW SCRAPS AT TOM HARRINGTON! RUSH!

sylv . . .

you will note that i have omitted the "ester" for i wouldn't want to have her name dragged into this. the names of "ester" and a. randall crapo must forever remain sacred in our hallowed correspondence. especially the latter. a. randall is latter perfect and so on far into the o'keefe script.

my dear sir;

perched here in my stuffy summer quarters, an antiquated,

musk-smelling trap overlooking several ounces of gull-dung on the sill i place my posteriors snugly into the underslung cane-bottomed chair to answer your recent memo. you, ever the playboy, sylv, have done it again. several old salts, who have passed through here with several hen-clams they are taking up north for stud purposes, bring word of your success on the high seas. these quaint old men of the sea relate queer tales of passing your vessel, california bound, on the lee side and swear tangy, nautical oaths that the laughs leaping out over the troubled waters, coming from the direction of the ship's concert gave raucous proof of your activities aboard. these jolly old tars added that as your craft slid away into the night passengers aft could be heard singing "16 men on weaver's chest. yo! ho! and a bottle of sal hepatica!" i ask no further proof of your ability to generate and control the mob spirit on land or on sea, sir. having concluded their strange table, a toast was drunk to you in bilge-water, and the mariners threw several false udders to their hen-clams and trudged away.

now that you are astride your mound of kelp it is only natural that you should fancy yourself a male lorelei and in this guise i am not agog to scent the lure buried under verbs and punctuation marks in your scroll. the siren in you peeks out from behind a paragraph having to do with the new packard series. you write solely with intent to cause me to pry my saggy pratt from the jagged apertures of this cane-bottomed relic pore by pore lest my skin be torn through quitting my seat abruptly and little shreds of allen be left dangling from the cane as bait for radio fans and souvenir hunters.

since you have seen fit to hurl your clarion ogle to the four winds three of the winds return you this reply. (the fourth wind i am keeping to use up some alka-seltzer i found in this cranny when i checked in.) i would prefer not to become involved in your packard plans. many things have come to pass with the picture. the story was scrapped a week ago and a new treatment is being written by harry and jack yellen. i expect to come out around labor day to lend a bit of confusion to things in general and the shooting is supposed to start october fourth. if it were possible i would rather come out sooner but everyone at home is sick and i will have to wait here until the end of the month until my brother recovers from a severe spastic colon condition which has rendered him hors de another color and unable to attend to matters at home for my aunts. he has just had eight teeth extracted and the doctors finally agree that this wholesale gesture might result in clearing up his trouble. i hope so for i have had nothing but grief at home and might just as well have stayed on the program.

with work to be done on the story, upon arrival, and with conferences and other matters that may come up, after i report to the studio, i wouldn't want to have the added weight of your packard venture hanging over my head. the last picture i made we had confusion for several weeks before it got under way and i can assure you that the preliminaries stir up enough excitement without having to worry about a covey of scenes and grandpa snazy for good measure.

you must realize that i have other offers, sir, enclosed you will find a bid to function at a "weenie roast," for nothing, only last night. fat-legged little girls are coming for autographs and leaving sweet pea blossoms at the desk and people riding by in trailers constantly invite me to run along with them for a mile or so merely that they can say they listen every "thursday." yesterday the head barber leaned over to the fellow who was hacking at my locks and said "that's frank allen that guy on the radio." my fame is assured mr. w even though i do not find it possible to give packard a tacit sendoff.

i wish you well in this venture. when we arrive i shall call you at the office, the patio, or the sanitorium. portland sends her best wishes for your speedy breakdown and we know you will put it over with a fang . . . especially the ipana show. be of stout heart. life is short but commercials are long and paths of glory lead but to chet's office. hoping this finds you the same and with best wishes . . . you think i am . . .

MR. A——
but you're mistaken!

THE BAY VIEW HOUSE
Bay View, Maine

august 16th

dear mr. weaver . . .

the enclosed clipping from the "society pages" of the new york times has been called to my attention.

i knew the minute your back was turned that the office would go to pot. immediate action is called for mr. weaver! something has to be done!

no man can serve two masters! is william p. rousseau to be allowed to share his allegiance to young & rubicam with miss eileen p. o'connell? is the firm going to permit mr. rousseau to have two chairs at his desk so that the bride may be at his side during the hectic hours of the business day? will the married life of our mr. rousseau be "one sweet song" (which the office will have to clear by the way) if he insists upon having the bride spend her honeymoon at sundry "town hall" auditions?

these are questions that only you can answer mr. weaver. the time is rife for action! we are looking to you mr. weaver to put over-rated god hymen in his place. we are confident that you will put mr. william p. rousseau in his place, too. and while you are at it you may as well put the intended bride in her place.

i am writing mr. rousseau under his social security number and advising him that he has approximately betrayed his trust. i am suggesting that if he is found in the office shaking rice grains out of his hirsute growth he will be subject to dismissal. i am threatening him with demotion if he insists upon going on with the wedding and permits the guests to throw rice instead of "minute tapioca" the product that started colonel stoopnagle on the road to becoming a member of the landed gentry.

honi soit qui mal le showboat, mr. weaver!

hoping this finds you demented.

Mr. A—

1936 APR 24 AM

BOSTON MASS

PAT WEAVER—CARE YOUNG AND RUBICAM
285 MADISON AVE—

ALL BOSTON WEAVER CONSCIOUS BOY SCOUTS PRACTICED FORMING
TO SPELL OUT YOUR NAME HAD IT WEEVIL CORRECTED THIS ERROR
AND ALL IS READY YOUR ARRIVAL YOU WILL FIND KEY TO CITY
UNDER FRONT MAT—SUCCESS—

FRED ALLEN.

hollywood
june 29th
1940

dear sylvester . . .

i have been mulling over a variety of ways to thank you for
your kindness in bestowing your american tobacco company's free
samples on our little company as we departed your city. as i despatched from kansas city, everyone was put to work on your products. women and children were smoking "luckies" in the club car,
the porters were puffing coronas in the aisles, the brakemen were
lighting pall mall, after pall mall, using the long, lighted ends instead of lanterns. i was perched out on the observation car tacking and spitting and spitting and tacking as the winds changed
coming across the country. we arrived here a nicotine-infested little band if ever i have seen a nicotine-infested little band. how
to thank you for contributing to the curtailment of our life-spans
has bothered me since i saw the newly-baked depot at los angeles
in the offing.

finally, i turned to yesteryear for my inspiration. as you know,
in medieval times, when the jester has been made to rejoice
through some kindly prank of his king, the merry andrew

strummed his lute, retired to the rear of the regal outhouse, and composed an ode to his lord.

i have no lute to seize, i have no regal outhouse behind which i can retire for inspiration but i have a nice gingerbread apartment at the el royale. to cope with the circumstances and to get in the mood to write you an ode, i made a small lute, stringing a ping pong paddle with dental floss. i retired behind an overstuffed chair, twanged my dulcet lyre and composed a rondo which i have duly dedicated to you. you will find it enclosed.

you will be glad to know that i have had three days off and while i have been enjoying my rest the studio presented me with the two opening scenes of the picture just in case i thought of a couple of gags to add while i was relaxing. we start july 15th and celluloid history should be made by september 3rd. mr. benny is relaxing in honolulu and will return in two weeks ready to creep into action. we are hoping for the best but wish that we were in maine or on the poop-deck of your junior bremen.

portland sends her sunkist regards. we had her regards out on the patio until they started to blister. we brought them in to send them off red-hot to you. we trust that all goes well in your little world of coffin-nails and that you will enjoy a banner summer about the mizzenmast.

seasonal good wishes . . .

FA—

VAL EICHEN

Allen confided his observations and irritations during his broadcasting years to Val Eichen, a retired vaudevillian in East Hampton, Long Island, who followed the Allen radio show and wrote weekly comments on its progress.

October 5, 1932

Dear Val,

I am pleased to learn that the program is getting such excellent results in your house. Are you sure that you haven't confused me with the Sisters of the Skillet? I want to send your letter, containing the economiums to the Smithsonian Institute to make sure that it is all authentic before jeopardizing what is left of my reputation.

It is a tough grind Val and I only hope that I can keep the thing going and up to a decent standard. The Marx Brothers have four authors and now they have to go to the Coast, on a picture, so the Standard Oil people are going to pay additional wire charges, for the broadcasts, and the four writers will probably get expenses, etc. Peall has four authors, Billy Wells, Joe Cunningham, Andy Rice and Dolph Singer, I think. If the fellows who write these programs, listen in, the comedians are assured of a big audience.

As you know the Roxy opened for the new season and it is the talk of the town. I say "The Talk," advisedly, it is more of a murmur. The joint is so big that May Worth came backstage, with one of her horses, during rehearsal and Roxy looked up and said "My God! we're not even open and we've got mice in the joint." They say he has multiplied everything by ten. If it is good he has it ten times as good and if it is lousy then you get it ten times lousier at the new house. Doc Rockwell came on the opening night and looked so small from the front that two women from the Gerry Society came backstage, after the show, to see if his Mother had a permit for him to be up so late.

You must know Roy Atwell, who does the jig-saw talking on the program. He has been a good Lamb for years and was a big man in shows a few years back.

I hope you are right about that big contract that is coming to me. I have been doing Zeno so long that I would like to be an Ajax when they're paying off just to see what it's like. Under separate cover am sending you a fan photo—the picture can be used as a fan during the Summer months, makes an excellent flooring for the bird-cage, can be used to set under hot dishes and if cut up small enough makes an excellent starched-effect confetti which is useful if the local laundry is giving a presentation of Tiny Tim with the snow scene.

Nothing else exciting. Hope that you will enjoy a Happy New Year and don't ever kick a panhandler . . . it may be

Fred Allen

March 20
1933

Dear Val,

Your card came today. I have owed you a letter for some weeks but no doubt Mr. Rattray explained my position to you. My position, when he called as I remember was sort of a crouch. I was attempting to fit the answer of one joke to the question of another. On your recommendation, Mr. Rattray and Mr. Sullivan were provided with tickets to the broadcast and later Mr. Sullivan's little girl was the lucky recipient of a picture of Portland. There is no charge for this service, Mr. Eichen, and I hope that we shall receive any future business you may be contemplating in our line.

The programs have been getting results and the sales of Linit have increased noticeably in the last few months. Naturally, the people who send in for a perfume container have to buy a package of Linit and since they have given out approximately fifty thousand perfumettes it is bound to increase sales. Having bought the Linit, I imagine the people will try it in preference to throwing it out and through this means new friends are made for the product.

It is too much for me, Val. I am all in. This is the nineteenth program, I think, and between routines for Portland and Atwell and the rehearsals and cutting and editing the material written by my co-author, it finally begins to tell. You want to know what became of Jolson and the others? At least, they are well paid in defeat. I am lasting longer but I'll never catch up to any of them from the money end. Still, it isn't bad. I have been living by my own wits for years and most of the others have to rely on writers and they're at the mercy of whoever provides the material for their assorted ventures.

That Brooklyn Eagle jig-saw puzzle looked like a Wasserman Test to me. Even the finished picture printed the following day looked like one of those they used in the lobby of the theatre at Hackensack when Harry Shea booked it. Ferry the Frog has dropped out of sight for sometime but he was finally found at the Acquarium. When things looked tough, he put on his toad suit and jumped in the tank down there. He was doing alright and would have probably been able to last through the Winter but the keeper saw him snapping at a dame in front of the tank and knowing that frogs are homosexual he became suspicious. Ferry was yanked out and was last seen snapping at flies in Mrs. Stanley's lunch room so perhaps she hired him as an insect bouncer instead of putting on a screen door.

General Pisano, the target marksman, isn't getting work because in these big movie theatres his rifles look like pistols. He is now trying to get Roxy's address and a cannon from the Government in hopes that he can get a showing date.

The enclosed correspondence from the Davey Tree people is self explanatory. It will help to prove that my time is taken up with asinine correspondence that prevents me from keeping in touch with my more intimate acquaintances. Am enclosing a five act bill which you can book into the house any Sunday it looks as though you will be lonesome.

Nothing else exciting. This is the first night I have had off in two weeks and I am spending it answering letters. It won't be long now when it gets so that I haven't got brains enough to go out and relax at a picture. Best for now.

F.A.

Monday

Dear Val . . .

I have been owing you a letter there . . . Old "Lazy Bones" . . . but instead of answering your last scroll I figured out where would I go if I was Val so I went to the rocking chair and fell asleep. Rumor has it that the caddy is making most of your drives and that you only putt when you are in the mood. Well, that's the way to be and it's great work if you can get it.

The programs have been going along swell . . . so far. Some weeks I get a kick out of them, Val, but after the two days spent writing them and two days rehearsing and cutting and consulting with the bosses about what is what you don't feel so funny when it gets around Nine o'clock on Friday night. There is always the feeling that you have to hurry for every second counts and we try to cram so much stuff into the half hour that we can't let down for a second. You should be around some night just before the broadcast when we are trying to take out forty-five seconds. The guy with the stop-watch and I am cutting out odd words and reading them so that he can dock exactly 45 seconds. By the time you get to the mike you're afraid to unbend or change a word lest the thing run over. You know at 29 minutes and 30 seconds you're cut off the air no matter where you are in a sentence.

I am always afraid that Atwell will say something that will have us cut off the air. Last week, on the second broadcast for the Coast, he said "I can lick my weight in wild-pratts" and I thought that would be the end but a few minutes later he came back with "I'll take off my goat and squirt" so it's no wonder that I am sagging at the temples and my step is halting, sir.

Have you heard the gag . . . Lee Shubert is going to present a show for the Shubert stockholders . . . the title of it is . . . Let Them Eat Jake.

It's funny about Ben Gross, the Daily News radio columnist. Last year, he never gave us a tumble but this year he has been very nice. If you want to keep your name in most of the N.Y. columns it is almost imperative that you have a personal press agent. I have none for I would rather cut up the money among the people on the program or give it to some guy to bring in jokes occasionally.

Tannen is signed for the Linit show which starts again on Sunday nights . . . sometime in October. He was only on the beer program for a few weeks. Radio is funny. In show business if your act was bad you smelled in all of the booking offices but in radio you can lay an egg on a macaroni program and some frankfurt maker will think you're the last word. I don't know a great deal about the Phil Baker program. For years, he helped himself to anything I had that was good but I don't know how he can hear me on the air. Still, all of his stuff is written and perhaps the authors do it. I haven't been able to hear him since I've been working ahead of him but during the Summer I thought his programs were very good. I heard quite a few jokes that belonged to me, in his routines and that may have influenced my opinion.

Well . . . to Hell with it . . . Live and let live . . . Hope everything is okay and that no one has knocked at the door to cause you to get out of the chair. If the mailman slips this in under the front door just wait there—a strong wind will blow it over to you . . . best for now . . .

F. Allen

October 8
1933

Dear Val . . .

I can use the gag about . . . "I didn't hear it until yesterday." I have the story filed away someplace but haven't thought of it for a long time. It is the same point as the Irish gag . . . He called me a hippopotamus three years ago but I never saw a hippo until yesterday . . . After a few months in this racket Val you get so that you can remember any story, gag, song title or point you've ever heard. I have thousands of gags filed away but I have to change them constantly since so many of our "favorite" comedians are taking them hot out of the books. Those bums don't ever listen to radio and don't know that those rancid gags have been told and told until loudspeakers are vomiting in the middle West.

F.A.

may 2
1934

dear val . . .

comrade rattray has written me in code about your indisposition. i have tried to decipher the code without much success so i am still not sure just what is going on.

i know that you have been a rabid allen fan for nearly three years and i have always been afraid that something would happen to you on that account. if you have been going abroad shouting allen praises you have possibly aroused the ire of a cantor fan. this is dangerous business, mr. eichen.

cantor fans are easily aroused and their fury knows no limitations. if a cantor fan takes a dislike to you, you are apt to be ptomained in a delicatessen . . . send your suit to a tailor and have it come back with the crease in the pants running around the side of the leg . . . find a stale blintz in your mail-box or undergo some other experience equally as embarrassing. i told you some time ago that if you thought the programs were okay to keep it under your hat where the discovery would have company in the form of dandruff . . . i felt that the world would eventually learn that i was on the air and then the cantor fans could worry as to how the news got out. if you think a penner or a cantor admirer put a pill in your beer to bring on your ailment, i wish you would let me know.

i can get revenge for you easily. simply by sending a couple of stale jokes to either of these fellows i can make them the laughing stock of the air. a stale joke would sound new in most of their routines and once their listeners had tasted a new gag they would demand more and then these merry andrews would have cause for worry. they have been reading almanacs to their listeners for many months with no one the wiser. i have even heard their studio audiences laugh when the boys read weather reports. if they have had anything to do with laying you low through contaminating any liquids that it has been your wont to quaff say the word and i will get busy.

i hope that you will soon be about complaining about the quality of your radio entertainment and then i shall feel that you are normal again. i am about three hundred letters behind here, at the moment, and the news reels don't look so hot for wednesday but when brother r told me that my east hampton fan and public was under the weather i had to skip everything and get down to business. do you want me to send another fan down to take over your work until you feel better or will you carry on there horizontally until there is enough breeze in the neighborhood to fly the allen banner as it should be flown . . . with its tatters away from the crowd.

best for now and i hope you will soon feel better, sir.

fred allen

sept. 21
1934

dear val . . .

glad to know that you liked the first show. i didn't think the program was as good last night. it wasn't my fault. about six p.m. we had to cut out several bits and a lot of the comedy to get the show down to the time. last week, the guest stars were dismissed at the rehearsal and this week they made up the time sheet forgetting that norma terris would add several minutes we didn't have on the opening broadcast. at the last gong the whole show was ripped apart and i had to work until almost nine to get it back together again. i didn't have anything to eat. i might just as well be a bum if i can't get time to eat when i'm working.

i really think that in a few weeks we will have as good an hour show as you can find for nothing on the air. i work five days a week on this one and unless i go nuts i think i can keep it up until the end of june. i know that if we can get the proper balance of comedy and music that we can make the full hour pass as quickly as the thirty-minute show used to go.

we are having atwell with us next week for one show. i have been trying to get them to put him on regularly with us and perhaps they will do it if everything is okay next week. i have an idea that we could use him as a weekly speaker explaining how to play golf, bridge, polo or anything that might come up. and if he can get enough money i hope that we can have him with us. i am a lousy boss. i am doing more work and getting less dough than any of the comedians. the people get more money on my show and it is a poor but happy little family. it doesn't make any difference though for i want to stay in radio if i can and this way if i can keep writing and putting on good shows i can probably get six months a year out of it.

jolson leaves in a couple of weeks and cantor finishes too. joe penner is the rage now but the baron and the chief were big last year. i don't want to be worn out and i figure if i give everyone a chance on the show and get good material that i can keep on going. you can let me know if i seem to be slipping and i'll take it on the lam for a few months until i can catch up on the joke books.

had a letter from lucy bruch. you may recall her from the pan time. she is teaching violin in frisco and has put on two new strings on account of the n.r.a. roy barnes was at the broadcast last night. i don't know him but he was there. let me know if you have any thoughts on the shows as it may take us three or four shows to get everything working smoothly.

hope everything is okay down there and that the groundhog won't be afraid to come out on account of the meat shortage on the island.

best for now . . .

Fred Allen

thursday

dear val . . .

after pulling more strings than a guy with a puppet act on the western vaudeville . . . i have emerged with four reserved tickets for our show on the seventh.

you will find them enclosed and i hope that i can write a good show between now and next wednesday so that the guests from east hampton will not return to east hampton and say that they finally had a chance to pull up the stockings of their idol and find that he had feet of clay.

we have thirteen more shows to go and i will just about come out even. i have enough acid going in me to turn all of the gold wedding rings mussolini took away from the married women of italy black, and my nerves are going up and down like the heels of any welterweight you saw in 1921.

i hope you explained to mr. rattray that i had to abandon all mail this year. the way things are now i have a choice—either i can have good shows or i can spend the time with letters and have a lot of humpbacked postmen cursing me around the country.

hope the kids will be able to come. if they like to laugh you had better tell them part of that opening routine you did in edmonton so that they can mull over the gags and laugh at them during our program.

formal regards and say "hello" to the william randolph hearst of east h . . . mr. rattray.

Mr. A.

7.

BOYS IN THE SERVICE

HARMON NELSON

dear harmon . . .

i just arrived home after a rehearsal and a conference. the program looks lousy, the writers look lousy, my agent looks lousy and about everything else looks lousy. i sat down and tried to figure out that things must be lousy for someone else and my thoughts turned to you. right now, i would rather be down there digging a straight ditch or investigating the stinking mechanics of a hopper than sitting here trying to decide where to start to re-write almost the entire program. well, that's life, i guess. you know which garbage goes into which can and i don't know which verbal dung goes into which bit.

i haven't seen any of the y & r boys since you left. harry von zell came over between programs last week but harry is one of the old guard and not afraid to be seen with an opposition account man. the younger element, the smiths, welches and others with the hair of executive puberty sprouting on their careers do not dare be seen in company that chet la roche would not approve. i would like to see chet in uniform. he would be telling the general how to put a commercial in between the bugle call and the next command. he would probably put the entire army on the kate smith show if it would boost the crossley.

if there is anything we can send you down there let me know. i have been confined for the past nine years . . . thanx to radio . . . and i don't know what people wear, use or need in other walks of life. if there is anything you overlooked making your departure with the twenty nickels or if there is any gastronomic delicacy you would enjoy i will be glad to send it on.

we finish the last week in june and i am going home. i have worked two years and am exhausted. if i don't go someplace and sit down soon i will run amok and probably go over and try to get a job working for rousseau. portland sends her kind regards and we hope that your year in the army will fly quickly so that you may charge again into the y & r confusion and get things under control. if the memos coming through are stacked on your desk for the next year you are going to have plenty of reading on your hands to get you up to date on inter-office matters. don't forget! if there is anything we can mail you . . . say the word! best wishes . . .

f. allen

old orchard beach
maine
july 16th
1941

dear harmon . . .

we are in receipt of your graphic account of things as they are below the mason hamlin line and in the cracker strata of society. i can see you now slumped back in a cane-bottomed rocker on the spacious veranda of some georgia mansion regaling your new-found southern friends with exciting accounts of your adventures in radio. "the night von zell stuttered during a sal hepatica commercial." the afternoon joe allen stamped in and demanded that cantor eliminate the entire sketch, etc. if those people think that army life is exciting i am sure that you are in a position to disillusion them and acquaint them with the facts. to wit; that radio is the greatest device yet invented to shatter a man's nervous system.

after your account of the "problem" and your assignment to k/p duties perhaps portland and i should send you a fanny farmer cook book. if you are going to be put in charge of refuse and thrown in close contact with the army cooks, you should have a knowledge of cooking and some dessert recipes up your sleeve. who knows, the commanding officer may accost you one morning and bark, "nelson, i want a bread pudding made and ready to serve for 600 men at noon." you will be in a hell of a spot. if you think of a cape cod, or a fanny farmer, recipe compendium will be of any use . . . advise instantly.

it must seem strange cutting down saplings to conceal trucks and scrubbing sooty pots after the kleenex era you passed through in the advertising agency business. i envy you the chance you have to get into perfect physical condition but i never could make the hikes with full pack and the strenuous training rituals. i guess radio has taken its toll for these days, i find myself winded after raising my hat to a lady acquaintance.

we are happy to learn that you have received portland's choice on occasion. last night, she mailed you some salt water taffy and some philip morrises. what you will do with salt water candy in georgia i will never know. we are stuck up here. it is rather a broken-down resort. there is no first-class book store since this is strictly a cartoon section. i doubt if many read and those who do confine their scanning to hymns and headlines. if we ever get to an outpost of civilization will pick up some other books. if i had the talent i would write a book about radio. what makes chet take bi-carbonate? or something like that.

there isn't much to do here. i am trying to work out some ideas for the fall and do a little reading. it is difficult though with relatives piling in and local fans coming to the house and accosting us on the beach. mark twain once wrote "obscurity and a small competence, that is the life most worth-while." i am sure that mark was on the right track. it is difficult to mind your own business when one is in what is left of the public eye.

wish i had something exciting to write. at the moment, i am pounding the corona and portland is making a salad in the saladotorium. that is the way it goes each day. i always seem to be answering letters and port always seems to be making a salad. some day we may reverse it to add a modicum of piquancy to the routine here.

if there is anything exotic you would like to make your talk of the camp . . . let us know. i know you can't use a lobster. potatoes and lobsters are the two outstanding products of this region. if there is something you can use i can go over to bidde-ford, which is the nearest metropolis, and send it to you. awaiting your word, portland and i send our best wishes and hopes that you are mastering your new craft without too much strain. the tide is coming in . . . i have to open the door. excuse me.

fred allen

T. J. SMITH

old orchard beach
maine
july 30th
1941

dear t.j.

madam and i are perturbed to learn that you have recently been a victim of an occupational ailment that has torn through the ranks of conscientious advertising men with all of the gusto of a memo. "can concords" or "sphinctor malagas," the medical term for les piles, are common among artisans who practice your craft. i think this recent epidemic of "pratt-neon," as these enlarged and glowing veins are termed around the john hopkins, has been brought on by the tendency of men like your chet laroche to economize on swivels. cheap swivels in office chairs are bound in time to lump the thin wood and cause a ceaseless touche to set in. the swivel is constantly "having on" at the executive's anus with vein-welts ensuing.

the aluminum drive will tend to curb this "pokeberry" scourge. if chet is defense-minded, apart from the atency's commercials, he will whip the swivels out of all young & rubicam chairs and give them to mayor laguardia. the sole function of the swivel in an advertising agency is the play it affords the executive, discussing an appropriation, mr. grimm is able to spin on his swivel and avoid the client's eyes while explaining what a radio campaign will cost or perhaps alibiing a low crossley. the swivel will never be missed, t. j. and without it you will find that your posterior-plums will not return.

we heard harmon last night and confidentially ham is better

than gabriel heatter. if your mr. harrington doesn't sign ham for a fall commercial, hitler and senator wheeler permitting, your mr. harrington is not the man i think he is. we have been in semi-constant touch with private nelson but portland is stymied up here. there are few shops and nothing to send him but salt water taffy or fried clams (which do not hold up well if exposed to a long journey, i am told).

convey our concern to naval lt. weaver. we didn't know that he had given up his post as a george washington hillbilly to mount the brine for uncle sam. weaver is certainly running the gamut and will certainly have some tall tales to tell his illegitimate children in years to come. the night his stop-watch caught while timing the benny program in boston, the night butterworth sent for his agent at midnight run-through of the packard show, the day he first saw mr. hill, the first time he figured out what the hell the tobacco auctioneer was saying and finally his cramming to cope with the jargon of the navy.

wish harmon and the naval lt. well for us. i hope we shall see them both this fall. re the introduction to h. allen smith's book, "low man," the reaction to same was swell. i may write a book some day. if i do chet had better resign. meantime, a long life to your ready wit, sir. i shall keep you in mind if we ever get tomasso guasi the bootblack back to finally perform that bit you were going to time on the air.

avoir, smythe!

f.a.

may
19th
1942

dear lieut . . .

this is the first chance i have had to answer your memo. through some process that eternally operates to hamper me from exercising free-will i was inveigled into appearing at a russian war relief banquet. you can imagine my surprise upon arriving at the dais to find seated there dr. lin yutang, the eminent chinese writer, and one thomas harrington, a young and rubicam despot. upon questioning mr. harrington i learned that he was to speak. the dinner proceeded, and i must confess that oscar of the waldorf had a bad night. the meat looked like something lucretia borgia had taken out of a chemical vat, the salad looked like a mess some rabbit had spewed and the ice cream appeared to be little frozen hernias in technicolor. i watched mr. harrington during the dinner. he ate about as much as a termite would put away in a quarry. i don't know whether it was speaker's fright or the food. i was hungry and ate everything but dr. lin yutang's menu.

after the principal speakers had bored the hell out of everybody the piece de resistance arrived. some 16 people in different professions gave their versions of how the russian situation might be expressed in each business. tom covered the advertising field and i posed as a radio humorist. tom didn't make me an offer after i had finished talking and i didn't ask tom to report for a bristol-myers audition the next a.m. either. this entire episode means nothing except to prove to you that you never can tell where you will meet a young & rubicam man. even on a dais. incidentally, mr. rubicam sent a check for $1000. it looks as though welch and van nostrand will have salary sobs shortly.

your explanation of the origin of "son of a gun" and "show a leg." i am not up on sea lore. i only know that privy councilor started during the reign of hen, the 8th. the court advisor had chronic diarrhea. whenever there was a matter of moment before henry and he sought the advice of his advisor he would shout "blowdown the privy and summon my councilor." hence, privy councilor.

the wing commander's talk on air etiquette augers well. those other lice have always used every foul device to gain their ends while the opponents wer stressing "fair play." even their fighting methods air and submarine are foul means of warfare. these matters should be settled man to man even under the carpet and given chet a hotfoot. i could have bored a hole through the ceiling and spat upon him. that would have been the nazi method. i, clinging to tradition, went in through the door and am now working for another outfit.

i haven't any good gags on tap at the moment. i am down to one writer and he has just gotten an extension. his wife lost her baby recently and spent some time in the hospital and the board gave him three months until she is strong enough to work, i guess. the other writer took a flight test at red bank last week. two days later, he moved out near the field and is now an instructor. trying to turn out around sixty pages weekly is drudgery and i have scant time for jinks, hi or low.

if you can use cigarettes, candy, cigars or chewing gum let me know. portland runs the commissary and we will be glad to make up a "satchel for smith" and skip a bundle for britain one week.

when you quit the service later on, i hope you will autograph an anchor for us to keep around the house. i think an anchor would add something to my room. an old keel would do but an anchor standing in the corner would look better. i still haven't seen weaver. tom told me last night that he seldom sees pat these days. gad, what a world. i can recall the days when i saw weaver on the hour. portland sends her best wishes and we trust that all goes well in your new world of knots and bells.

and now to the script, sir!

f.a.
180 west 58th

may 2nd/44

dear t.j.

i have owed you a letter for so long that if letters accumulated compound interest i would owe you a small tome by now. the last interview data on the jap prisoners was very entertaining. i hope you are keeping a mental diary for your postwar lecture tour which i assume you will open at the harvard club, with colored slides. i feel like an old fumfet. i have about thirty other friends scattered the hell and gone all over rand and mcnally territory. they all write, including weaver, of exciting escapades and interesting experiences and here i am with my high blood pressure worrying about a new way to present jessel as a guest this coming sunday. i will be like rip van winkle when the war is over. i will rush out on the street with my rusty typewriter and not know what the returning hordes are talking about.

i am this day in receipt of word from sylvester weaver. in my last communique to weaver i told him the name of your dingy. sylvester advises that some time ago he was in port with you. he added that he never associates with birdmen. he claims they are always looking down on others . . . from force of habit. the weaver wit is razor sharp and he will be the life of many a board meeting when he returns. i gave him some radio news. jack benny is leaving general foods and going with g.w. hill on the pallmall program this fall. benny has the seven p.m. sunday time sewed up and hill will get that along with the benny program. jack has lost dennis day who went into the navy this week but he has a new set of writers who have worked out well. there is some other gossip. don stauffer arranged the benny deal since don is now head of radio at ruthrauff and ryan. when jack van nostrand left the owi don hired him and now jack and don are around lining up shows for the new agency. they made me a swell offer but i am quitting again this fall. the doctor told me i should take a good rest lest my high blood pressure become chronic and since the writers are gone and two of the actors i can only see more headaches coming up in the fall trying to break in new writers and actors and attempting to maintain the high standards you set for the program when you held the whip hand.

recently a new 30 percent tax was levied on nightclubs and places serving drinks and having dancing and entertainment. it has knocked the hell out of business all over with the exception of the stork club and one or two other established places. i might also add that liquor is scarce and very expensive. a drinking man will do well to stay in foreign ports until the tax wave and scarcity blows over. i have been in touch with young & rubicam recently. shows are so scarce at the moment that all agencies are around trying to steal each other's programs. hubbell and joe moran are in charge of radio at y & r. tom harrington has left on a six month pass to look for his stomach.

from the executive side the picture is constantly changing. chet, i understand, has been quite ill and is supposed to be one of the big men in the blue network when he returns to action. from the entertainment side everything is the same. rochester is still stealing benny's clothes. cantor is still jumping on von zell and the mad russian and fibber magee is still saying "tain't funny" or whatever it is. perhaps, after your rugged life, these tid-bits of trivia do not interest you. radio has about ceased to interest me. i received a letter from a priest over in brooklyn who claims that our program is slipping. i am going to write and remind him that priests lay plenty of eggs with those sermons and they are still using the "loaves and fishes" and "the sermon on the mount" routines. a comedian has to hustle around and get new routines occasionally. after i write the letter i expect to turn lutheran.

portland joins me in wishing you well in your new profession. when you return we shall know you by your rolling gait and the billingsgate you will no doubt be using. good luck, sirrah, if there is anything i can send you or handle for you here . . . let me know . . . i have been trying to find a copy of the smart set anthology for months. if there is one aboard will you steal same and send it on. until another day . . . i am . . . you are . . . he is . . .

the olde chieffe

fred allen
180 west 58th

beverly hills
california
august
11th . . . 1944

dear t.j.

congratulations on your new executive position with the fast growing organization that is doing so much to relieve the various advertising agencies of their top executives. your letter caught up with me out here in beverly hills. i am here to make an independent picture. i came out last fall to make it but complications set in and i returned to new york and the program. this season, i have given up the program and no kidding. charles cantor, john brown and fallstaff have all moved out here and minnie pious alone remains in n.y. if i ever start again and hope to work in the east it seems that i shall have to train an entire new crew to handle my mots bon and mots not so bon.

i have been working daily with morrie ryskind on a screenplay. most of it seems funny to me but god knows what will happen to much of the dialogue before the picture is finally completed. we hope to start after labor day and i should be back east around the end of october to languish over the winter. last night, i performed on one of the "mail call" programs written and produced by the tom lewis army radio unit here. i met bill morrow and bob welch on that job and am enclosing a picture of private welch. he is the only man who looks the same with a gas mask on as he does without one. tom lewis became a father this week. an eight pound son was born to loretta young. we met them after church on sunday and later had breakfast with them. the following day the baby was born. portland and i are taking no credit, merely stating a fact.

wednesday night i came home, after a hard day at the quip, and found a note reading "lt. weaver will be at the bar at 5 p.m." we contacted the lt. and he had been home for four days with liz. she is working in pictures here and lt. merely called us to say "banzai," or something, since he was leaving for miami and his "ship" at six a.m. the following morning. the lt. looked the same or perhaps a trifle thinner but his mood has not altered and he is looking ahead to post war days when he will be at the helm of his tobacco outfit and wield the ship over his tobacco auctioneers mr. f.e. boone, of lexington, kentucky and "speed" riggs of points south.

now that we are in beverly hills i am out of touch with your set in new york. speaking of sets mr. van nostrand mailed me a copy of the "smart set anthology." this book is scarce and i suggest that you keep yours against the day when some collector may offer a fancy price for same.

it must have been a pleasure to meet hank fonda without having to sit through an entire 20th century-fox masterpiece to catch a flitting glimpse of him. i saw a photo of caeser romero at the wheel of some sea-going tub. it seems the armed forces are doing strange things with some of our hollywood favorites. also read about your favorite evelyn waugh doing some military duty for the british. i read one of his books and it seemed to me that his humor was forced. i must be wrong, or perhaps i had an early waugh effort, for sally benson and several others speak highly of brother waugh's books. 12 years of radio may have dulled my critical facilities. i will check on the recent waugh works and let you know. i am also behind with my new yorker reading in recent months. the draft grabbing the writers, work, high blood pressure treatments, etc.

chet laroche is now the head man at the blue network. he wrote me asking me to have lunch. he seems to think that this country needs a new will rogers but i am sure that a will rogers today who attempted to make fun of labor, and the various men in power, would find his sponsor's wares banned and his career in jeopardy. chet may be trying to get me knocked off.

your popcorn enclosures give me a good idea of the type of fun "the boys" want. unfortunately, i haven't been able to play any camps or do much entertaining for the benefit of service men, apart from giving 800 tickets to the canteen in n.y. weekly, and i am not hep to the style of gag that bob hope and some of the others wend around the camps and battle stands.

we expect to be here until october 15th at least. if there is anything i can send you . . . let me know. if you are eating weevils in the flour and want some sort of sauce to flavor same i may be able to dig up some potent relish to kill the weevil taste. portland joins me in good wishes and we hope it won't be too long before you will be back with your feet on a desk.

good luck . . .

> fred allen
> beverly wilshire hotel
> beverly hills, california

may 11th/1945

dear t.j.

i am in receipt of all of your communiques. i have been indolent about the quill in recent weeks. the draft board is taking fellows from the show each month and i never know where i am or who will be left every thirty days. it has made more work for me and naturally this cut down on the letter output which was quite formidable in quieter times. am glad to know that you finally received the books and scripts. i also sent you five pounds of hard candy before the new ruling went into effect. as you perhaps know, we cannot send packages overseas unless specific articles are requested by a person. i guess you have to get an order from the commanding officer and then the order is taken to the post office and after it is okayed the parcel will be accepted. if there is anything you want and you can furnish me with the authority to send same i shall be glad to get going.

tonight, you will be glad to know that we are taking lt. sylvester weaver and mrs. weaver plus jay van nostrand and mrs. van nostrand to dinner. pat showed up out of nowhere last sunday at the broadcast. he has been at sea for some months and looked tan and fit. he also reeked of beverage which leads me to believe that our forces are receiving their rum rations as usual.

the little world of radio seems to be going back to the moronic and morbid statue it enjoyed some twelve years ago. there is talk that major bowes' program may go back to a full hour. this will be a step ahead in radio's march of progress. nothing seems to change in this frustrated industry and it seems to me that you can return any time and pick up what you were doing and be right in tempo with the doings of the day. our show has been doing well all season. it is hard to find guests now and all of my writers have gone one by one. i am down to one myopic gentleman and another chap who expects to feel uncle sam's hand on his shoulder this month. i see ham nelson every few weeks. i make recordings for his army radio outfit when they take one of our programs to be rebroadcast for a certain area.

i only hear from him when he needs something in a business way but he seems to be well and busy about his tasks.

i am supposed to give up the program this fall. the doctor has told me that my blood pressure continues to rise and that unless i take a prolonged rest he feels that i will invite a chronic condition. i am planning to abandon the show after june and go to hollywood to make a picture in the fall. if i avoid the weekly aggravation that goes with the writing and accumulation of the weekly rubble my pressure may go down and another day i may be able to return to the microphone as fresh as the proverbial daisy. there may be a little trouble with the sponsor but the cemeteries are full of men who didn't know enough to quit and i may establish a precedent if i leave at the height of my success. the word height here is used loosely. i fear that i have passed my peak despite anything you may have read in dr. pitkin's book "life begins at forty."

portland and i are still leading the same cloistered existence. i live like a louse inside of a clock—every hour, every day it is the same movement and the same routine. after eleven years i guess i should be used to it but in the days of capt. grogg we had some fun. today, it is drudgery. guest stars are non-existent, writers are fast disappearing and everything is getting confused in my estimation.

we hope that you have everything under control. the news has been very good here the past week and i hope that it won't be long before what is left of the world can get back to normal so that we who are left to cope with the sordid business of living can get about our business. i should really have written this on a v-mail envelope but i am long-winded and when i look at one of those little pages it seems that i couldn't even get the punctuation on a page. this may take a little longer but at least there will be something to read.

don't forget . . . if there is anything you want, that i can send, let me know. portland and i send best wishes and news that lamb is scarce and the man at the golden horn has been forced to lump his shishkabob???? into a deluxe dinner which now costs $2.75. this is news and it isn't good news. when you have time send me another communique.

good luck . . .

> fred allen
> 180 west 58 st.
> new york city

BILL MORROW

> november second 1942

dear bill . . .

i hate to bother you but wish you would do me a favor.

i went to see sig herzig's show one night last week. it was dull as any side of a roundhouse. after the play?? had been on for some twenty minutes the feminine star made a comedy?? exit and fell on her pratt. the star?? (male) came down to the footlights, out of character, and announced that uta hagen had been hurt and the curtain would be rung down for a few minutes.

after a ten minute wait the curtain went up and a character

who hadn't appeared in the play up to that time stepped down to the lights and announced that he knew the audience. he added that miss hagen was hurt quite badly and that they had sent for a doctor. if the audience would be patient he would let us know developments as soon as he could. the curtain came down again.

about this time i remembered that i had met "looney" lewis on broadway the night before. he asked me to come into the central theatre and see his new tab show. "looney" said "try and come in before thursday. i am doing a couple of cute bits i think you'll like." since mr. herzig's show didn't seem to be making any impression on me i told portland that we might be better off if we adjourned to the burlesque joint and got a small order of "looney" and his tableau.

we left mr. herzig's farce?? and went to the central theatre. we saw mr. lewis do about four creaking burlesque bits and some other material that was as old as dinosaurs. lewis is the first burlesque comedian i have ever seen spit dirty water into the second comedian's face. most of them spit water but it looks clean. this water "looney" spit was black and seemed to have suds mingled in with the h20. it was the last show; perhaps the comedians were spitting soapy water on each other to enable them to wash up while they were doing the bits. we weathered the show and came home.

now, here is the favor, bill. i am enclosing the two stubs from mr. herzig's show?? am also enclosing the two stubs from the "looney" lewis show to prove we went there, also, the program marking off miss hagen's name since she fell on her pratt and screwed up my evening. if you see mr. herzig around will you see if you can get my $6.60 back? if not, mr. welch might like to make up this amount. regards.

fa

feb. 29
1942

messrs. welch, lawrence et morrow . . .
gentlemen;

when your letter arrived i smelled a rat, not a lone rat, mark
you, but a covey of the rodents (genus mus). later this concentrated mousey odor was traced to the mailman who had b.o.,
halitosis, denture breath, under arm reek, and foul feet. the reason
i suspected the rat fume as emanating from your missive is because
the only time i ever hear from you messrs. welch et morrow is
when you need a fast spot for mail call, command performance or
one of your other cantatas. when i opened your billet-doux and
found that a brisk preface for your book on radio writing was
wanted i felt that you hadn't let me down.

as you may suspect i have been having a hell of a time getting out my own command jubilee every sunday. money has no
value here in the east. if you want a guest and the guest happens
to have a radio program he wants no dough to appear with you.
he will swap an appearance. in recent weeks i have been a stooge
on duffy's, information please, the quiz kids and this saturday i
am on truth and consequences. the only break i have had so far
came when mr. anthony agreed to come on our show and didn't
want me to appear with a fresh grief routine the following week
on his show. all of this entails extra work and i have little time for
letters or other so-called, in my case, writing. as usual with requests
of this sort there is a deadline involved. if you will let me know
the latest possible date the preface can be in i will try to work out
something. i do not want any money for my efforts, if efforts. i
think the book will have a limited appeal and i doubt if the con-
tributors will receive a great deal. books of this sort are not unlike
actors running a benefit for an actor or an actors' organization.
actors raise millions for the red cross, march of dimes, etc. but
when the friars or the n.v.a. put on a show for some needy actors
nobody gives a damn and the tickets are bought by other actors

who one day will be destitute themselves. i think this book will be purchased by relatives of the chaps who have contributed, the chaps themselves and perhaps by some budding radio writers who are now employed in shipyards and similar defense plants. so much for the book.

advise mr. morrow that i am leaving for kansas city with three ruptured friends to get in on that free truss bonanza. i am enclosing a news item for friend morrow. 4-fs with hernias are being taken in the army here. you can't get in without a hernia now.

tell bill if he is stuck for gags i can give him one about the ungrateful sardine who wouldn't help his poor old mother out of the can and another one about the dog with the sweet tooth who would only bite people with diabetes. i have some other clean ones which i know you can't use on those army shows. and while i think of it i had a letter from a soldier up in alaska who heard the command performance we did for your army outfit, the big xmas show. he said he couldn't understand much of the talk but he knew i was on the program because he saw my name on the label on the record. who does your recording, the baldwin locomotive people?

tell bill that h. allen smith is starting on his new book and he is still raving about his visit with bill fields. nothing much is happening around here. the mayor has started a drive picking up delinquent girls on broadway at night. if this keeps up several sinatra fan clubs will be in jail shortly. liquor is scarce and with the new tax the drinking man will have to write a letter to his congressman. the white collar worker who likes a high white collar on his glass of beer is going to have to cut down on food if he is going to maintain his 1942 drinking quota. all of the shows are packing them in. crowds follow any actor with grease paint on his collar to find entertainment. three men with jaundice were pulled into the hotel lexington by the manager who promptly opened an hawaaian room in what was formerly the ladies privy. ned sparks left for philadelphia yesterday with a new musical show which proves that show business is booming.

well, to hell with this. i have a new writer locked in a closet. i am going to let him out for a run around a copy of a tree grows in you know. this writer was with hope for some time. i spoke kindly to him the first day we met and he broke down and cried. apparently, it was the first kind word he had heard since he had started his career in radio.

i trust that all of you hail fellows are still well met and that you have the goose hanging high enough to keep it from dragging. pay my respects to merry men morrow, beloin and the bulging al lewis. and to you mr. welch may i say that new york hasn't been the same since you left. you can construe this in any manner you see fit. mrs. a wishes to send a kudo, she rented from variety, to tempy. i may see you this summer but i doubt it since my eyes get worse each week. if we do come out we must repay eddie for that night at his house. i think we should all gather in bill's hollywood knockerbocker suit and break a cheese fondu.

excuse the brevity, etc.

name the song before the gong!

l.s.m.f.t.

i'm talkin about slip covers!

i love to spend each wednesday with you. not with me.

regards . . .

F.A.

january 1st
1945

dear bill . . .

this is the first day of the new year. my head doesn't seem to have any bones in it. i seldom drink these days but with 1944 checking out i took portland over to see the old year out with a couple who have bad eyes. we finally saw the old year and most of the guests out and today i am home feeling as though i had just spent two years in the bladder of a dinosaur.

the package of gum arrived okay. thanx a lot. gum and cigarettes are scarcer around here than they seemed to be in hollywood. most of the cigarettes are sold under counters. today, when you see a humpbacked guy going down the street you don't know whether he has some spinal ailment or whether he has been bent over under the counter all day sneaking cigarettes to regular customers.

since i have stopped working i have been busier than i ever was with the show. have written a couple of magazine articles, a book review for the times and i am doing four guest shots this month. i have a couple of offers to write a book and am supposed to talk to allen smith about it in a day or so. have talked to allen a couple of times but haven't seen him. i don't know whether you saw him while you were here, or not. he bought a house up in westchester but doesn't move until next spring. i guess he expects to get in some serious writing once he is located.

the picture i made opens here soon. an independent picture apparently has a tough time getting a theatre in new york and i guess ours will have to wait its turn. if you see it out there wish you would let me know what it looks like. confidentially, in my opinion, it isn't too hot. the scene jack and i have went better than anything else at the previews but a lot of other material is pretty thin.

haven't heard anything from "bully boy" welch. give him my regards. i hope you both will have a happy and prosperous annum, i don't know but you may have some solution. if there is anything i can do for you here in new york . . . let me know. i think brother benny will be here in a couple of weeks to play some camps. the march of dimes people asked me to play three cities with jack but i have some guest shots that conflict. if you see bill fields tell him i'm sorry we couldn't have that dinner with mr. fowler. expect to give the morris office my business shortly and may try to get another picture in the spring. if i don't hear from you before will see you then. good luck.

f. allen

july 4th
1945

dear bill . . .

i think i owe you a letter. you wrote me last st. patrick's day. i haven't been waiting for another holiday to answer your rousing missive. the nimbus of hubbub that has hovered over me for years finally closed in this spring and i had to abandon all extraneous activity.

you asked me to mention jimmy starr's book. i had that "corpse came c.o.d." in no less than ten scripts and it lasted until sunday. i had the book thing dragged in, naturally, and sundays it was cut. it got to be a gag and i think the sponsor suspected that i had a piece of the book. if you see brother starr you can tell him i bought a copy of his book which is probably more than a lot of people who mentioned the book did.

i spent last evening with h. allen smith. he has just finished his new book. buddy desylva did the preface and h. allen feels pretty good about the book's chances. he is taking it in to the publisher tomorrow. he now has a contract to assemble an anthology of humorous pieces. this will take a little doing as it requires plenty of reading to dig up matter that will be fresh in a book of this sort. allen has been on the vehicle for months and looks swell.

will you get word through to sgt. welsh. i owe him a letter. advise him that i have no intentions of writing. we are leaving here july 13th and will arrive in your city on the 16th, i believe. i tried to get out of that picture deal i had but mr. skirball is in production and wouldn't hear of my defaulting. he came on to n.y. with morrie ryskind and morrie is trying to get the story into shooting shape. i am supposed to work with morrie for three weeks on the dialogue and then we are giving demille three days to get out of town.

as is my annual custom i have retired from the air for a season. i haven't any writers, all of the actors have moved to hollywood and the doctor told me that it will do me a lot of good to either get in another racket or to go and hang around with some nuns for a year.

jack haley is here on the alert. he leaves with his uso unit any minute. he played camp shank last night and was a big success. ben blue is around trying to get a unit together with ann sheridan. they have been here three weeks with no material but i think they opened someplace last night. someone told me that jack benny was in chicago. i thought he might be coming here. there is a rumor that jack is finally going to outdo hope. jack is taking eight midgets with him overseas to give shows in fox-holes. there is also another rumor that the pepsodent company has a contract with eisenhower to keep the war going until hope's contract expires. what will hope do when the war ends? pepsodent is worried. so far, we haven't been able to get a reservation at the beverly wilshire where we will have to live this time, if we can get in there. we can get in the town house and the beverly hills hotel but without a car we will be better off at the bev-wilsh. (this is code) we may end up with two sets of waterwings bobbing around in someone's pool until we can get indoors.

trust that all goes well in your unit. nat hiken and bob weiskopf are out at 20th with the winged victory outfit but the colonel got rid of irving lazar and brother landis the two who really got the show started with moss hart last summer. god knows what will happen to the boys unless they get with some other swivel group.

will see you later in the month if all goes well. regards to typhoid mary if you see her around.

fred allen
180 west 58th

montauk, long island
august
4th
1945

dear private morrow . . .

where the hell are you? i can't get sullivan's column down here and have lost track of you and broadway rose. a surf-fisherman passing through here trying to get some bait without using any of his coupons told me that he had seen in sullivan's column that you had been able to get out a few days to help mr. benny with his african unit. another man who drives through here with a trailer brothel on his way to a coast guard camp told me that he had seen in sullivan's column that mr. benny had left for africa. i can't get sullivan's column down here and believe me, private morrow, without sullivan's column you don't know a thing.

as you suggested in a moment of grape-abandon i wrote bill fields. i received a long letter back sending his regards to his highly-regarded friend bill morrow. he also regaled me with an account of his trial. some fink writer sued bill for using the snake story, the rattlesnake holds the guy by the leg and rattles for the police. bill lost the case and had to pay six grand to the writer plus lawyers' fees. he is still pretty mad about it. i offered to look the gag up for him and get an approximate idea of its age but bill said it was too late. he had paid off and he says "my estimation of the learned and ancient profession hasn't changed one iota." bill is good and mad at lean gag writers and lawyers. it is too bad that you cannot be out there to console him.

bill gave me some advice on high blood pressure. he says i should take a rest. bill says "remember the story of the irish soldier named kelly. his captain said to him 'kelly, you've killed enough men today you can lay off tomorrow.'" bill is starting to speak in parables. somebody has got to take his words down. if someone hadn't taken down the early parables the world would have no bible. bill may be giving us the sequel to the bible if somebody will get out there and take this stuff down.

i sent you some pin-up pictures before i left town. did you get them? what the hell are you doing? i am at gurney's inn, montauk, ny. it looks as though the picture deal is off. i will probably be in n.y. all winter. do you think mr. benny will return with a couple of ubangi writers? if you get time and if anybody has time you have time . . . drop me a line. regards.

fred allen
gurney's inn
montauk, n.y.

ANTHONY V. SAUPIOS*

december 4/44

dear tony . . .

after four months in hollywood we arrived back in new york last week. you can imagine my surprise, after entrance to our apartment had been gained, to find a stack of mail on top of which rested an enormous coconut. i didn't realize it was a coconut with scabbard complete at first glance. i thought it was a bowling ball someone had left out in the rain and it had gotten a bit lumpy. then i thought perhaps it was an old y basketball that had congealed in the cold air of the big gym. after portland and i had waded through the hundreds of letters, papers, bills and charity requests i took a good gander at the wooden goiter and found that it was a coconut with your name on it. the coconut is still here. i don't know how to open the thing but the milk is still rampant inside and one day i am going to borrow a couple of termites and have them eat a small hole in the outer shell. if i can get a screwdriver into the hole i may be able to pry the husk off and test my few remaining teeth on the coconut meat.

* One of Allen's handball-playing friends at the West Side YMCA in civilian life.

we appreciate your thought of us in your jungle surroundings and if any teeth are broken we will send you the bill.

with our mail there were two packages. one was from "french mike" containing an ashtray made from the end of a large shell. i haven't heard from mike since early last summer and had no idea where he was. the ashtray has an italian insignia on it so i gather that he is in italy at the moment. i have established contact at the y again and all is about the same. "jack the ripper" passed away. i don't know whether you knew jack, or not. he used to go into the wrestling room with a small punching bag which he attached to his head and if he had an audience jack would bounce the bag with his head to the amazement of those assembled. jack continued to box and exercise and eventually had a heart attack and passed away at the pre-social security age of 60.

the rest of the members seem to be in about the same shape. joey has high blood pressure, the same affliction i have. he weighs 217 and really should take some weight off but handball doesn't seem to reduce him at all. mickey, last new year, resolved to run 1000 miles this year. he had monthly sheets torn from a calendar with the number of miles he has run each day. he expects to finish to 1000th mile this coming friday. the y is supposed to have a cameraman there and i am trying to get the picture company to send a cameraman to take some pictures of mickey completing his final mile. i have another fellow who has promised to put mickey on the air if he wants to go on some radio program. frankie recently knocked out some ex-marine who was employed as a watchman at the j.p. morgan company. it was the first fisti-cuffs ever engaged in by morgan employees and a few days after the fracas frankie was called in and given a raise. tote-basket mike is still the same. since he has replaced mr. quint, as head of the tote basket dept., mike has been having labor and executive troubles but last week we pried him away from his duties long enough to play a few games of handball. the gym is still deserted and i guess it will remain that way until the war is over. i am going to boston tomorrow for a complete physical examination and may have to stop exercising shortly. i have given up the radio program this season and it is a little confusing after all of the years i kept running around to suddenly find myself getting up mornings and wondering what to do during the day. i may try to write a book or do some other writing to keep occupied. i can't very well make any plans until after i hear what the doctor has to say.

we finally finished the picture out in hollywood. i saw it last week and unfortunately it isn't too good. this is my personal opinion. it is treason to imply that a picture is bad until it is finally released and everyone knows about it. when the picture gets to new york i may have to hide for a few weeks until the whole thing blows over.

we finally had winter show up all of a sudden this past week. it has been down around 24 degrees all week and people are shivering in the streets and all we need is some snow to make it look like a genuine winter. with the manpower shortage it seems that some of the charitable organizations are going to use lady santa clauses on the streets. kids will have to be more gullible than ever to accept kris kringle with a big bust and lipstick under the whiskers.

trust that all is going as well as can be expected in your section. i hope it won't be too long before you can get back home for good and we can get the y back to normal with the old familiar faces and the handball courts so crowded you can't get a game. recently i sent some books to a friend of mine in the pacific. if there is anything i can mail you write me at home and i will be glad to function. i expect to be in new york all winter and if my blood pressure goes down i may start back working late in the spring or next fall. portland joins me in sending our best wishes and hopes that you have everything under control.

good luck . . .

fred allen
180 west 58th st.
new york 19, n.y.

july
17th
1943

dear tony . . .

your card has made the rounds. it followed me up to boston and missed me there and then it came on down to montauk where portland and i have come to try and get a little rest for a few weeks. we'll certainly get it here. none of the guests seem to be under eighty and there is nothing to do but eat, sleep and sit around on the beach. the coast guard has stopped all fishing which eliminates any change from the dull, albeit restful, routine.

it's funny, when gene goldman came back on furlough a few weeks ago he was asking about you. i told him that you were studying and i thought that perhaps you were preparing to go into some special branch of the service. i was surprised to learn you were already at camp upton. i didn't think you would finish school until the end of the summer. if you want gene's address it is a/sgt. e goldman, 16th comm. sq. gp. x. apo 462, minneapolis, minn.

am in touch with french mike, as well. he has been in africa for some time. recently he has been in the hospital with malaria but is out again and apparently as good as new. he complained that he had all of the cigars and cigarettes he wanted but he couldn't find matches. i sent him a lighter and have just received word that it arrived okay. lighters are hard to find and i finally had to go to dunhills so mike is wandering around africa with a beautiful silver lighter which will probably be stolen the first time he sets it down.

before i left the city "tote-basket mike's" front tooth came out which caused a minor disturbance in mr. quint's department. mike claimed that it air-conditioned his mouth which made him more comfortable but when he opened his mouth he looked like a burlesque comedian. franky found a clinic on park avenue where dental work was done at cost and when i left mike was debating visiting the clinic to have his gap replaced with some plastic replica of an incisor.

i was supposed to go to hollywood but it looks as though my trip is off. my high blood pressure has had me running to the doctor all winter. he finally told me that i should rest for at least six months and if i don't improve over the summer it looks as though i will be a bum until the first of the year. i wouldn't mind not working if i could go to the gym but i am not supposed to exercise which makes me feel like an old man. what i need is a year in the army away from all of the headaches and troubles that go with radio. some routine of this sort would fix me up, i know. for the present though it looks as though i am doomed to lay low and see what happens to my pressure over the summer. we hope to stay down here in montauk until labor day. it is restful and all that but it is also pretty dull after hopping around the way i have for the past twenty years.

hope that all goes well in your new environment. let me know where you go. i assume that you will soon leave upton for some special branch of service. mail at home will be forwarded. this montauk address may be changed if the weather gets bad or if it finally gets too deadly to stand.

best wishes . . .

fred allen
180 west 58th st.
new york city

8.

THE LAST YEARS

THOMAS E. CONGDEN

march 19
19th   50

thomas e. congden—

i am sorry that i cannot accept the yale record award.

in this country today we have 5,000,000 unemployed. i am
one of the 5,000,000.

if you give me an award how will the other 4,999,999 unemployed feel? in addition to relief payments and unemployment insurance they, too, may want awards.

this could result in rioting on the yale campus, further
jeopardise the economic structure of our democratic form of government and cause the marshall plan to backfire.

i never look a gift horse in the mouth but i am not averse
to looking an organization in the motive.

what you propose in effect is to exchange the effort ex-
pended in the preparation of an alleged humorous speech of ac-
ceptance, a trip to new haven and sundry hours of my time for
a covey of negative tributes, a brace of boolas and possibly a chorus
of the whiffenpoof song.

had you thought of me when i was a practising humorist, i
might have reacted. now that i am unemployed my presence on
your dais could only be construed as an affront in retrospect to
ogden nash, s. j. perelman, henry morgan and al capp—earlier
recipients of the yale record awards.

sincerely—

fred allen

THE CAPE CODDER

july
12
1950

dear editor—

you are the editor of The Cape Codder. i am a subscriber.

when a subscriber writes to an editor it is usually to complain about the paper's editorial policy, the small-sized print used in the help-wanted columns that is keeping nearsighted people, who are out of work and have no glasses, from finding jobs or to berate the editor for misspelling the name of the subscriber's wife in the news story that told how the subscriber's wife fell off a stool at a howard johnson stand and spilled 26 kinds of ice cream on her burlap ensemble.

my purpose in writing this letter is not to condemn. i have no desire to add another gray hair to your editorial cowlick. i merely want to despatch a kind word to you and to your little gazette.

to me The Cape Codder is a friend who comes to my door each week bearing tidings from the cape. the affairs of the outside world find no place in its columns. The Cape Codder chronicles only the happenings on the cape and the gossip and matters of moment to its denizens.

what other weekly gives you news and items such as these? (i quote from recent issues)

"now is the time to protect pine trees from the destructive turpentine bark beetles."

"albino woodchuck shot by frank hinckley in cummaquid."

"the striped bass struck in at pochot beach, orleans, sunday."

"cranberry clinic to be held july 12 and july 18. cranberry growers will meet to discuss bog problems."

"mildewed sails can now be prevented easily and inexpensively."

what other journal gives its readers pieces comparable to "orchard twilight," "the june woods" and "campin' on the island" by somebody who signs himself l.r.j.—colorful memories of happy yesterdays and tributes to fauna, flora and secluded nooks and crannies discovered by l.r.j. in strolls about the cape?

what other paper comes out on thursday to enable you to finish its contents and have its pages ready to wrap up a fish on friday? the answer is—no other paper.

until i subscribed to The Cape Codder i thought that a cranberry was a cherry with an acid condition. i thought that a seagull was a thyroid pigeon. i thought the mayor of cotuit was an oyster. today, thanks to The Cape Codder, i know why the pilgrim fathers, who had the entire continent available for their purposes, chose to land on cape cod.

enclosed please find check for another year's subscription. may you and The Cape Codder trudge along down through the years enjoying the success you merit for a job well done.

sincerely—

> fred allen
> the belmont
> west harwich
> massachusetts

JACK NORWORTH

> august
> 25th
> 1951

dear jack—

your note and the "cusp-a-door" mike brochure arrived today. i hope that before you go into production on a large scale you will have some research done to enable you to check on the chewing tobacco market today.

some years ago, when i worked for the chevrolet people, i saw a set of statistics on tobacco chewing that were frightening. these figures proved that tobacco chewing had fallen off 102.9

percent. this meant that not only every man, woman and child in the country had stopped chewing but that 2.9 people who were thinking of taking up the habit had changed their minds.

according to the chevrolet report tobacco had fallen off because of the automobile and the paved road. when a man drove a horse his speed was low enough to permit him to chew tobacco and spit a low wet curve in the breeze that would clear the horse and the buggy. the increased speed of the automobile introduced a hazard. when the driver leaned out of the car and spit the occupant in the back seat suddenly acquired a tan bib. in many cases, if the speed was high enough, the driver would receive his brown charge right back in his kisser. the paved road presented another problem. when a tobacco chewer walked with a lady along a dusty road he could turn his head and void suddenly. there would be a tiny puff of dust and the pool was covered before the lady could sense what had happened.

i had to quit chewing but not because of above reasons. i have high blood pressure which for some reason known to the medical fraternity does not go with tobacco chewing.

hope you are well. the next time we get out to the coast i will make another attempt to catch up with you. meantime, watch your step with this "cusp-a-door" mike proposition. you may have to import "wetbacks" to start chewing to take your stock off your hands.

regards—

> fred allen
> 180 west 58th st.
> new york city 19

ARTHUR MACKENZIE

Allen took haste to send the following letter to Arthur MacKenzie, his putting-green friend at the Belmont on Cape Cod, after reading a news report about an attempted burglary at MacKenzie's Ford agency in Cambridge, Massachusetts.

Saint Max's Church
Cambridge, Mass.

July 1, 1952

My dear Mr. MacKenzie:

I am writing you to help me rectify a grave injustice that has been done two fine, upstanding young men who are members of my parish.

On Monday morning, June 30th, at an early hour the Cambridge police reported that Bobby Anthony and Donald Tarud had been found prowling about the MacKenzie Motor Company showrooms. These two innocent youths were charged with attempted robbery and sent off to prison.

A terrible mistake has been made. God help us, Mr. MacKenzie! As the pastor of St. Max's Church it is my duty to appeal to you as a Christian brother, Mr. MacKenzie, to beg your aid and to explain to you the circumstances that led to the plight these two clean-living, upright young men find themselves in today.

Mr. MacKenzie, as God is my judge, this is the true story:

Bobby Anthony and Donald Tarud are altar boys at St. Max's Church. At two a.m. on Monday last I was awakened by a Mr. Doyle pounding on the rectory door. Mr. Doyle in a state of extreme agitation gasped that his wife was dying. He wanted a mass said—it was urgent. I rushed into the church—there were no candles. I couldn't say a mass without candles. Also, I would need two altar boys. Raising my cassock I dashed out into the street. I saw two lads coming home from a Boy Scout rally with their bugles and wigwag flags under their arms. These boys were Bobby Anthony and Donald Tarud. I explained my predicament—an emergency mass and no candles. Bobby Anthony said he thought he could help me. His aunt ran a Tea Shoppe and brought her candles home every night. Bobby said he could take a few candles —his aunt would never know. Donald said he would go home with Bobby and get some matches. Since they were both altar boys I asked them to hasten back to assist me at the mass for Mrs. Doyle. The hour was late. I said I would leave the rectory window open. When Bobby and Donald returned, to save me the trouble of opening the rectory door, they could step through the window.

I didn't know, Mr. MacKenzie, that Bobby was nearsighted. Bobby's nearsightedness is responsible for this distressing dilemma. Coming back to St. Max's with the candles, Bobby saw an open window. Thinking he was back at the rectory, Bobby climbed through the window. Donald followed him. The rest we know, God save us! The burglar alarm, the police, the sordid stories in the papers. The fault is partly yours, Mr. MacKenzie, if you had closed that open window when you left your showroom on Saturday evening this ghastly blunder could not have been made.

I know you are a good man, Mr. MacKenzie. The poor of my parish, here in Cambridge, often speak of your generosity. They tell of the Shriners' Parade, on the hot day, when you took off your fez and put it on the head of a little old lady who had sunstroke. They recall the Christmas you put sugar on 200 doorknobs and gave them to poor children for lollypops. They speak of the Rotary Luncheon when you passed your chicken a la king out the window to a passing tramp. And your greatest philanthropic gesture, Mr. MacKenzie, the day the widow in East Cambridge had trouble with her Ford and you, without charge, personally fixed the widow's rear end.

Your heart is as big as my parish, Mr. MacKenzie. Do your duty. Call the police and tell them the true story. Demand that they release my altar boys, Bobby Anthony and Donald Tarud, two harmless young men who stand charged with attempted burglary.

God bless you, Mr. MacKenzie.

Father Fred Allen
Pastor of St. Max's Church

P. S. If you cannot have the boys released can you arrange to have them tried before some crooked judge you know in Cambridge?

JACK EIGEN*

dec. 25
1952

dear jack—

this is the first opportunity i have had to acknowledge the receipt of your recent book "the story of jack eigen." i don't know how the book is going. if i knew that you were putting it out i would have suggested that you put a few portholes in the book and try to sell it as another "caine mutiny."

if you haven't heard of me lately i had a bad summer. i had one foot in a mortician's hand for two months. i had a hard time getting him to let go. i thought i was going to go permanently bebop. i was going to be cool indefinitely. fortunately, i escaped and expect to be able to do some work after the first of the year.

i know you have been doing better than hopalong cassidy out there in chicago. when portland and i came back from california last june the conductor on the chief told us that he lived in chicago and heard your program every night when he was at home. many friends of ours in chicago tell us about you when they come to town. hope you will continue to stay hot during the winter for when the summer comes around the weather will take care of this problem.

things are the same here in new york. winchell is suing the n.y. post and the n.y. post is suing winchell. i guess they ran out of names to call each other and hired a couple of lawyers to get some new material.

the roxy was closed up for several weeks. they reopened this week with the stage turned into an enormous skating rink, replacing the stage show with a skating spectacle is taking a great chance. if you don't like the picture you don't have to bother with the roxy—you can see all the skating you want at the rockefeller plaza rink and you don't have to buy a ticket.

* Chicago disc jockey.

the cinerama is the biggest thing in town. if you haven't seen this you are in for a treat when it opens out there. after you sit and look at those enormous cinerama pictures when you step out on the street fat jack leonard looks like georgie price.

danny kaye opens at the palace in january. the stage show playing this week will be held over to act as ushers during the danny kaye run. the strand is closed. they lose more money when they're open. most of the picture theatres can make more money closing up. johnny ray is at the capitol. the capitol is freezing his tears and selling them to the roxy for ice. the capitol will make a profit this week if the roxy pays its ice bill.

portland joins me in a happy and good new year for dorothy and for you. "life is uphill—carry on!"

F.A.

NEAL O'HARA*

jan. 15
1953

dear neal—

i am sorry that i cannot be without you tonight at the clover club dinner. when i came to boston in 1945 to speak at your inauguration i felt like an accessory after the fact. the minute you became president the clover club was doomed. i predicted that the dais would be made into a raft and donated to L street, the food concession turned over to howard johnson and the hearty camaraderie of the clover club members presented to the russian delegation at the u.n.

i can see you now as you were sworn in. when three lumps came up in your throat, word swept the hall that you were fraught with emotion. i know that those three lumps were only your adam's apple and two martinis olives. as you fell into office i didn't know whether you were a man addressing the clover club

---

* Boston newspaper columnist.

dinner or a soul resigning from alcholics anonymous. i said to myself "this man may be a live wire but he has blown a fuse. the
clover club will start going downhill faster than park street near
beacon."

but the years proved that the clover club survived and defied
extinction.

i had a few jokes, you may be able to fix them up and start
off your 33rd year in the club with something different.

bill cunningham predicted that general macarthur would
never get into the white house. bill said that the country would
never elect a president who starts combing his hair from under his
armpit.

the senate finally approved charles e. wilson. the senators
were suspicious of any man who had two million dollars when he
arrived in washington.

television is thriving. bishop sheen's sponsor is making a new
tv set for the clergy. it has a stained glass tube.

texas is still the state abounding in opportunity. in one small
texas town they found oil in a cemetery. 400 dead people became
millionaires.

in hollywood, california, a tea shop failed. the owner of the
tea shop had 100 candles left over. with the 100 candles he
opened a church and is doing very well.

since i cannot be with you, neal, i want to congratulate bill
bullins, the new president. i want to hail you as the new bernarr
mcfadden starting your 33rd year as a member and i want to wish
the clover club many wonderful dinners to come.

fred allen

PAUL MOLLOY

Paul Molloy, Chicago *Sun-Times* radio-TV columnist, received mail from readers in 1953 asking if Steve Allen and Fred were related. He sent it on to Fred and received this reply:

dear paul;

    i have just returned to the city to find your letter and the enclosed postcard from one of your readers which inquires whether i am the father of steve allen.

    since i have first showed my face on television, i have been receiving fan mail of this type. people have been writing in to learn if i am steve's uncle, if i am the father of the panel folks on life begins at eighty, and if i am the star from one of the old movies.

    one avid tv fan wrote and asked me if i was extinct. this last card was sent in care of the smithsonian institution.

    obviously there is something wrong some place. people who see me on the street are always stopping me to say, "you sure look a lot better than you do on television." my doctor assures me that i look normal for my age, and recently one of our local eddie fisher fan clubs mailed me an application and asked me to become a member. and you know that they are not letting old men into the eddie fisher fan clubs.

    since i look pretty good at the moment, i think the trouble that prompts people to ask me if i am steve allen's father, or if gabby hayes is my other son, originates with the people themselves.

    i checked on one tv owner who claimed that i look pretty wrinkled and found that a small piece of corduroy had fallen over his tv tube. this man was seeing me through the corduroy and naturally i was coming out pretty wrinkled, and a little baggy on one side.

    another old lady who wrote in asking if i was ethan allen using the name of fred was checked and we found that she had put her glasses down on some scotch tape. she was looking through the sticky side of the tape and wondered why she couldn't take her eyes off of me when i was on the screen.

an old gentleman living on a farm, we found, needed glasses. his eyes were so bad he couldn't locate the tv set in the room. he was looking out the window all day and wondering why a lot of his neighbors were suddenly on television.

just advise your readers that if i look wrong, i am okay. the trouble must be with them.

f.a.

HAL KANTER

A gifted writer and producer of radio, television and moving picture comedies, Kanter was the creator of the first George Gobel show on TV at the time when these letters were written. Just before Allen's sudden death in 1956, Kanter was corresponding with Fred about a TV comedy idea in which Allen was interested.

MEMO FROM

FRED ALLEN

To: H. K.

i have been sitting around in my turtle-necked tallis worrying about your guests for the coming season. i think i have come up with something. what about larry naker? larry was cured—freed from the bondage of alcohol by tv—but recently, after seeing three beer commercials and a roma wine spot announcement larry went back to his sinful ways. you can open the season with larry naker if you want a new face. let me know.

DEAD STOCK
REMOVED

SANITARY TRUCKS

JOPLIN
RENDERING CO.

---

nov. 26
1954

hal—

if you are interested—these people remove studio audiences on short notice.

regards—

f. allen

(Enclosure)

Could you give me the information on the following?

1. Are Ed Sullivan and Fred Allen brothers? If so, what is the family name?
2. Is Fred Allen the father of Steve Allen?

Thank you,
Mrs. L. D. Lemon
Ashland

feb.
11
1955

hal—

you have to admit that television sets people to thinking.

F.A.

may
20
1955

dear hal—

as your friend i advise you to sell your typewriter, consign your files, (if any) to your incinerator (imagine if all of the comedy writers burned their files and a "laughing smog" set over all of southern california) get back your dues from the writers' guild (if possible) and give some serious consideration to taking up a new profession. the day of the writer is done. the enclosed clipping tells the story. abc-tv won't assign writers to the henny youngman-rocky graziano show. they want it ad lib. you know as well as i know that youngman and rocky couldn't ad lib out of a drowning episode (youngman would never think of "help" unless he had heard somebody else say it first.)

all of these economy vogues get started in the east. it may not be long before you will report with the script some morning at rehearsal to be informed that the gobel show is dispensing with writers. as soon as your producer, mr. o'malley, learns about the youngman-graziano idea, he will follow suit. he will convince george that all he needs to kill the half hour is a brisk session of o'malley kicking it around with george, letting the quips fall where they may.

i don't know mr. o'malley but my aunt used to say "never trust a man you catch looking at you through his eyelids." a man who can do this is thin-skinned and barely able to contain himself. when i went to kindergarten i knew a man who looked like mr. o'malley. he used to hang around the school at recess, he used to whip out a beanshooter and siphon the jelly out of little boys' jelly doughnuts. i don't say that this man turned out to be mr. o'malley but i am warning you. if henny youngman and rocky graziano start ad libbing not only the writer will be through but abc-tv may find itself turned into a frozen custard dispensary.

F.A.

june
7
1955

hal—

if you didn't believe me when i warned you to unload your typewriter i call your attention to the enclosed clipping.* you may remember bill morrow. some years back, he was one of hollywood's top writers. the minute he heard about the new henny youngman and rocky graziano ad lib show he turned his corona in and obtained a polaroid. obviously, he is doing very well in his new profession photographing his friends. this might suggest something to you. a small motel, selling pizzas in the back, may be a thought.

i haven't been able to start working on my autobiography. mort green and george foster, who have been working with goody all season on the berle show, are turning their office over to me and i hope to get going next week. mort and george are going to the coast to work on the johnny carson show for a couple of months.

there are so many distractions that i never have any time for myself. in recent weeks i have made two trips to boston, written a treatise on the city of new york for the garroway show, a piece on will rogers for the nbc tribute to will on his birthday anniversary, went to stroudsburg for dinner and have just finished a piece on herman wouk for the book-of-the-month club news, a small magazine published by the book-of-the-month club. herman's new book is the selection for september. all of these things have been cuff jobs so you can see why i am a trifle frayed and haven't been able to start my book. forgot to mention that i read george axelrod's new play. he wants me to do a part but i don't think it will help the play or me either. you had better think before you start casting me in your picture. portland and i will be here all summer let me know ahead when you plan your eastern trip.
regards.

fred allen

* A photo of Bing Crosby taken by Bill Morrow.

august
11
1955

hal—

happy to know that you have checked niagara falls and zion canyon and they are both all set for the coming season.

i have stumbled upon an angle for you and the show. you can top the $64,000 quiz with your own gimmick. give bibles away every show. if you blow your present sponsor, pet milk, look at these other sponsors available—cemeteries, funeral homes, trailer sales companies.

do not treat this lightly. you want good will and there isn't enough to go around.

FA

(Enclosure)

There is NO substitute for GOOD WILL in business
. . . GOOD WILL is a Company's *biggest* asset!!
Good morning, Mr. Sales Manager:

Radio shows have set, and are setting, the pace in give-aways. And the only one we ever knew of who objected to this type of show was Fred Allen. Certainly we, as well as your listeners, would not turn down a genuine guaranteed value free offer.

We know of no offer that you can make your listeners that will have the universal appeal of a HOLY BIBLE. A Holy Bible that cannot be purchased in book stores . . . that cannot be duplicated . . . and represents the finest in religious art reproductions as well as having all the Bible Helps that are so necessary for inspirational Bible study. You can bring this HOLY BIBLE to your readers either as a free gift from a sponsor or at a ridiculously low price as a station promotion.

First, let's explore the sponsor angle. Churches, Cemeteries, Funeral Homes, Used Car Dealers, Real Estate Firms, Trailer Sales Companies, Insurance Firms and many others use "Good Will" appreciation items. Items that are designed to last over a long period of time and are either "Thank You's" for past business or an invitation to future business. Many of these "Good Will" items do not last as long as anticipated and/or are not designed to be consistently used. In either respect they do not do the job for which they were intended and the donor purchased them.

september
3
1955.

dear mr. kanter—
i have been working as a
toreador down in mexico.
i have been doing very w
ell and have become quit
e popular with the fans
who attend the biggest b
ull rings.
recently, as i turned my
back to reach for my c
apella with which i inte
nded to despatch the bul
l (el toro down here) he ho
oked me with his horn. i
ignored the bull's gestu
re, snapped up my a cape
lla and despatched him.
several americans who sa
w me accept the horn say
that i must come to holl
ywood and go into the ad
vertising game. if i can
take the horn, i can lau
gh off the finger.
what do you advise, amig
o?
a dios, miguel pedro

december
21
1955

dear hal—

sorry you will not be able to work on the "morningstar" screenplay with herman wouk. i do not know whether you have ever met him but he is a wonderful fellow with a lot of talent that he hasn't even used yet. the last time i saw him he told me that milton sperling was going to produce the picture for warner's. bennett cerf told me last night that herman was going to replace him on the "what's my line" panel while bennett is away in california. while bennett was talking he told me that he was going to be on your show. (if this is news to you—don't quote me.) if herman is going to set on the panel, how can he go out to the coast to work on the screenplay? do you think that bennett is reliable?

the electronic creative slave has to bow to the machine. we did over 780 shows and most of the air waves that were pregnant with our jokes and clever lines finished up caught in the crotches of pigeons, sparrows and flamingoes who dared too far north. only a machine can cope with another machine. remington-rand is trying to cross sam perrin with a dynamo and come up with a machine called "funivac." this will be an electric brain that will write comedy scripts. you merely pull a lever 35 times and the machine lights up for ten minutes and spews out 35 scripts, enough for one season. the remington people tried mating phil sharp with a small dynamo and the test machine came up with a chromium ulcer. the company knew the machine was practically human and threw phil out of the plant. only two writers have ever beaten the electronic age. george bernard shaw, he died before the age got going well. abe burrows, who quit when duffy's tavern was going well. shaw never sold the rights to anything he had ever written. maurice evans told me one time that the old man, when he was ninety was collecting ten and fifteen thousand dollars weekly from royalties coming in from around the world. one season for you is enough. it is fun for one season but pictures are easier and more credit accrues in the easier medium.

have been working hard on the book. i have completed seven chapters and am hoping for the best. if you haven't had a note from goody recently—am enclosing one. he didn't capture me—i got away.

happy new year.

fred allen

feb. 10
1956

dear hal—

i haven't been able to cope with your recent letter. i not only do not remember stanley adams, whose quote was aired by the reporter, i don't recall any writer on our show who was paid $1500 weekly. how brother adams sandwiched me in there between henny youngman and berle will call for some explaining when i catch up with him.

goody ace is non-existent as far as i am concerned. jane has been down in miami and he has been commuting. i think they knock off the perry como show in two short days. goody takes a long ride in the subway with a tape recorder and comes back to the office with the dialogue for the show. in the office they have an old berle junior writer who works with kindergarten blocks. this block man reduces goody's dialogue into words that perry can understand and pronounce. you can appreciate the amount of time goody has to himself during the week.

i liked the benchley book. i assume you meant the one his son nat wrote, the biography. i thought it had been rather hurriedly assembled and i thought, knowing bob, that he deserved a masterpiece on which sufficient time had been spent to stand as a permanent tribute to a wonderful man.

bennett cerf returns to the what's my line show tomorrow. if there is anything to report on his jaunt or experiences i will send it on. bennett rarely says anything until he has sold it in written form in one of his many columns.

only two items to call to your attention. i attended the reuben friedman services in philadelphia. you remember reuben's book "the emperor's itch." rube not only spotted napoleon's scabies he had a list of people in television who started scratching themselves as of now. warn hollywood writers not to be too cocky with the collapse of the ad libbing team henny youngman and rocky graziano. we have two men who may scale the heights abandoned by rocky and henny. last night during the performance of "fanny" a small fire probably set by the management in the basement caused smoke to seep up through the orchestra pit. with no writers, nor script that was evident to audience, alan carney stepped down to the front of the stage and said "There's nothing serious, everything's under control." assuming this to be a straight line ezio pinza, another solid ad libber, replied, "all right everybody, let's go on with the play." if this type of ad libbing catches on not only will the writers all be out of work but goody's block man will be writing all of the broadway shows.

if you do eventually come east—let me know ahead if you are interested and i will get sid perelman and al hirschfeld for dinner or organize an outing to the old roumanian with a set of unreliable characters.

portland joins me in best wishes. i am finishing chapter 9 and will be happy when i get the book together. god knows if i will ever live to go over the whole thing to cut and polish it. tv is sure progressing. last week, i heard bishop sheen quoting lou holtz.

fred allen

february
22
1956

dear hal—

there has been a slight delay in the delivery of the bennett cerf scroll. it arrived yesterday, today is a holiday and i think that bennett is doing some lectures later in the week. i will make the personal delivery on sunday. this will prolong the suspense and lead bennett to think that you are an unappreciative heel who never acknowledges gestures. just when he is around calling you all of the anti-emilypost specimens i will present him with your letter. with your letter, on sunday, i will carry a big suspensory in case he wants to hang his head.

you are rushing purim out your way. next sunday, feb. 26, is purim here. also, on friday next, light candles 5:28. portland and i have been preparing for purim. portland is experimenting with a new seasonal delicacy, a combination hamantaschen and pizza. in the traditional hamantaschen along with the prune, poppy seed or chocolate nut fillings portland sprawls a few anchovies. adding the anchovies if you have some of the hamantaschen left over after purim you can flatten it out and make a small pizza or a large pizza depending on the amount of hamantaschen or the original size of the hamantaschen, you had remaining. in the purim spirit i took out my shofar and blew it around the house for a few hours to have my lip ready for passover. i play the only cool ram's horn in town and word must have gotten out. i had a call from steve allen. they opened the benny goodman picture at the capitol uptown and the national winter garden downtown. steve asked me to double for him. he was over in the capitol lobby blowing the clarinet and i was down in the national winter garden lobby holding a jam session with three other cool shofar cats.

enclosing a copy of "the great bartender." if you are planning any jewish dialogue for the g show write to p.o. box 8, liberty, missouri. "oui va" and givault" are a couple of samples that will have old box 8 crammed. get your order in early.

the steve allen picture opened well except for one notice, in the times. arthur treacher is a tonic to be taken without shaken on any occasion. arthur has been lecturing recently. i may look into that field next season when i am through with the book. finished chapter 9 yesterday. am taking a day off to write letters and catch up with a few things.

f. allen

march 4
1956

dear hal—

a few of the boys came over this afternoon with their shofars and we had a ram session. i appreciate the pick you sent on but i have quite an assortment from my old banjo days. when my lap became tender suddenly i had to give up the banjo and take up the shofar. i have a pick three feet long that i used on the bell rope at the local church up in boston. i was the only carillonneur playing by pick. when i played i kept the studio audience in the belfry to give me plenty of room for my pizzicato work. your man, george gobel, or "lonesome who's this," is a plectrum beginner or an embryo plucker as we used to say in the game.

am enclosing a few news items. mr. robert e. lee chambliss, the birmingham garbage collector, who was fired for "conduct unbecoming a city employee." what the hell could a garbage man do to conduct himself provocatively?

i have a theory that if a giant plunger was placed on top of radio city and pressed down suddenly 90% of all television would go down the drain.

new york now has a detail critic; mr. jack o'brian having run out of facets to pan has gone into reviewing the artists' makeup and making suggestions. he has run out of venom mid-season. i knew he couldn't last. he started off the season panning everybody, writing on his stomach and coiling as he wrote to get the snake's point of view and to replenish his venom. but he overdid it. if your show comes east—check on your man's makeup.

i have finished chapter 9 and am half way through 10. if i ever finish this book i may go in for bongo tightening. lindy has started segregation. with the chicken dinner the dark meat is served on a different plate. carry on.

fred allen

(This letter was written three days before Allen's sudden death on March 17, 1956.):

march
14
1956

dear hal—

if my book was finished i would be happy to talk over the tv idea. i have a definite commitment—a double commitment—that obligates me to deliver the completed epic to the sat eve post and the little, brown co. i have only finished nine chapters—am completing the tenth this week—and will need four more chapters to abandon my author phase. when the 14 chapters have been completed i will have to go up to boston to go through the entire book with the editor for cutting and polishing. since i am not a writer i find that, closeted with my pencil and lilywhite paper, i can only hack out from 800 to 1200 words a day. going at this speed, unless my life span holds out, i may never finish the bloody tome. "treadmill to oblivion" used up all of the radio years and the editor is coming over next week to try to devise some way to enable me to squeeze a chapter or two out of radio without repeating. if things go smoothly i doubt if i can finish the cutting and editing before december. i have no deadline. the story will only be sold once and with my limited vocabulary and lumbering pace i want to spend as much time as i require to do it well.

any writer, who has the skill and opportunity, should protect himself in television. somebody recently told me that on the "i love lucy" residuals jess oppenheimer is getting 10% of the $30,-000 desi is catching. with all of the shows you have done the past two seasons you could tremble in your old age in affluence.

one of the reasons i started the book was because after 19 years of radio success and drudgery i found that the tax dept. had most of the money and, after i put "two for the money" with goodson and todman and then lost it through sickness, i decided to take it easier. photogenically i do not come off too well and i didn't want to analyze the medium for my purposes with intent to do my own show again. some time ago i talked with henry morgan about doing a weekly discussion about the news. henry was eager but it was the book again. i promised to talk to him later. when i finish with the book i will talk to anybody who will talk to me. i appreciate your offer and would rather be associated with you than anyone else i know. the next time we meet we can talk about it. meantime, i am going to madame vine not in the trailer.

fred allen

JOHN STEINBECK

june
2nd
1954

cher jaques—(you are not hearing from any mono-lingual jerk)

portland and i have just returned from a fast trip to california. as you perhaps know leaving california is always construed as a gesture of effrontery by the chamber of commerce. the chamber stoutly maintains that california is god's country and they have the screwball assortment of religious sects out there to prove it. we fended off being converted and arrived home yesterday to find your letter.

i am alerted and leaving my head out of the window drooping, pending the arrival of pat convici bearing new best seller.

as you know i have not been in touch with my godson, john steinbeck junior, through circumstances beyond my control —(the rift in the family lute)—my normal acquaintance was gelded in the bud and john, jr, and i remained strangers. it is only in recent months that portland has re-established contact with his mother and taken dinner with her on several occasions.

during john, jr.'s brief span his godfather has survived one coronary occlusion and one cerebral spasm. i will try to parry the reaper until such a time as my godson is informed that there is a supreme being available for the believing and that there are spiritual forces rampant in the world for guidance and help.

i am only familiar with the godfather's obligations as defined by the catholic church. here they are—

"it is the duty of the sponsor, in virtue of his office, to take an interest in his spiritual child, and to take good care that he is instructed in the duties of a christian life and that he lives up to it, as in the ceremony he solemnly pledged himself for this." (if the parents die or neglect the child's catholic education this duty falls to the lot of the godfather or godmother.)

how this works in john, jr.'s religion i do not know. in the catholic faith the parents naturally supervise the religious training of the child. while the parents live the god-parents are available but semi-dormant. the god-mother remembers birthdays and makes occasional presents and, if not watched, her maternal instincts cause her to hover. the god-father is on call for moral support and material and spiritual help if an emergency arises.

you can advise me about john, jr's religious bent. also, his artistic hopes. if he wants to be an actor between frank loesser, abe burrows and you he should be able to find a vehicle for broadway.

we do not plan to go to europe this summer. little, brown is doing a book containing a collection of our old radio scripts. i have to supply introductions for some 25 chapters. i start tomorrow—god knows when i will finish—if ever.

i met burl ives out in hollywood. he said that he was out there to work in "east of eden." i didn't know that it was going to be filmed this summer.

hope elaine and you will have a good summer a good fall and a good half a winter.

portland joins me in best wishes—

> fred allen
> 180 west 58th st.
> new york city 19

JAMES THURBER

West Cornwall
Connecticut
August 29, 1961

Dear Portland:

I am sending you two letters from Fred to me and my letters to him, including one written to Fred in Heaven as soon as I finish this note.

I shall never forget Fred's warm greeting to you on the Allen radio show: "Portland!" and your answers. In my aging but still unclouded memory, everything you and Fred said to each other was somehow akin to the Sweetheart Duet from "May Time."

With much affection and deep appreciation.

Cordially yours,

James Thurber

August 29, 1961

To Fred in Heaven:

I have just sent Portland the letters that you and I, old boy, exchanged a few years ago, years that seem to me in some ways yesterday, because the memory of you is still so vivid in my heart, and in some ways a hundred years ago, since any time at all without the sound of your voice or the sight of your words on paper is bound to seem a century in length. This will, of course, be called sentimental, and it is, but there is a sincerity of friendship between men that must have a touch of sentimentality to be true.

In 1957 I brought out a book called "Further Fables of our Time," during the writing of which there you stood, one afternoon, silently reminding me of many things, including those unforgettable crows of yours who were scared so badly by the scarecrow that they brought back corn they had stolen two years before. That afternoon I wrote the following fable:

The Crow and the Scarecrow

Once upon a farm an armada of crows descended like the wolf on the fold. They were after the seeds in the garden and the corn in the field. The crows posted sentinels, who warned them of the approach of the farmer, and they even had an undercover crow or two who mingled with the chickens in the barnyard and the pigeons on the roof, and found out the farmer's plans in advance. Thus they were able to raid the garden and the field when he was away, and they stayed hidden when he was at home. The farmer decided to build a scarecrow so terrifying it would scare the hateful crows to death when they got a good look at it. But the scarecrow, for all the work the farmer put in on it, didn't frighten even the youngest and most fluttery female. The marauders knew that the scarecrow was a suit of old clothes stuffed with straw and that what it held in its wooden hand was not a rifle but only a curtain rod.

As more and more corn and more and more seeds disappeared, the farmer became more and more eager for vengeance. One night, he made himself up to look like a scarecrow and in the dark, for it was a moonless night, his son helped him to take the place of the scarecrow. This time, however, the hand that held the gun was not made of wood and the gun was not an unloaded curtain rod, but a double-barrelled 18-gauge Winchester.

Dawn broke that morning with a sound like a thousand tin pans falling. This was the rebel yell of the crows coming down on field and garden like Jeb Stuart's cavalry. Now one of the young crows who had been out all night, drinking corn instead of eating it, suddenly went into a tailspin, plunged into a bucket of red paint that was standing near the barn, and burst into flames.

The farmer was just about to blaze away at the squadron of crows with both barrels when the one that was on fire headed straight for him. The sight of a red crow, dripping what seemed to be blood, and flaring like a Halloween torch, gave the living scarecrow such a shock that he dropped dead in one beat less than the tick of a watch (which is the way we all want to go, *mutatis*, it need scarcely be said, *mutandis*).

The next Sunday the parson preached a disconsolate sermon, denouncing drink, carryings on, adult delinquency, front page marriages, gold on Sunday, adultery, careless handling of firearms, and cruelty to our feathered friends. After the sermon, the dead farmer's wife explained to the preacher what had really happened, but he only shook his head and murmured skeptically, "Confused indeed would be the time in which the crow scares the scarecrow and becomes the scarescarecrow."

Moral: All men kill the thing they hate, too, unless, of course, it kills them first.

* * *

Another of my favorite lines of yours that keeps coming back to me was when you said to the bald bass fiddler in the orchestra, "How much would you charge to haunt a house?" You still haunt my house, Fred, a benign, cheerful, happy, and inspiring ghost, and you always will until the day that I join you, Bob Benchley, Bill Fields, Fanny Brice, and the others whose humor and comedy helped to keep me going and still do. Humor and comedy are no longer what they used to be, Fred, when you were on earth with those others.

Make reservations for me up yonder, yeah? God bless you,

As ever,

Jim

november
19th
1953.

dear james thurber—

i want to thank you for sending me a copy of "thurber country."

you will not lose the royalty on my cuff volume. i had bought a copy before yours arrived. this will prove that i am not psychic.

if simon and schuster have done their job well i should be the only man in the world with two copies of "thurber country."

my lawyer will see you shortly about the inscription you have kindly added to my copy. you cannot be my greatest admirer since i am your greatest admirer. this is a form of adjective incest rarely practised except by broadway columnists.

many years ago, harold ross wanted to try and make a writer of me. i told harold that when i saw what you were writing i planned to insert my quill back into the fowl.

who knows—if the foot had been on the other shoe—today you might be doing a lousy television program and i might be mailing you a copy of my new book "allen country."

   sincerely—

                 F

             Edgartown, Mass.
             August 20, 1954

Mr. Edward Weeks
The Atlantic Monthly
8 Arlington Street
Boston 16, Massachusetts

Dear Mr. Weeks:

It was great news to learn that Fred Allen has written a book. Any year that has a book by Fred Allen is a good year, no matter what else happens.

Fred Allen's hilarious, and sometimes chilling, eighteen years in radio may have been a treadmill for him but it was a flight for me more interesting than Lindbergh's. I say "chilling" because of the sharp sketches and anecdotes he puts in about some of the human gargoyles, such as Echo men and Molehill men. I love to see vice-presidents and other advertising men taken apart and nobody can do it better than Fred, because he saw them with one of the clearest eyes of our times and is probably the one man who wasn't afraid of any of them. You can count on the thumb of one hand the American who is at once a comedian, a humorist, a wit, and a satirist, and his name is Fred Allen, and I wish he could come along in person with each copy of his book, but we can't have everything in this world.

Thanks for sending me the proofs and giving me a chance to say these things, any or all of which you may use in any way you see fit.

March of Trivia:

I think he means "censored" when he says "censured Billingsgate."

My own Portland tells me that Beef Strogonoff is not made with milk, as Fred says, but with sour cream.

Best luck to you and Fred and the book.

Cordially yours,

James Thurber

august 30, 1954

dear james—

how do you make a living? you must have saved your money. how can you donate the time filched from your allotted span by wolcott gibbs and ted weeks? i have it from an unreliable source that without your help two issues of mr. gibbs' "fire islander" could never have appeared. more of your valuable time has been frittered away by permitting mr. weeks to unload his galley proofs of my treadmill to oblivion at your tent flap.

i appreciate your kindness in wading through the proofs and sending your comment to master weeks. you are right about "beef strogonoff" being made with sour cream instead of milk. i think the number jack benny rendered was "the bee" sans flight and bumble. i know the rimski-korsakov "bee" but the jack benny "bee" was a b "bee" sort of a standin around the musical hive.

to repay you for your co-operation i promise to withdraw again from the writing craft. this is my final book. thanx again.

F.A.

West Cornwall
Connecticut
September 3, 1954

Dear Fred:

I got a letter from Weeks in the same mail with yours in which he threatened to change "The Bee" to "The Flight of the Bumblebee" but I have wired him to lay off. What we don't want is a book by you with additional musical titles by me. At my age I can really screw up a galley proof. At least I didn't change "Love in Bloom" to "Love in Bloomsbury." I am musically illiterate anyway, but I do know that Joe Venuti is the greatest violinist and that Walter Huston was the best vocalist, not counting Bert Williams, for Fred Allen in his rendition of the Titwillow parody.

It's easy enough to say you're only going to write one book, but I hope you'll find yourself doing another one before long. Don Stewart used to say unhappily, "I think I'm going to have another book." He went through change of life, however, in the early thirties, but he had had about eight. You haven't told the whole truth about yourself and there must be something you're holding back, such as a chapter on how to survive certain actresses you've appeared with. Which reminds me of Howard Dietz's "A day away from Tallulah is like a month in the country."

I've been writing some stuff about Ross, a great character who, as Gibbs says, is hard to make believable. He once said, during a discussion of Willa Cather, "Did he write 'The Private Life of Helen of Troy'?" He shared Sam Goldwyn's belief that Wuthering Heights was something that wuthers. After his daughter was born he said to me, irritably, "I think of a woman as having daughters and a man as having sons." He was scared to death of having too many female hormones. He was pleased when

Jack Dempsey turned up with two daughters. It's hard for me myself to believe what I have already written about Ross. He was one of those rare guys who, when they can't do it at all, can do it better than anyone else.

Your mention of David Freedman reminded me of some remarkable stuff Ken England told me about him. Ken had been one of his stable of writers. I liked the one about the time somebody demanded some timely jokes about Technocracy and Freedman told Ken to get out the fat man file and make changes like this: "A fat technocrat was waiting for a streetcar when . ." Ken said that Freedman used porterhouse and sirloin instead of sleep and nature rebelled and killed him for this heresy. Forty steaks in place of forty winks won't work apparently. I know you got a lot of stuff in your book that I couldn't get around to before Helen's voice gave way again, but she is a professional editor and reader and gets around to most of it, and will get around to it all when the book comes out.

Well, I've just survived another vacation there on the Vineyard, with boats and willow trees flying through the air. During the height of the blow a middle-aged woman said to me, "This is not good for my high blood pressure." Her husband then complimented me on having written "Showboat" and asked me where I got my ideas. I told him I stole them.

Did I ever tell you how Max Eastman garbled some stuff I told him about you for his book "The Enjoyment of Laughter"? My favorite creatures are still those crows of yours that brought back corn they had stolen two years before. Me, I haven't enough strength left to give back ideas I stole two months ago. Right now I'm doing a piece involving the mythical political courage of the late Will Rogers, based on the prevalent statement "If Rogers were alive today, he'd be put in jail." Actually, this bosom friend of senators and congressmen was about as daring as an early Shirley Temple movie. I am, too. Hoping you're the same,

    Affectionately yours,

                    James Thurber

HERMAN WOUK

In 1936, shortly after he was graduated from Columbia, Herman Wouk joined Fred Allen's writing staff. For the next five years he and another young man, Arnold Auerbach, served as Allen's assistants in preparing the scripts of the weekly comedy show. After serving as a naval officer in the Pacific, Wouk launched a highly successful career in the postwar years as a novelist and dramatist, producing among other work the best-selling book, *The Caine Mutiny*.

may
third
1951—

dear herman—

sorry it has taken me so long to write and tell you how much portland and i enjoyed the caine mutiny.

since i gave up my program it seems my days have no pattern. my brother has been back in the hospital and between trips to boston and a few guest dates here i never seem to get anything done.

i think your book is excellent. the chapters describing the storm at sea and the court martial are really wonderful. the queeg character is a perfect portrait of a weakling rampant and the love story is sustained well.

it just occurred to me that since you are no longer in my employ i have a nerve turning critic at this late date.

i know the book represents an enormous amount of work and i hope that the financial returns will repay you for the labor invested in a project of this magnitude.

one satisfaction i imagine a writer enjoys is the knowledge that as his talents develop he has something that cannot be taken from him, but satisfaction alone will not sustain the writer and his family. if there is any justice you will be richly rewarded for this effort.

arnold's show closed while i was in boston. i was sorry that its run was so short, and sorry, too, that i missed it. i heard that arnold and harold had some fine things in the show.

trust that you and all of the great neck wouks are in good fettle. portland joins me in best wishes.

fred allen
180 west 58th

fred allen
june 17th
1951

dear herman—

laston told me that you had taken a house at fire island. subsequently, i had a note from art buchwald saying that he had seen you in paris. i thought you were still in europe until your letter arrived.

it is good to rest occasionally. success is something to cope with today. as soon as you have arrived at a point where attention is focused on you it seems that hordes of maggoty little characters ooze out of your days to waste your time. today, there are so many pressure outfits and so many scurvy nobodies who somehow survive themselves through using other people for their negative purposes.

i have discussed this with john steinbeck on several occasions. it seems to me that a fellow who works hard to accomplish something has a problem to maintain the standard he has set for himself. after his initial success he should have the time and the privacy he needs to enable him to continue to do good work. the writer's time is certainly worth more than the time of even a group of drones at some luncheon or some dynamic jerk who is attempting to use the writer to attract an audience for some fund-raising event.

the public has no time to waste on a failure. if you are a success you should have no time for the public since by comparison collectively the public is a failure. mark twain wrote "the skin of every human being contains a slave." also, "on security

and a competence—that is the life that is best worth living." mark
expressed my sentiments many years before i was able to make
them known. i have always felt that the creative person derives
most of his pleasure from his work. when he requires relaxation
he can seek company.

i have the solution. if i could only write, i would be all set.
we are going to do a quiz show on film next fall. with film you
can talk an hour and cut all of the weak matter. we have done
three auditions. i have a lot of freedom and the auditions worked
out well. with a little luck we should be able to kill a season with
this charade. i did the amateur and round table ad lib routine
for several years in radio. once i get back in that field again it
shouldn't be too hard.

we are leaving for the cape next week. if we start to make
weekly films in august we may come down to fire island some
day. i liked it there. the week-ends were noisy but the rest of the
time it was quiet and it should be an ideal place to work. hope
all goes well with your family and the book. we will see you
this fall, if not before, meantime—best wishes—

"the chief"

august 28
1951

dear herman—

i appreciate your kind letter. i had rather a bad time. on two
or three occasions i seemed to have a content of 60 percent ecto-
plasm. how i ever fended off the poltergeist trend and assumed
full dimension again i will never know. possibly a wonder drug
might have been brought into play.

the fanny brice book is very interesting. i have just finished
the proofs of "tallulah" that richard maney boswelled. the public
doesn't care how the words were welded. if the subject matter
has interest that seems to suffice.

on several meetings h. allen smith has suggested that i try a
book. after i did the preface to his "low man on the totem

pole" i was hot in writing circles. allen volunteered to help me. john steinbeck said that he would do a preface for me if i would attempt a random collection of experiences in show business. others have hinted that i should try to write but i always felt that they were trying to get me out of radio. i always seemed to be too busy to ever start.

if i have to stay out of tv and radio for a long rest i would be interested in attacking a book. i have never done any concentrated writing. as you know radio meant weekly deadlines and pressure. ideas were needed in profusion. if you knew the medium the crude craftsmanship could be escape notice with a few passages of music, some loud sound effects and the imagination of the listener generally confused. all of the things i have written have been short, staccato sentences. there was never description or extraneous words. years ago, humorous writers grew at a leisurely pace. today, a career can be finished in a few years. in radio, the fellows who stay in and have talent become charlatans and hacks. hollywood, too, is crammed with writers who might have developed but who didn't.

i would like to talk to you about the project. you can call me or send me a card with your number and i will call you. glad to know you are making good progress with your next story. mutiny is only your beginning. see you soon.

fred allen

august 13
1954

dear herman—

your friend mr. wolcott gibbs is obviously a name-dropper. he wrote me a letter and lowered your name into his opening sentence. that will explain the appearance of my piece in the fire islander. mr. gibbs promised to send me a copy of the paper the week the piece was used. after waiting for two weeks for the paper to arrive i sent him a note and one dollar enclosed to send me a copy. he returned the dollar and said that i was lifetime subscriber. i still have not received the paper. i am thinking of withdrawing as a contributor. i don't mind not getting paid for my product but i resent being ignored. i may go over to the shull group next summer.

fire island is wonderful for your purposes if you can avoid the social group. gene fowler had a house there years ago and he told me once that he did more work there than he was able to do in the city. i guess the middle-part of the week is quiet and good for working purposes. the week-ends bring the people who can only kill their time by taking up your time. if the people who cannot do anything would all go in a corner of the world and outdull each other, the creative people could get more work done.

i am looking forward to your new book. the income from "the mutiny" should enable you to take as long as you want on the next book. if the subject is one that you have "well in hand" you have the knowledge, the skill and the depth to bring your treatment of it to life for the enjoyment of the reader.

my book is called "treadmill to oblivion." little, brown will publish it in november. it really isn't a complete book. it is the story of radio show. a radio program is not unlike a man. it is conceived. it is born. it lives through the experiences that fate allots to it. finally, the program dies and like man, is forgotten except for a few people who depended on it for sustenance or others whose lives had been made brighter because the program had existed. as the story progresses chronologically there are excerpts from some of the better shows and odd routines of min's, claghorn's, etc. the little, brown people are enthused about it but i guess ink and enthusiasm are the two commodities a publisher requires. the book could have been better. if i could write better or if there had been more time. i will appreciate your opinion of the effort when it shows up in november.

if the pilot film we have kicked around the agencies is not sold i may try to do an autobiography during the winter. i have never spent any length of time trying to write. working on this radio book was pleasant and i would like to attempt the other even if nothing comes of it.

hope your chores will soon be completed temporarily. success is wonderful up to a certain point. it consumes your time. it infests your days with leaches who want to promote you for their selfish purposes and eventually, if you try to cope with the demands, it affects your health. i have always felt that when i was a failure nobody bothered me. when i became a success the people who were trying to use me were failures according to my new standards.

i know that sarah and the children are well. hope you will finish the summer and the book in super-fettle. portland and i will see you later in the fall.

life is uphill—carry on. (charlie cantor—an old epigram made up by him.)

fred allen

september
18
1954

dear herman—

i appreciate your comment on the galleys of "treadmill to oblivion." helen said that she was going to ask ted weeks, at the atlantic monthly, to send you a copy of the proofs some weeks ago. i told her i thought it was an imposition unless she sent you a note asking, whether, or not, you were busy. the bloody proofs caused me sufficient embarrassment. brother weeks sent them to john steinbeck, james thurber and allen smith. allen was the only one i would ask as a friend to cope with the book. john and james wrote very nice comments and allen smith sent me a note telling me his reaction.

this season is rather confused. nbc has no time available for the show we auditioned last may. i have a number of guest dates set and little, brown will probably stir up some activity when the book appears. if i have time available i may think about trying to write another exercise. when i see you we can talk about it if there is no other subject to discuss. i think i explained the lack of time with treadmill. it was impossible to relax or think the problems out thoroughly. if there is a next time i will make sure there will be no rushing.

am enclosing a column from the east hampton star. the paper is owned by a lady i have known for many years. her daughter has been living in paris and writing a weekly column for the paper. her paris columns have been very interesting. this summer she has been visiting her mother and this column was written on the boat back to europe. it is a funny idea. watching the storm in the "caine mutiny" with a real storm tossing the boat in the opposite direction.

i imagine you are back from fire island. we didn't go to the cape this summer. the hurricane went through the section we usually visit and blew away an entire section of the beach. when hurricanes come to the cape you can sit in hyannis and watch the resorts go by. hope it missed fire island this year. hope your book is finished. will see you anon.

fred allen

january
8
1955

dear herman—

sorry you have had to lash yourself to your manuscript to ride out the gale of cutting. that is one consolation you have doing a book. if you were writing a tv play you would have been on the air ready or not. i hope it goes smoothly from now on.

"treadmill" has been going very well. you and james, the thurber, were responsible for getting it off the ground with your endorsements. the first advertising budget was small but it was used mostly to plug you and james. when the reviews started coming in they were all good. i thought that little, brown would advertise more to take advantage of them. when they didn't do anything about the notices, with the holidays coming on, i paid for the times and tribune ads all through december. i went on as many radio and tv shows i could get on to plug the book and i guess the cumulative effect of the assorted elements plus the fact that we sent out almost 3000 xmas cards, using the little, brown mailing list to reach the jobbers and book dealers, and the same number of new year cards advertising the book got things rolling.

i have been thinking about doing an autobiography. tv, and the things i get to do in the medium, is too hectic. after over 20 years i should be entitled to an off year to try to write. if i can't make it come out i can slink back into tv and forget my writing ambitions here as i take a dim view of the future at the twilight of my career.

portland and i expect to be here all winter. whenever you are available—give us a call—meantime, a new year better than ever.

fred allen

fred allen

feb. 20–1955

dear herman—

a few more sessions and we might be able to bring smalltalk back. during the samuel johnson days they had big men enjoying smalltalk. today we have small men enjoying big talk. the "coffee house" (in expresso form) is thriving in new york. if we can interest arnold and a few more worthy conversationalists we may found a new set of boswells, pepys and wits to restore the pleasant art of conversation to the esteem it enjoyed in london in the spectator days.

the last time i wrote brother gibbs was to send him your address. i told him that if you were available that if he wanted to have lunch, and he would give me a day or so warning, i would be happy to host the venture.

if you know how to reach him, or have any day that is better for you, just give me a ring.

regards—

august
2–1955

dear herman—

glad to know that the piece i wrote about you for the book-of-the-month club magazine looked okay. it seemed quite long, as i remember it, but the gentleman said that he would try to use all of it, if possible. i haven't heard anything from him since so don't know what happened. i hope they will send me a copy of the magazine for that month.

i am sure that the book-month selection assures your marjorie morningstar an enthusiastic critical reception. i don't know anything about books but it would seem to me that the woman market should far exceed the male. that doesn't work either otherwise caine mutiny would have been on the wrong end of the potential.

my appendectomy came from no place. no symptoms, no pains, no high blood count until the last minute. fortunately, i went into the hospital because of the july 4th week-end. the doctor said that if there was any trouble it would be difficult to obtain nurses and an open-all-night surgeon. after all these years, i sure thought that i would arrive at the utter-mckinley patio with all of my equipment. i guess it is as jesse crawford once said, "you never can trust an old organ."

i have started my autobiography. i have one chapter finished and the second chapter almost completed. i am working in a little office that mort green and george foster use for writing during the winter. when they come back from the coast i will probably give it up. when you come back to town i will ask you about the place you had. if i stay with the book i will have to give up everything for a year, or so, and i will have to get a routine. enjoy the island. it has been terrible here in the city. call us when you come home. best wishes to all wouk extant.

                                                                fred allen

                                                      116 East 68 Street
                                                      New York 21
                                                      March 18, 1956

To the Editor of The New York Times
Dear Sir;

The death of Fred Allen, America's greatest satiric wit in our time, brings to mind Hazlitt's elegaic paragraph on the Restoration actors:

"Authors after their deaths live in their works; players only in their epitaphs and the breath of common traditions. They die and leave the world no copy . . . In a few years nothing is known of them but that *they were*."

Fred Allen was an eminent comic actor. But without a doubt his great contribution to life in America came in the marvellous eighteen year run of weekly satiric invention which was the Fred Allen show on radio. His was the glory of being an original personality, creating new forms of intelligent entertainment. He was without a peer and without a successful imitator.

His knife-like comment on the passing show of the thirties and the forties came from sources no other comedian had access to. He was a self-educated man of wide reading; he was a tremendously talented writer; and he had the deep reticent love of life and of people which is the source of every true satirist's energy. Fred's wit lashed and stung. He could not suffer fools. In this he was like Swift and like Twain. But his generosity to the needy, his extraordinary loyalty to his associates (in a field not noted for long loyalties) showed the warmth of heart that made his satire sound and important.

Because his work was a unique kind of comic journalism the written residue might have suffered the usual fate of journalism. Fred fortunately preserved a fraction of it in that fine volume of Americana, his recent book, "Treadmill to Oblivion." When he died, he was working on his autobiography; the portion he completed will be published.

But the few writings he left will give future generations a dim notion at best of what sort of man he was. In Fred Allen, the voice of sanity spoke out for all Americans to hear, during a trying period of our history, in the classic and penetrating tones of comic satire. Because he lived and wrote and acted here, this land will always be a saner place to live in. That fact is his true monument.

Herman Wouk